LOVE
&
MONEY

LOVE & MONEY

A Life Guide For Financial Success

Jeff D. Opdyke

WILEY

John Wiley & Sons, Inc.

Published by John Wiley & Sons, Inc., Hoboken, New Jersey.
Published simultaneously in Canada.

For general information on our other products and services please contact our Customer Care Department within the United States at (800) 762-2974, outside the United States at (317) 572-3993 or fax (317) 572-4002.

Wiley also publishes its books in a variety of electronic formats. Some content that appears in print may not be available in electronic books. For more information about Wiley products, visit our web site at *www.Wiley.com*.

Library of Congress Cataloging-in-Publication Data:
Opdyke, Jeff D.
   Love & money : a life guide for financial success / Jeff D. Opdyke.
      p. cm.
   Includes index.
ISBN 0-471-47658-7 (CLOTH)
      1. Finance, Personal.   2. Couples—Finance, Personal.   I. Title: Love and money.
   II. Title.
HG179.O638 2004
332.024'0086'55—dc22   2003020202

Printed in the United States of America

10   9   8   7   6   5   4   3   2   1

For Amy and Zachary.
My two best friends, from A to Z.
Without your love, the money doesn't matter.

Acknowledgments

As a writer for a daily newspaper, you come to accept as a fact of everyday life the notion that someone else is going to look at what you've just written and express their own opinions about how to tell the story in just a little better fashion and, thus, massage your copy—or rip it to shreds and paste it back together again in a new order. But until you sit down to write a book, you never realize just how important those people are at helping you shape what you really want to say.

To that end, I owe huge thanks to Airié Stuart, my editor at John Wiley & Sons, Inc. She saw the vision for *Love & Money*, and the promise of a book designed to help readers navigate the financial challenges of their own lives and of living life with another person. Airié bolstered my enthusiasm for this book and tolerated me throughout the process. Her thoughts and her ideas have made these pages substantially better than they would have been without her much-appreciated commentary.

I must also thank Denise Hughes, a financial counselor in San Carlos, California, who befriended me and who spent untold hours sharing with me her knowledge of the psychology of money, both for the Love & Money column I write and, in particular, this book. Her generosity, humor, and ability to describe how our noggins operate has greatly benefited this book and allowed me to better understand how money flows through all our lives directly and unconsciously.

Any success I've had with the Love & Money column I write for *The Wall Street Journal Sunday* stems in large part from standing on the shoulders of my friend Tara Parker-Pope, whose Balanced Life column set the tone and set the standard for what personally reflective journalism should be. She has been an unending source of help, ideas, and words when my own words and experiences failed me. I still owe her a ton of money from all the quarters I've borrowed through the years to buy my Pepsis.

David Crook, the editor of *The Wall Street Journal Sunday* deserves much thanks for giving me a chance at writing a column and giving me support along the way. I also have to thank Mike Allen, the bureau chief who first hired me all those years ago in the *Journal*'s Dallas bureau, for taking a chance on a guy in holey jeans and a T-shirt. He taught me the art of napping under your desk and, better yet, how to write with conviction. Edward Felsenthal and Neal Templin, my editors at *The Wall Street Journal*'s Personal Journal section, have graciously tolerated me writing the Love & Money column when, instead, I could be home at night writing another PJ story. Neal, you'll notice I didn't take a dig at you as did our curmudgeonly officemate Jonathan Clements in his book.

Wesley Neff, my agent, deserves recognition for helping me secure my first book contract. For that I am eternally appreciative.

Many personal finance books rely on hypothetical examples to demonstrate the financial lessons of life. I can assure you that every anecdote in these pages is rooted in the experiences of friends, colleagues, acquaintances, relatives, or numerous readers of the Love & Money column who have willingly allowed me to use their stories to illustrate the choices and challenges of managing your money and your relationships. I thank you all. In particular I want to single out Jack and Colleen Evans and Melissa and Mike Williams, two sets of longtime friends who, through the years, have provided thoughtful commentary on their life and their experiences trying to manage their families and their money.

Three people have provided the bulk of unwavering support and help throughout this entire journey, from the column's beginnings through the culmination of this book. My wife, Amy, and my young son, Zachary, have endured and tolerated more time without Dad than a wife and son should have to. I appreciate your patience more than you know. More important, you both have been a never-ending source of ideas and love, and for that I'm extremely lucky and blessed. You are both as much a part of this effort as I am.

Finally, there is Larry Rout, who edits my column for the Sunday edition. I do not possess a vocabulary rich enough to express how much he has improved my writing, my ideas, and my life. A column focused on the intersection of personal finance and personal relationships was his brainchild, and the gratitude I express to him here for offering to me the job of columnist cannot begin to truly capture my heartfelt appreciation.

More important, he has been a friend throughout my career, benevolently guiding my path, serving as a role model for the father I someday hope to be. If ever a book deserved a second byline, this is it, and it belongs to Larry.

Contents

STAGE THREE
The Kiddie Years: Big Dollars for Little People

STAGE FOUR
The Middle Years: Reevaluating Your Life

STAGE FIVE
The Later Years: Planning the Future

Introduction

What is personal finance if not personal?

So much of what you read about "personal finance" is about the *finance:* how to invest in up markets or down; the right retirement moves now; when to refinance your home; the best ways to save money and how to save more; how you, too, can become the millionaire next door.

Lost in all this finance is the *personal*—the ways in which our money weaves through our lives and the ways in which our lives merge into our money.

Exposing the interplay of love and money is my motivation for writing this book. Consider this your road map to better finances and, ultimately, better relationships. My aim is to get you to put your financial life under a microscope and to look at your money, and the decisions you make about money, in a different light. By examining money in ways you've never done before, or by considering the financial implications of your decisions in ways you've never considered before, my bet is that you'll gain a better understanding of how money matters that arise every single day play a role in the relationships you share with your spouse, children, parents, even friends.

In doing so, you'll learn to live better financially, to talk more effectively about money with the people important in your life, to deal with financial problems more productively, and, yes, to have more money. Right now, maybe you and your partner are at cross-purposes in some aspect of your financial life. You might want to help out a financially ailing parent, while your spouse balks at that prospect. Maybe your partner wants to unite the family's finances into a single joint account, but you fear losing autonomy over your life. These issues are like a mutual fund that carries a high fee. That fee—in this case, conflict—is a burden that impacts the money you accumulate over time. If you can just cut the cost somehow, you'll be so much better off financially.

In *Love & Money* terms, cutting those costs means learning what stands in the way of the harmony you seek. The suggestions that arise throughout the following chapters may seem incremental individually, yet in aggregate they make a huge difference in how you're spending, where you're investing, and what you're saving. They will help you improve your relationships in numerous subtle and not-so-subtle ways.

I know. *Love & Money* is the offspring of a popular *Wall Street Journal Sunday* column—also called Love & Money—that I write and in which I lay bare my financial soul, as well as that of Amy, my wife. There's nothing we won't divulge. Through dating and marriage, we've been together for nearly two decades. In those years, we've struggled with financial issues that have strained our relationship, and sometimes still do, such as an ongoing debate about whether to have another child. We've excelled in matters that give us confidence about our future, such as beginning to plan early for the retirement we envision together. We have argued, we have agreed, we have yelled, and we have discussed issues rationally. The issues you read about in this book may become heated discussions in your life. As did my wife and I, you will come to realize that you are experiencing what many others have in dealing with the day-in and day-out drudgeries and frustrations of managing money.

Along with shining a light on my own life, I also have invited friends, family, colleagues, and thousands of readers from every corner of the country to weigh in with their thoughts on the same issues I have confronted. They have done so in large numbers, offering me an often unfiltered glimpse into the real money culture of our society—a culture that frequently has little to do with traditional notions of personal finance and much more to do with everyday anxieties about the way money flows through our lives.

Readers like Bonnie, in central Florida, often see slices of their lives unfolding eerily similar to mine. Like my mom, Bonnie says her mom is "a financial mess." Like me, Bonnie was raised by her grandmother who bailed out Bonnie's mom time and again. Like me and my wife, Bonnie and her husband "have spent an untold number of hours throughout the years discussing the unpleasant likelihood of having to support my mother" because she likely won't be able to support herself. Like me, Bonnie "knows how this will work out when it's all said and done, but I am not looking forward to it." Instead, like me, Bonnie is left feeling "just a high level of angst."[1]

Bonnie's story reflects a simple fact: We all face many of the same financial quandaries. The only difference is that each of us sees those quandaries through our own lens. That's the strength you can derive from this book. These people have either dealt with the very issues you're worried about right now or were prompted to deal with them after reading a particular Love & Money column. No matter the case, they have shared their lives with me, in turn giving me a unique database of advice, lessons, solutions, and personal anecdotes that stretch from one coast to the other—and in some cases circle the globe.

Because of this bond with readers, I have learned enough about love and money and relationships to write a book. These pages reflect not only my own life, but the experiences of friends and readers everywhere, in every stage of life. *Love & Money* addresses the problems you face today, and it's a book to return to time and again as new chapters of your life unfold. The issues you confront early in your life—such as the basics of saving and spending and accumulating debt—are dramatically different than those you face when you become a parent and your financial priorities shift. Those days, in turn, differ tremendously from later years, when you earnestly start looking ahead to your dreams for retirement.

Love & Money, therefore, is segmented into broad life stages, with each stage divided into chapters that represent some of the universal issues you'll deal with. Some are big issues, such as the question in Stage Two about whether a bigger paycheck equals greater power in a marriage. Some are troubling issues, such as the Stage Four challenge of dealing with the financial incompatibilities between you and your partner that neither of you foresaw but that years later loom large in your relationship. Some are seemingly simple issues, such as the Stage Three realization that paying your child an allowance can be really tough—not on your kid, but on you.

At the end of each chapter is a Dollars & Sense section offering practical advice and, in some cases, resources to help you achieve in your own life the results you seek. Some are free, online resources; some are exercises you can try at home; others are books that do a fine job of expanding on topics important to building a strong financial life. I'm not advocating that you spend more money on more books, but some subjects demand far more space and explanation than I can give them in these pages.

The common thread running through every chapter is the overlooked role that communication plays in our financial affairs. We all like to think that money is, well, just money. The truth is that money is tied to a host of emotional issues bundled up inside us that are themselves the true seeds of financial discord arising in our relationships. We hear all the time that money is a leading cause of divorce—a fallacy you'll read about in Stage Two—when the truth is that our inability to *talk* about money is the real culprit.

Certainly, tackling the emotional aspects of money is incredibly tough. After all, we're just not raised to openly discuss our dollars. Consider the conversations we all have with friends and family members. We gab about the most intimate details of our lives—our fears, our vices, our aspirations. Talk of our sex lives is often no more shocking than inquiring about the weather.

But money? We don't go there. Our finances are just too personal.

I still remember a friend telling me over lunch one day that while she eagerly anticipated her wedding, she was scared to death of talking to her fiancé about financial issues—though she recognized that such issues must be addressed. "I just know," she said, "that I'm going to inadvertently come off as some kind of money-grubber if I start asking questions about his money, and what his expectations are of our finances, and my desire to stay home at some point and raise a family. So I just avoid it and hope he brings it up."

Because of such reticence, personal finance remains the last bastion of privacy, a deep secret that, like our bank PIN, we dare not divulge. That silence has real consequences. By being secretive about our money, we create chasms in our relationships that can seem impossibly large. We keep the peace by keeping quiet. It's just easier that way. All the while, though, the chasms grow and the financial strains build.

There's little wonder why. It's difficult, bordering on impossible at times, for people to fathom the financial actions of another, because they can't even begin to understand the divergent definitions of *money* that separate all of us. Yet such fundamental understanding is a central tenet of building a successful financial life in which everyone affected feels secure and confident about money. A family simply cannot strive toward common goals if no one openly talks about the destination . . . or the journey.

The biggest problem in bridging these chasms is that no one wants to equate love with money. Doing so seems crass, because we want to believe that neither has anything to do with the other. They do, though. We all fight about money just as we do about love, because both are passionate subjects that kindle our emotions. How you manage the financial conflicts that arise—and they will—determines how successful you are in preserving love. It also determines whether you effectively keep your financial life on track or allow the discord to breed contempt, anger, and frustration—maybe even divorce.

Let me give you a small example of what considering money from a different viewpoint can do for your life. Though Amy and I have been together for a long time, we never had a clue about what the other wanted from retirement. One day, I asked Amy to write out her list of dreams and wants and necessities for when she retires (all of which you'll read about in Stage Five). I did the same. It turns out we both want a little loft in Vancouver,

British Columbia, a city we both love to spend time in and where we'd like to spend long stretches of time when we punch out at work for good. I never knew that about her. Based on that common ground, we opened a special savings account to begin squirreling away a few dollars so that we might one day buy our dream loft. Maybe we will never get there. Maybe we will. Whatever the case, that one little exercise—tell me what you really want from your retirement—could mean we live a far more satisfying old age than we otherwise might have. A potentially life-altering change stemmed from one small conversation, one of dozens of similar exercises you'll find scattered throughout these pages.

I want you to shine a light on your money and put it under the microscope. Instead of relegating it to some dark, hidden corner of your life, pull it out of the shadows and open it up to truthful, honest reflection. I want you to learn, as I have, from the lessons of so many people out there who are in many fundamental ways just like you. By understanding how you and your partner differ on your very personal views of personal finance, and why, you can learn to more effectively navigate the financial divides that separate you—and to do so with greater insight. That knowledge will do far more to promote a sense of financial success and security than the next hot growth stock ever will.

The truth is, even after all these years together, Amy and I still often disagree on our finances, not just as they relate to us, but to our young son, our aging parents, and our friends. Our differences, as in many marriages, play out in hundreds of ways, big and small. Some are obvious; some are not so obvious. In the best of times, the outcome of our conversations is that we make each other think about an issue in a new way. In the worst of times, we find it taxing to agree, and we know there's still an issue for which we've yet to find a compromise, something we will have to face again later.

That's okay, though. Arguing is simply passionate proof that we care about where we're going. As you continue to search for common ground with your loved ones, or at least an acceptance of other views when some particularly divisive financial matter pops up, this book will help you see what others are thinking on the same issues. Whatever you ultimately decide on these matters, resist the sometimes unrelenting urge to just brush them under the rug and hope they go away.

They won't. At the end of the day, love and money, like all of our relationships, are intimately intertwined.

STAGE ONE

The Formative Years

Financial Fundamentals

Many years ago, I rushed into my editor's office at the newspaper where I worked. A major earthquake had just wrecked the capital of El Salvador. I told my editor that a photojournalist down there would have a great opportunity to capture the rescue efforts under way as teams from across the world descended on the devastation of downtown San Salvador. In my editor's office at that moment was one of his longtime friends, a well-regarded newsman from a national television network, who looked at me and said very simply: "Then why are you standing here? Go."

That was October 1986. I was in college, working for the student newspaper.

By "in college," I mean "dirt poor." I never had much more than pocket change, certainly not enough to afford the $400 ticket. My grandparents, who raised me and with whom I lived during my years at Louisiana State University, did not have that kind of money available, either. Being that this was a state-funded institution of higher learning, the student newspaper certainly wasn't going to send me on a Central American junket.

What I did have was an American Express card. Without telling my stepfather, my mom had listed me on her account as a co–card holder, an effort to school me in some money management skills. I was to repay every purchase on time, and she implored me to use the card wisely so that trouble would befall neither of us. Until the temblor, I don't think I charged a single item. Now, though, a plane ticket into a disaster zone seemed to me a very wise purchase indeed. I dashed over to the student union travel office and plunked down my plastic to grab the first flight out of New Orleans. The next morning I was winging it to Central America—with no clothes save for those on my body, a camera bag filled with gear, and a grand total of $28 in my pocket (not enough to rent a hotel room, so I slept on a couch in the lobby of the Camino Real Hotel). Basically, I made a hugely unwise financial decision. I acted on impulse—this trip would be great for my budding career, I rationalized, so it was therefore worth the price.

That was my introduction to money. Sure, I'd earned and spent money before that; after all, I was 20 years old at the time. I had a checking account—though I rarely balanced it successfully—and I had earned meager paychecks cutting lawns with my neighborhood buddies, Mike, Jim, and Ian; flipping burgers one summer at McDonald's; bagging groceries for more than a year at Kroger; and, at this particular point in my story, snapping photos as a staff shutterbug for the LSU yearbook and daily newspaper.

But I did not understand money, aside from the most rudimentary concepts: You earn it; you spend it; you never have enough of it.

The El Salvador incident perfectly illustrates how so many of us deal with money—and why so many of us make a hash of our personal finances. I didn't have the cash to pay for the ticket, so instead I relied on a credit card. Yet I had no viable plan for addressing the debt when the bill arrived, no savings to draw down, and no way of repaying the debt promptly from my paychecks, since those had never amounted to squat. As I said, the student newspaper wasn't going to foot the bill. But I figured, why worry about money I didn't need to repay for several weeks? I can deal with that tomorrow; getting to El Salvador is what I need to do *today*.

Of course, you see the problem here: Tomorrow always comes, and by then you're not worried about the bills you accumulated yesterday but the bills you're racking up today. Soon enough, all of this amasses into one big financial mess that you don't know how to deal with.

That big mess is what Stage One is about. Before you can worry about money and relationships, you need to understand money and yourself. The rapport you have with your money is the single most important financial relationship you will build, since only you have control over how you spend, save, accumulate and manage debt, and plan for events months or years into the future. Stage One centers on understanding each of these basic financial matters so that ultimately you can apply them to your own life and the relationships you have with others.

Love & Money starts with your budget. Now, before you tense up, as do most people when that *B* word is tossed out, I'm going to show you how to skip budgeting and instead build a spending plan. The difference is more than words. Budgets look backward and confine you to historical patterns. Spending plans look forward and each month allow you to foresee spending and saving priorities, giving you control in meeting your wants and necessities. Spending plans are proactive; budgets are reactive. By creating your own spending plan, not a very difficult task, you'll quickly gain a stronger grip over your financial life.

Doing that, getting a firm grip on your finances, allows you to better control your debt, an insidious piece of our financial being. Debt can be benevolent, providing access to an affordable home and affordable transportation. Or debt can be malevolent, sucking you into auto leases for flashy cars you otherwise could not afford, or accumulating expenses for random purchases you ultimately don't need and for which you don't have the cash in the first place. Every store you shop in these days offers its own branded credit card, and, hey, if you sign up right now you get 10 percent off your purchase. Soon enough, you have a piece of plastic from every merchant in the mall and enough bills rolling in each month to wallpaper a room with statements. If you aren't careful, you begin to feel that your debt really defines who you are.

One key to erasing debt and avoiding it is to curb your discretionary spending. All those throwaway purchases you make every day—the four Pepsis, midmorning and early-afternoon lattes, snacks, magazines, newspapers, even the inexpensive restaurant meals—seem like minor purchases. Their cost is generally insignificant in relation to your income or other big expenses like housing and insurance and car payments. Plus, these tiny purchases are a nice way to reward yourself without spending a small fortune.

But here's the fine print you never read: Add together all your small purchases, and you know what? You've spent that small fortune. If you can begin to control your spending, you can begin to control your debt, and you can begin to stash away more of your income for the things in life that really mean something—like, say, financial security.

I know lots of people in my life who earn fat salaries but have no financial security whatsoever because they have nothing set aside. Some don't even have savings accounts. They live a couple of paychecks shy of financial ruin. Hard as they try to shove that fact from their consciousness, the possible predicament constantly needles the back of their mind. To create the most basic sense of financial security, you need an emergency savings account you can rely on for, well, an emergency.

What, though, is an appropriate sum to have saved? And how does your sense of security define the amount that's right for you?

All of this you'll find in Stage One.

Before we get there, let me say something about the past—specifically, childhood. For all of us, our habits—good and bad—stem from our history with money. How we saw our parents handle their money and how they allowed us to handle our money as kids define how we interact with money as adults and how we interact with our own family financially.

For instance, growing up with grandparents on a fixed income had a dramatic effect on my view of money today. My grandfather was a mechanic-turned-tire-salesman who retired without a pension. My grandmother grew up in a Mississippi orphanage, never had anything, and thus struggled to provide more for herself and, particularly, her family. As a purchasing agent for a chemical company she supported the family on a salary that never topped $30,000 a year—and typically was a good bit less. We lived on a tight income, and I came to see money in terms of the obstacles that frustrated her every day. We never took family vacations, except for weekend fishing trips with my grandfather or maybe a couple days once a year staying with relatives in Jackson, Mississippi. My most vivid remembrance of money as a kid was listening to my grandmother in somber moments bemoan that her attempts to salt away a little money, however meager, were continually dashed because, she complained, "Every time you save a nickel, someone takes a dime."

Amy, my wife since 1992 and a part of life since my freshman year in college in 1984, sees money from a different perspective. We grew up in the same south Louisiana town, Baton Rouge, and our financial surroundings were similar in terms of income. Her dad worked jobs similar to my grandmother's; her mom worked in a credit union. Dinner out, even at a local cafeteria, was an infrequent occasion for her family. Nevertheless, Amy saw money through the eyes of young parents inherently optimistic about tomorrow and heading into their peak earning years. She saw the family's finances blossom, instilling in her confidence about her own financial future.

Because Amy and I often see money so differently, divisions run through many of the most basic facets of our finances. I fear never having enough; Amy grows frustrated at not spending what she knows we can afford. That's an inherent conflict in our viewpoints.

There's nothing unusual about any of this. In fact, it's actually the point of my little story: You, me, and everyone else have different sets of experiences with money that we draw upon every day, usually unconsciously. That history is who we are every time we open our wallets or go to the bank to deposit our paychecks.

You might come from a family where Mom always berated Dad for his screwball get-rich-quick ideas that always crumbled. The money invested vanished and the bills mounted. You look back on that and chuckle at Dad's goofy notions. Then your spouse walks through the door, excited by a hot investment tip, and suddenly you're in a tizzy. Your spouse was just sharing an idea, but a childhood money memory raced through your unconsciousness, and now you're that little kid again, raging inside about your parents' money troubles and worried that this is just another chance to lose money the family needs.

Remember that as you read through this stage of *Love & Money*. If you can identify your hang-ups about saving and spending that stem from your childhood, you can begin to better address the fixes you need to make.

By the way, regarding that $400 I spent on the ticket to El Salvador . . . my mom was livid with me for racking up a charge I couldn't afford; my stepfather was livid with my mom for giving me access to her credit. In the end, I paid back as much as I could, but she ate a majority of the cost. As you might expect, she also confiscated the AmEx card.

A year later, American Express offered me my own credit card.

I haven't missed a payment yet.

CHAPTER 1

Budgets Are Like Diets—Everyone Cheats

Developing a Spending Plan

Budgets are useless.

Okay, that might be a bit hyperbolic. After all, I'm pretty sure budgets help lots of people gain control over their financial lives. I don't happen to know any of those people, because all the people I know hate their budgets, refuse to make a budget, or insist they have no need to live by a budget. Melissa, my wife's best friend from Louisiana, won't even use the word. "*Budget*, to me, sounds poor," Melissa says. "I grew up not having a lot and having to shop at discount stores, and I can't get over that in my head. So I look at *budget* and *poor* in the same light."[1]

Certainly, the two words aren't synonymous. In fact, if you adhere to a budget you're more likely to reach a point in life where you're wealthy—or at least comfortably content, not poor. If you live according to your budget, then by definition you live within your means, and if you live within your means, you're not amassing a load of debt by living the high life. You're probably much more careful with your spending, and you're probably able to set aside a few dollars that, ultimately, will give you a sense of financial security. I believe in all of that. I even aim for it myself. So do most of the people I know.

Still, none of those folks follows a budget. Or if they do, they do so thinly at best, because in reality people do not want to feel constrained by the spending restraints a budget demands. It's only human nature that you want to feel in control of your own money; you don't want to feel your budget has control over you. Here's a conversation I had with a friend about budgeting:

ME: Hey, I'm writing about budgets and . . .

FRIEND: Why do you always bring up budgets? You know I hate budgets. I don't even like when you talk about budgets. I don't follow a budget because it's my money and I should spend it like I want. You know this. So why are you asking?

That was the actual budget discussion, in its entirety.

Amy and I have had a budget for all the years we've been married—sort of. It's a very pretty budget, with heaps of numbers highlighted in more than a dozen pastel colors denoting all sorts of categories. The harsh truth, however, is that our budget is all but worthless because we've never really adhered to it. Fixed costs are not a problem, because they don't change and are easy to plan for. The real problem we face, and which many people I talk to struggle with constantly, is managing all those fungible, variable costs in our life. The restaurant meals, the personal expenses, lunch during the week, snacks, impromptu trips to the beach or the mountains or wherever, the unexpected need to replace a tire, the seven DVDs you buy on sale to go along with the new DVD player you snapped up on an impulse while shopping for a $5 extension cord at Wal-Mart. Those are the costs that typically derail a budget.

Indeed, Amy and I were frustrated each month because we were unable to save the money our budget insisted we could if we would just live within the bounds of its variable parts.

We tried to alter our budget to make it more amenable to our life. We changed the way we allot money to categories and how we allot money to one another. We tried giving each other an allowance. We've saved receipts and tracked historic spending patterns to structure our budget around what we typically buy. For several years, as you'll read in an upcoming chapter, we operated on a system of joint and individual checking accounts. In part, that was supposed to force us to more effectively live within our budget because it would limit what we each could spend on ourselves from the joint account—basically, all those personal and discretionary purchases during the day that are the bane of budgets.

All of that was to no avail. Every month we faced the same scenario: We spent more than we wanted to, eroding what we could be saving and never really having much to show for all that we were spending.

At some point you realize that sitting down to pen a budget is the easy part. Putting your plan into practice is where the process goes awry. More often than not, you feel annoyed by the fetters of a budget, and you feel lousy about your inability to follow it when you continually overshoot your bottom line. Ultimately, you reach a moment where all you want to do is take your budget out back, bludgeon it with a bag of coins, and leave it a quivering heap of submissive numbers.

There has to be a better way.

. . .

Budgets are a big deal in the world of personal finance; they are one of the primary building blocks of financial security and financial planning. Basically, a budget is your road map from wherever you are to wherever it is you hope to go. Of course, lots of people read maps about as well as they read Sanskrit. If you reflect back on your knowledge of Bugs Bunny cartoons, you might recall that many a time the wabbit popped up in some unexpected locale only to realize yet again that he should've taken that left at Albuquerque.

That's exactly how it is with budgets—you hang a right in Wal-Mart instead of a left, and soon enough you're spending a couple hundred dollars on that DVD player instead of checking out with just a cheap extension cord in your bag. But not taking that right is tough. You work hard to earn a paycheck, and you'd like to spend a little on enjoying your life. Trust me, I know. I bought my DVD player on a whim while walking around New York City one day, just because I felt like watching *The Maltese Falcon*. (I bought the DVD, too, along with a couple other movies that looked interesting.)

One or two similar purchases and suddenly you've blown your budget for the month. That doesn't necessarily mean you're spending more than you bring in, although that is certainly one of the more extreme results. More likely, you have the cash flow to cover your expenses, but you're just not getting ahead financially; you're not saving what your budget says you should be able to.

After so many false starts and restarts through the years, Amy and I eventually gave up following our budget with any real precision. We began using it mainly as a signpost that we were at least attempting to move in the right direction. In lamenting our seeming inability to live according to the rules of our budget, Denise, a friend of mine who is a financial counselor in northern California, suggested that the problem with our budget may be the budget itself.

"Spending is often about values. When you try to adhere to a budget, you might feel you're doing without because you value what you want to spend your money on in the first place—but your budget says you can't," she told me. "So you feel like you're being deprived by your budget. And you end up hating your budget, so you give up on following your budget. There is a better way."[2]

Amy and I began following some advice Denise offered. We abandoned our budget completely. In doing so, we began to save more of our salaries than we had in the past, and feel more in control of our finances. Better yet, we don't have to deny ourselves the pleasures of spending on what we really want or what we like to do as a family. Her suggestion: Replace your budget with a so-called spending plan.

In truth, a budget and a spending plan are similar. Yet they function very differently and are based on two distinct philosophies. Before I detail how a spending plan works, though, let me first explain why I think budgets don't.

Amy and I live within our means, yet we blow our budget every month. That's odd to say, but it's true. We know, because our pretty budget shows us that after paying all the fixed costs in our life and after accounting vaguely for variable costs like food and restaurants and personal spending, 20 percent of our take-home pay should still be unaccounted for.

Oddly enough, we always manage to waste precisely that 20 percent during the month. The thing is, we know that money is there, a cushion we can push into without overshooting our income. Yes, if you're thinking we have a problem with spending discipline, you're absolutely correct. We do. But we're not so different than most everyone else we know. Unless you're a Buddhist monk, you probably do not thrive on self-denial, and that's exactly what a budget demands: You must deny yourself the privileges you know you can afford.

That's not the biggest problem, though, because you should be able to buy, within reason, what you can afford—and most people do. The biggest problem is that you go out and buy what you can afford today . . . and then you go buy what you can afford tomorrow and next week and the week after that, too. Suddenly, when the month ends, everything you could afford has consumed everything you earned.

To make a budget work, you generally have to learn to deny yourself over and over and over again every day of every month. That $3 a day you save by skipping your morning Starbucks fix will amount to nearly $800 over the course of a year, if you can just muster the discipline. In many ways budgets, like diets, are about deprivation. Sure, it doesn't have to be that way, just as diets don't have to be only grapefruit and cottage cheese. Still, "doing without" is the general mind-set, and psychology plays a huge role in how we all deal with our money. Once you feel deprived of what you can afford—and what you want to treat yourself to—it won't be long before you chuck your budget completely to reclaim your money.

"Keeping a budget," says Andrea, a New York friend who refuses to follow one, "is just another set of rules that are no fun and that we'd really just prefer to ignore. People just don't want to feel constrained in any way."[3]

Thus, to me, budgets are useless.

. . .

To build the financial life you want, you do need to live within the framework of something budgetlike; otherwise, you lose track of your spending—never a good thing. The spending plan is my answer.

Here's the difference: A *budget* generally looks over your shoulder to base future spending on historic patterns—say, for example, the $388 a month Amy and I spent, on average, for groceries in the past year; a *spending plan* looks ahead to estimate spending on what you want to achieve, say, for example, no more than $400 a month on groceries. Yes, in large part that's just a game of semantics. But that's part of the point, because "words have a dramatic impact on how we react to things," says Denise.

Whereas a budget tells you how you're going to live your life, a spending plan lets you diagram the life you want to live. Essentially, you're in control and *you*, not your budget, make the choices. The upshot: You might really want that $3 Starbucks jolt every morning, and you're more than willing to cut $15 from your spending elsewhere just so you can begin every day well caffeinated. The result is that you're much more likely to stick to your plan because you're feeling no hardship. It's like dieting on everything you love to eat.

That doesn't mean you can have everything you desire. You have to choose what's important to your life. If you want to spend your money at Starbucks, then by all means you should do so—and the best part is that you can and still live within your plan. Just admit that Starbucks is your priority when you determine you want to take a vacation and you realize you don't have enough money saved to afford the trip you want.

By actually planning your spending each month, you can look ahead to the costs you have and the expenses you foresee. In doing that, you immediately see how your wants jibe with your monthly income. Since a spending plan isn't set in stone like a budget often is, you can reconfigure your plan on the fly each month to strive for some specific goal or need you have at the moment, and you can do so without screwing up the rest of your spending.

I detail the nuts and bolts of a spending plan in the Dollars & Sense section that follows. Let me share the basics really quickly. At the start of each month, Amy and I sit at the kitchen table and zip through a prepared list of potential expenses—everything from the mortgage to our son's allowance—filling in what our known costs will be and jotting down what we expect to pay for less certain items, like family meals out or extraneous expenses for our son or personal expenses during the workweek. We then match the total against the income we know we will generate for the month. If the costs are higher, we can systematically pare unnecessary expenses; if the income is higher, we have a target to aim for, money that we can shovel into our savings account at the end of the month.

What we most like about a spending plan, and what makes it so workable, is the flexibility we've gained. One month, for instance, we needed to buy $900 in airline tickets for a family trip to San Diego. The spending plan allowed us to pencil in the cost that month, actually making it easier to meet our goal because we consciously cut other unnecessary expenses. That seems trivial on the surface, but it has deep implications in terms of the way most budgets work. Previously, we would have simply gone about our life, more or less following our quasi budget, and bought the tickets along the way, only to realize at month's end that we not only spent what we normally spend, but also another $900 on top of that—blowing our budget yet again. With the spending plan we not only didn't blow the budget, we were able to save money and still afford the trip.

Friends of mine in Seattle, Jack and Colleen, have followed something similar to a spending plan for a couple of years. They began doing so just after Colleen left her job—a move that halved their income—to become a stay-at-home mom when their first daughter was born. Before the change in lifestyle, they tried to live within their budget, but routinely failed because they would do things like go to the grocery store and spend $50 on food for just a meal or two. A spending plan changed their focus because they realized that "a budget imposes limits, and no one likes limits," Jack says. "Our spending plan, though, gave us boundaries. It didn't tell us what we couldn't buy; it just allowed us to see the ramifications of what we wanted to buy so that we could make a better choice or make cuts elsewhere to get what we wanted."[4]

The big surprise, Jack says, is that "with Colleen at home, we figured there was no way we'd be able to live well on one income. What we found, though, is that we could afford to live on one income once we got into the pattern of using a spending plan." One of the benefits, Jack notes, is that in having month-to-month control of your spending, "you have a much better ability to chip away at any debt you have, and you can better budget for long-term savings because you plan for it each month."

In fact, Jack says their spending plan gave them such awareness about their money and what they choose to spend it on "that we realize we could have been in a much better financial position after all these years because of the spending we did without really paying attention to our budget. Our spending plan forced us to pay attention."

Dollars & Sense

Budgets take discipline, and that might just be their biggest wart. Most of us simply don't possess the kind of self-restraint necessary to follow a budget without feeling deprived and resenting it. For that reason, most budgets, like most diets, are doomed to fail. Sure, you might be principled for the first couple of months, but at some point you slip off the budget wagon and it's all downhill from there.

Take a hard look at the reasons why you continually fail to live according to the rules of your budget and I'll bet you find your rationale stems from a feeling that you should not have to deny yourself what you know you can afford. You don't like the sense that you're handcuffed financially, and you probably hate the self-loathing that often arrives at the end of the month when once again your spending has failed to track your budget.

Kill your budget. Instead, consider a spending plan.

People at first don't always catch on to the mind shift that separates spending plans from budgets, since both, essentially, seek the same end. Think about it this way: Does it make more sense to steer your life by looking through the front windshield to see where you're headed, or is it smarter to drive while looking in the rearview mirror? With a spending plan you're looking ahead to exactly what you *have* to spend money on this month, as well as what you *want* to spend money on this month. With a budget, you're looking over your shoulder at what you typically have spent money on in the past.

Just because you spent $219 a month last year eating out doesn't mean you have to budget for that going forward. You might determine one month that you're willing to skip the restaurants in favor of a weekend at the shore with friends. In managing your money proactively with a spending plan, you have far greater flexibility to swap one cost for another before the month even begins, effectively affording your fling by planning for it, working it into your spending for the month, and consciously avoiding other costs you know you can skip to make the trip possible without impacting your finances.

Consider how that same trip typically filters through the average budget: You know your weekend getaway will cost $200, so you set aside that money in your head and you figure you'll just work it through your budget by cutting out some other expenses along the way. Here's the problem: We humans have a wonderful ability to compartmentalize. Once you set aside that money mentally, to you it's already saved and ready to go. The result is that you generally spend as you normally would during any given month, and suddenly you've blown your budget without even recognizing it. When the trip arrives, you realize you don't have the cash you thought you had set aside, so you pull out a credit card to pay your costs, starting a whole new series of problems. Now you've thrust this month's outlay into next month's expenses, even though you've earmarked those funds next month for a new set of tires your car desperately needs. You see how quickly you can lose control of your budget, and you grow increasingly annoyed by it.

The reason it works this way is because we generally don't interact with our budget on a regular basis, meaning we lose touch with our money and where we're really spending all of our dollars. If you're like most people, you create your budget and monkey with it only if something dramatic happens to you financially. Perhaps your salary goes up or down or some major fixed cost changes—maybe you buy a new house or move to a more expensive apartment. You basically build a budget and then play with it only to get an idea of how some new arrangement impacts your cash flow.

A spending plan is all about continual interaction, and I don't mean that in a painstaking sense. I know people generally don't want to muck around with money constantly and would rather go about their lives. Still, just as you would tend to a garden to make sure it's not choked by weeds, you have to tend to your money to ensure your finances aren't choked by bloated spending patterns you might not even be aware of. Honestly, Amy and I spend less than 30 minutes a month, total, on our spending plan.

There are a number of ways to incorporate a spending plan into your life. Several books and systems exist, including *Money Minder*, by Karen McCall (www.financialrecovery.com), and *Couples and Money*, by Victoria Collins, a certified financial planner and a psychologist who employs a cash flow management system not unlike a spending plan.

You don't need to spend any cash, though, to create your own spending plan. With a little effort, you can build a plan of your own.

- The first step is to track your spending for one month. That means recording everything you spend money on, from the donut you buy on the way into the office to the book of stamps to your car payment. Everything. Log it all in a small notebook every day, or keep a basket into which you stuff every receipt for every expense. You'll need this to create customized categories for the costs you typically have.
- Don't edit your expenses during the month. Just spend as you normally would so that you can build an accurate profile of how money flows through your life. Once you've accumulated a month's worth of expenses, draw up a list of various categories they fall into. Be specific. Some expenses we all have: housing costs such as a mortgage or rent, groceries, electricity, telephone, water, clothing, haircuts. Others are more specific to your life: satellite TV; magazine subscriptions; breakfast, lunch, or dinner away from home; prescriptions; manicures; movie rentals; cell phones; car payments; school tuition; veterinary care; a weekly shoeshine. The list is long. Don't forget to include regular savings and investing, even if the amounts are small.

- On a spreadsheet or on several sheets of paper, list along the left margin major expense categories, such as Home, Food, Self-Care, Transportation, Entertainment, and so on. Then divide those into individual subcategories into which your dollars generally flow. (Under Home, for instance, you might have rent/mortgage, property taxes, electric, maintenance, phone, etc.) Alongside each expense category, pencil in what you expect to spend that month (and I highly recommend a pencil; I promise there will be lots of erasing early on). To the right of the categories, create four columns: "Week 1," "Week 2," "Week 3," "Week 4." Jot down under the appropriate week whatever you spend in a category. This gives you an instantly visible indication of where you stand. If you plan to spend just $300 on groceries one month and you see that by Week 3 you've already gobbled up $275 worth of chow, you know you're either spending too much on those supersized bags of double-stuff Oreos or you're underbudgeting a major cost in your life that you've not paid much attention to in the past. The weekly checklist gives you clear, immediate running commentary on your real costs for the month and allows you to better gauge how well you're following your own road map.
- At the bottom of the page, detail your expected income for the month.
- On a separate sheet of paper, tabulate all of your expected expenses for the month. To the degree that you can, look ahead to irregular and special expenses you know you'll have—for example, car insurance or a vacation—and factor a proportional amount into your costs for the month so that when the bill arrives you've got the cash to cover the cost. (The more you work with your spending plan, the better you'll be at planning those infrequent costs. If you really want to prepare, set the money aside in a special savings account that you tap just to pay for irregular, though known, expenses.)
- Add up all of your financial resources—basically, add to your expected income whatever amount of cash you have in your wallet and in your checking account at the moment. This represents the entire pot of money you have to spend for the month.
- Compare your projected expenses against your total resources for the month. If your expenses exceed your available money, you must rethink your spending. Cut back the extraneous costs for things you know you can live without. If you want to allocate that $15 to Starbucks, go for it; just cut that cost elsewhere, perhaps by reducing DVD rentals or restaurant meals. If you're income is greater, then earmark that money for savings or investments or paying down any debt you might have.
- At month's end, balance your actual costs against your projections to gauge how well you managed your money for the past 30 days. At the

same time, prepare next month's spending plan. It doesn't have to be identical to the previous month's; you may have a special expense in the upcoming month—airline tickets, for instance—so plan for it now by curtailing some other costs for one month.

Once you create your spending plan, strive to live with the boundaries you've set. Remember, there's fluidity to your plan. If you realize you're not going to spend $200 this month eating out, you can shift that money to some other expense you'd rather make, or just shovel it into savings for a later date.

If you find you can't stay within the plan, then you need to address that by taking a hard look at where you're spending your money and why. You'll begin to see patterns emerge. Maybe you go shopping on the weekends every time you get bored, ringing up purchases you otherwise don't need. You'll see exactly how you get yourself into debt through overspending in various categories.

For partners, a spending plan is a great tool for creating financial intimacy. The plan demands communication, since both partners must speak up for what they expect their expenses to be for the month. If when combined, your expenses exceed your dual income, "then you need to negotiate with each other to balance competing financial priorities," says Denise, who notes that a spending plan saved her from divorce. Her husband, she says, "has needs and wants that exceed our income by double or triple most months. My pattern has always been to hold back and have conversations with myself about my needs and wants, but never to verbalize them. I would build up a rosary of resentments in my head because he had so many needs and wants. What I learned from doing the spending plan is that so do I. It was my work to get them out, express them, tell him what I needed and wanted. When I started to do that, a shift occurred for both of us. This tool helps prevent conflicts in a relationship."

Now let me warn you: Initially, you might feel as though your spending plan is a budgetary prison by a different name. Give it a few months. You'll realize that it's all about financial freedom—you have the freedom to spend however you wish without any guilt because you've already given yourself permission to buy what you've planned for, and you know you can afford it without hurting your checkbook, your savings account, or your credit card.

Ultimately, you'll likely notice what Amy and I learned quickly once we axed our budget in favor of our spending plan: You gain greater peace of mind about your finances and greater control over your money.

Go out back right now and bludgeon your budget. It's useless.

CHAPTER 2

Are We What We Owe?

Controlling Debt

Ask a few friends and if they're candid you'll quickly realize that many people see debt as the communicable disease of personal finance. No one wants to catch it, so everyone is leery of getting too involved with someone who's got a bad case of it.

That's what my friend Debbie says she has faced for much of her adult life. Over lunch one afternoon, she and I were talking about her new job and small pay raise, when she divulged what she said was her biggest financial fear: "I'm concerned no one will marry me because of my debt."[1] Her obligation at that time was in the neighborhood of $20,000. Part of it stemmed from student loans, the rest the result of poor credit card management in the early years after college. Debbie lamented that, having moved into her thirties, "I should have $20,000 saved, not be on the opposite end." The trouble isn't in paying off the mound she owes; she pays that back to the degree she can each month. No, Debbie's dilemma is in coming clean when she finds a man she likes.

"With the people I date," Debbie says, "I hide my debt because I don't want to scare them off. Debt is almost like VD in a relationship; it's this dirty little secret in your life that you can't disclose until you have to."

Until that lunch, I'd never thought about debt so nihilistically. Debt is so visible, so easily obtained, and often such a necessary part of our lives when it comes to buying a home or a car that it seems a bit puzzling that debt could be perceived as such a stigma. Even in my own marriage I brought in more liabilities than assets—about $10,000 in combined car and computer loans—while my wife, Amy, brought all cash. As we were dashing to the altar, neither of us ever thought to discuss our finances, let alone debt. Indeed, after I recounted my lunch with Debbie, Amy told me that going into our marriage she saw the relationship as "a package deal. So we share everything."

That's the way it is for most people early on. Love conquers all and debt is rarely powerful enough to get in the way. Or so I thought.

On the ride back to the office that afternoon, I realized that Debbie's fears were worth pondering. Maybe I was too naive about my debt when I was still single. Maybe Amy should have taken a more critical view of my debt when we began dating instead of seeing it as just another element in the package. Maybe I should have taken a more critical view myself and initiated a discussion about my debt with her. At the very least, Amy probably should have known how much debt I was on the hook for, since it was sure to impact our life to some degree if we were to get married. My monthly obligations to the bank, after all, would preclude us from saving as much as we otherwise could have or spending on other things she might have wanted to pursue.

Debbie's fears raised an intriguing question I'd never pondered: *Are* we defined by what we owe?

Debt itself is not a problem. Debt, in fact, can be good. Debt provides the leverage we need to buy big-ticket items such as homes and cars. Otherwise, we're all on the 100 percent down, $0 a month payment plan, and if that's the case, then suddenly we're a nation of apartment dwellers all tooling around in used Yugos.

No one can argue that taking on a mortgage to buy an affordable home is unwise, since home ownership creates wealth over time. Likewise, you can't really argue against student loans, because the earning power created by an education will pay off the debt over time and generally provide better opportunities in life. Assuming some debt for a car makes sense, too, since a car provides the mobility to improve your life.

Debt makes substantially less sense when, for instance, you lease an auto to drive a status symbol that you could not afford with a traditional loan. The same goes for using gimmicky financing, such as principal-only loans and low-rate mortgages that adjust upward over time, so you can buy a bigger house in a better neighborhood. (Basically, if you ever find yourself employing financial hocus-pocus to fool your brain and your wallet into believing a purchase is affordable, a strong likelihood exists that you should probably be shopping elsewhere.)

The really big debt issue is consumer debt, the debt you collect on your credit cards. Such debt often indicates poor money management skills, because behind just about every mound of debt, you'll find lurking bad savings habits and habitual spending problems typically tied to a lack of self-discipline. Those are tough character traits to admit to, because at the core they represent a misguided sense of entitlement. You think you deserve this and that, so you buy this and that, and you rationalize your need to buy it *now*, maybe because it's on sale, which is certainly a sign from the gods that you should buy it, or maybe because you worked really hard this week (unlike everybody else in the workforce) and deserve a little treat. If you don't have cash, no worries; you can always whip out the plastic. All the while you're unfazed by the ramifications to your financial life, or if you are concerned, the ramifications aren't deterrent enough to alter your ways.

When you're single you can get away with spending foolishly—for a while at least—and not worry about accumulating debt, because you have to answer only to yourself, and, hey, you can always con yourself into believing you're worth every penny you spend on the consumer debris that makes you happy.

Here's the problem, though: The habits you establish while single are the habits that carry across into your relationships, and that's where "debt can get in the way of a budding romance," says Becky, a reader in Minnesota. Before she met her husband, Becky dated numerous men "who were in big, major debt." She says she "felt like a Sugar Mama to these guys." Those relationships died in short order, because, Becky says, "having made sacrifices to get my money, I felt like I would have to be the strong one in the relationship." Becky realized she wanted in a partner someone who could be her financial equal.[2]

Preparing for the future, and future relationships, is critical to your success with money when it comes to love. Being equal in terms of income is not a necessary prerequisite. Being equal in terms of outflow, though, is a necessity. By that I mean that you and your potential partner must be equal when it comes to knowing how much money flows out every month and where it's going. One person cannot act as financial gatekeeper while the other blithely accepts that everything is progressing smoothly just because he or she hasn't seen or heard about any problems. You want to avoid at all costs the possibility that hidden debt is a factor in your life. To prevent hidden debt (or any other hidden matters) from wrecking your life or your future life, your finances need to be as transparent as gin.

Gina, a woman I know in northern California, never talked much about finances with the man she ultimately married. Other than his penchant for eagerly paying for friends' meals and drinks at bars and restaurants, Gina didn't notice her guy's debtor ways. Once married, she figured he could easily manage the family's finances because, well, he managed millions of dollars in his budget at work. In that context, she figured, how difficult could it be to manage a relatively small family income?

An emergency several years into their marriage opened her eyes to a huge and hidden problem brewing in her life.

Gina lost the family checkbook. To thwart any potential thievery, she closed the account, opened a new one and contacted creditors to let them know of the change, too. That's when she learned that her husband had opened a dozen credit card accounts in his name. Nearly all were maxed out; many had cash advances taken out at high interest rates. Her husband had amassed a total of nearly $35,000 in credit card debt secretly. He was making only minimum payments on the bills. Worse, Gina learned, was that even though she had no authority to use any of the cards, never knew they existed, and had never signed for a single purchase, "I was responsible for half the debt."[3]

Because her name was not on any account, though, the creditors would not share any of the details with her about the spending patterns. Regardless of where the money went, Gina had to repay more than $17,000 for purchases she never made. The law mandated she pay.

In most states, creditors view debt as common property. If you or your spouse ring up huge amounts of debt, either openly or clandestinely, chances are high that you're both on the hook for paying it off, no matter who had a hand in accruing it. That's not so bad for wayward debtors; they get to skip out on half their purchases. You don't want to be on the raw end of that deal, paying for what you never bought. By the way, Gina shortly thereafter filed for divorce. The 18-year-old marriage "already was rocky," she says. The discovery of the hidden debt "had me reeling."

At some point in a relationship, circumstances force debt into the open, often in ways you never expect. In Gina's case, it was the lost checkbook, which she attributes to "a guardian angel making it so that I could discover the truth." With my friend Debbie, the truth emerged when a guy she was dating invited her on a diving trip to the Caribbean. Instead of hiding her reality, Debbie was honest and told the fellow that she couldn't afford the cost and, wisely, that she couldn't put the tab on her credit card because she already had too much debt to deal with. That revelation, brave in the context of a budding affair, nevertheless sealed the fate of that relationship. Debbie's frustration was that she wasn't looking for someone to step into her life and bail her out. "I'm capable of paying off my debt myself," she says. "If a guy wants to help, great. If he doesn't, great. I just want someone to come into my life and not worry about my debt."

We all like to think, as Debbie hopes, that in the intoxication of new love no one cares about credit card bills and overpriced auto leases and student loans and the sundry debt we accumulate. As my wife said, it's just a part of the package you accept when you're in love.

She's right; it *is* part of the package—and that's precisely the problem.

When the intoxication of new love fades and the realities of life set in, the debt that seemed a nonissue quickly can become a source of frustration and strain in a relationship. If you don't deal with it productively beforehand, especially if it's hidden, debt inevitably will shred your relationship.

There are ways of handling debt proactively. The most honest approach is to straightforwardly acknowledge that you have X amount of debt in your life and here's what it stems from. If you're ashamed because your debt is the by-product of an overdeveloped impulse to "just charge it," then you have to come clean with yourself and any potential partner in your life. You have to admit you have a spending problem, and then you have to confront it. You can hide assets in your life that no one will ever know about, but you can never hide debt; someone, the creditor, always knows what you owe, and at some point that debt will come out into the open in your life.

Christie, a longtime friend of mine, recalls that she and her boyfriend had been struggling with their relationship for years and began drifting apart. He was closed off and moody. She was "certain he was having an affair." When she could take no more, she confronted him. It turns out his sullenness had nothing to do with another woman and everything to do with the mountain of debt he had accumulated. Once that news was in the open, his worries began to fade, their relationship improved, and Christie was able to help him find ways to pare his debt. She helped him see that his problem was his credit card and thinking that he could live now and push the payment into the future.

"When you have a bunch of debt," Christie says, "this is how you think: 'I'm hungry; I can either go eat sushi or have Mexican. On a credit card piled up with $10,000 in debt, $70 is the same as $20, so I might as well eat what I really want, so let's have sushi.' You just don't realize how much that sort of mentality continues to destroy your ability to get out of debt."[4]

Certainly, debt doesn't destroy every life or every relationship. Yet debt, even in small amounts, breeds outsized aggravation.

Melissa, Amy's best friend since high school, started dating Mike in college. He was paying for his education partially through student loans, which amounted to about $5,000 by the time he graduated. In college, as singles, Mike's debt didn't mean anything to Melissa. It didn't impact her life; it was his issue, and his debt didn't affect her happiness with him. She never gave Mike's debt a second thought.

However, as I keep saying, debt has a way of sneaking up on your life.

Melissa ultimately married Mike. Suddenly, his debt meant a lot in her life. Melissa essentially became custodian of the debt shortly after they married. Mike decided to return to school to pursue an MBA full time and was no longer earning a paycheck to service his loans. The reality of Melissa's life became very different than her vision of it.

Her recollections of the period: "I'm getting up every morning to go to work and he's sleeping in, and I'm paying for his debt and his car and his gas and our apartment." In very short order, Melissa realized that a spouse's debt "becomes both of your responsibilities when you get married, and ultimately you both end up sacrificing. But I had a hard time with it, and I had some animosity about it all."[5]

The angst and resentment of that period is past, and Melissa certainly doesn't regret the marriage. Still, she says that having gone through the process, she realizes she should have thought more clearly back then about what taking on somebody else's debt really means. It means you, as a nondebtor, are now burdened by debt payments that affect your life. Even if you ultimately are not responsible for a penny of the payback, your partner might be unable to contribute as hoped to the relationship's finances because part of his or her salary is already earmarked every month for debt repayment. That could mean the two of you can't afford the things you otherwise looked forward to, perhaps a ritzy vacation once a year or the ability to save for a house as quickly as you'd like. You also may end up as de facto custodian, as Melissa did, when your spouse heads back to school or loses a job. In the worst case, you could find yourself in a situation like Gina's, where a partner with a spending problem racks up a bundle of debt on the sly, or even openly, and you're ultimately responsible for repaying thousands of dollars for which you never received any benefit.

Looking back on what she has learned, Melissa isn't sure she would enter another relationship involving meaningful debt. "I've worked too hard to deal with that, and I know what I want" out of life, she says. "I wouldn't want to risk not getting there because of my husband's financial obligations that I didn't create."

Based on Melissa's comment, I asked Amy: "If you were to go into a relationship today, would you marry a man in debt?" With years of postcollege life behind her, her answer is more complex now than "it's a package deal."

Amy wouldn't immediately dispatch such a relationship. Neither, though, would she submit to it without knowing substantially more about the source of the debt. Is the guy living a lifestyle beyond his means on the good graces of MasterCard? Does he have an unmanageable gambling habit? Is it, say, a med school loan and he's on his way to becoming an orthopedic surgeon? The answers to these questions play a big role in what ultimately may be expected of you, the partner without debt. Likewise, these are the questions a potential partner should be asking before committing his or her life to you, the person saddled with debt.

I asked myself the same question I asked Amy. After all, I was the beneficiary of a partner who willingly accepted my debt into her life and ultimately used her cash to pay off my bills. My immediate thought was that it wouldn't matter, that my affection for someone would pardon any concerns about her debt. I'd like to think that her debt is something that I could overlook or, at the very least, deal with constructively.

Yet, I'm not necessarily convinced I believe myself. Yes, debt is manageable, and two people committed to one another can handle it and eradicate it over time, just as Amy and I did. However, I see the issue a lot like Amy and Melissa do. There's a complexity to debt that two people should address before committing themselves to one another. No matter where you are in life, you have invested a lot to get there. I'm reticent to risk it all, to possibly be forced to start from scratch again financially if a new relationship failed, or if I were thrust into a debt situation that I knew nothing about and that I might be called on, by law, to remedy.

Ultimately, Debbie has reason to worry. For better or worse, we are what we owe.

Dollars & Sense

Debt may be a common theme in our lives today, but when you listen to the voices of people across the country, you hear the same refrain: The best way to come into a marriage is with both partners debt-free.

Denise, my friend who counsels people struggling with financial problems, notes that a number of financial behaviors can lead to debt trouble. These are key behaviors to keep an eye out for, either in yourself if you recognize you have debt issues or in your future partner:

- *Instant gratification.* Much of our consumer culture is built around the concept of "buy now, pay later." My mailbox is stuffed daily with credit card applications offering huge lines of credit, in addition to mailers and catalogs from a variety of merchants urging me to buy now—be it rugs, furniture, cars—and make no payments for nine months or a year. Such ploys seem enticing, almost like getting something for free, if only for a while. Yet in falling for such pitches and applying for more credit, you are chronically spending into the future. That's a road to increasing debt and, ultimately, increasing stress that leads to resentment in a relationship.

One solution: Live on the "buy now, pay now" plan. Pay cash for what you want to buy, and if you can't, then save until you can. The added benefit of this is that you often find that by the time you save the necessary funds, you don't want what you originally couldn't live without. If you really want this item, consider a three- to five-day grace period; if you still want it badly enough, reevaluate how you can save to afford it. If nothing else, keep in your wallet every credit card receipt you accumulate each month to remain up-to-date on how much you've rung up. Then pay off the bill in full when it comes in.

- *Poor money boundaries.* The example of this trait is going to dinner with friends, ordering a $10 meal that you can afford and then agreeing to split the tab equally among everyone because you don't want to appear cheap—even though your portion now amounts to $35. Or maybe you succumb to purchases you know you shouldn't make, usually on impulse and usually on credit. Chances are, you probably rationalize those purchases, too, convincing yourself that it's a great deal or that you deserve it. If so, debt problems await you, if they aren't already a part of your life.

One solution: Stay true to yourself and your wallet instead of going with the flow when you're out with friends. In general, create a monthly spending plan for both necessary costs and a reasonable amount of mad money, and abide by it. That will impose on you the financial boundaries that will force you to live within your means. The truth is, despite those clever marketing mavens at credit card companies, you really *can* leave home without your American Express, and not everything Visa can buy is priceless.

- *Seeking an emotional fix.* Sometimes spending has nothing to do with buying and everything to do with how you're feeling. If shopping or spending money helps you medicate some fear, anxiety, anger, or other emotion, there's a good chance you'll amass a tidy fortune of debt—or at the very least not save adequately—because of purchases you never wanted or needed in the first place.

One solution: Replace shopping with other activities, such as walking, athletics, working out, journaling your thoughts, or just calling a friend. Support groups exist to help understand, control, and redirect your underlying emotions.

Living within your means is at the core of the debt issue. However, for many people—men and women—living within your means is a lost art. Sometimes, debt, and I mean unsecured credit card debt, is simply about poor money management skills; more frequently, says my counselor friend Denise, "It's about something emotional."[6]

Solutions exist to help curb the urge to splurge, and some are really simple. Denise knows a woman who was shopping for flowers when she became so overcome by the beauty of orchids that she loaded up her cart with about $300 worth of plants. Instead of rushing to the checkout line, she wheeled around the store for another 20 minutes to ponder the expense and its effect on her finances. When she walked out, she was empty-handed—and proud to have demonstrated discipline over her money.

If you're in a relationship that's moving toward marriage, a good way for you and your partner to gauge one another's indebtedness is to examine each other's credit report. That might seem a bit offensive or even too private, but, look, you swap body fluids before you say I do; you should be willing to swap a couple pieces of paper that will give you peace of mind about each other's fiscal fitness. You can obtain copies of your own credit report online from web sites such as www.equifax.com or www.myfico.com. You'll pay a few dollars for the privilege, but it's worth the cost.

When you're dating, take a keen interest in how your potential mate handles money and, particularly, debt. That means paying attention to several indicators: How frequently does your partner pull out the credit card, and does the combined cost of the items exceed what seems reasonable for someone in that income bracket? Do you notice an abundance of spontaneous spending, particularly on credit? What emotions does your partner display when the credit card statement arrives? Agitation and frustration can be signs of stress over the inability to pay. Does your partner make only the minimum payments? Do several credit card bills arrive each month? If you can answer yes to a number of these questions, you must make sure you know how much debt your partner has and the plan for paying it off.

I know several women who have insisted that a fiancé extinguish his debt before agreeing to walk down the aisle. Becky, the reader in Minnesota, talked to her fiancé before their wedding to understand how he had gotten himself into debt and his plan for getting himself out. Together they set a goal that he would cut his debt in half by the wedding day, and he did. Shortly thereafter, Becky says, he was operating on a cash-only basis, and one morning told his wife that he "loves to wake up each day and not live paycheck to paycheck," as he had been doing before. "It was one of the sweetest things he has ever said to me," Becky says.[7]

Ultimately, to effectively control your debt requires that you know what you can afford and what you can't. More important, it requires that you know when *not* to buy what you can afford.

CHAPTER 3

Small Change Is Real Money

Managing Your Spending

Every morning on the way into the office, I pop into a deli to grab a Pepsi. I never think about this cost; it's only $1.40, sometimes $2.49 if I grab a croissant, too.

Yet that morning habit is a metaphor for something far larger than a cheap and unhealthy breakfast: It symbolizes the discretionary dollars we all blithely toss off and that are rarely factored into our spending. They're minor purchases—nothing on par with a mortgage or car note or electric bill—so we easily spend, figuring, why sweat small change?

Yet small change has a habit of becoming big dollars over time. The effects show up every month when you're sitting at the kitchen table, wading through credit card bills and bank statements and mumbling to yourself: Where did all the money go?

Controlling spending is one of the three key traits to improving your overall financial health. The other two—saving and a judicious use of debt—flow directly from an ability to keep your wallet closed. The problem tends to be that although you can see the hit you take to your pocketbook when you buy a new car or drop a bundle on clothes, you don't typically feel a similar impact when you spend a few bucks here and there on little things, like a soft drink or a movie or a magazine, even though this might be the tenth magazine you've bought in the past two weeks.

Fresh out of college, I earned $315 a week in my first job at a small newspaper in northeast Louisiana. I had no discretionary spending worries—mainly because I had few discretionary dollars to spend. I hewed tightly to the meager budget written in pencil and taped to my refrigerator door. Through the years, though, my family's budget has become increasingly intricate. No longer scrawled in pencil, I moved it to a spreadsheet painted in a rainbow of pastel colors that track all sorts of items. As mentioned in Chapter 1 it's pretty—but a bit meaningless. All it really does is catalog our income and fixed expenses and some routine variable costs. After that, the numbers grow hazy.

My problem is common. We all let the small expenses of our daily lives slip through the cracks because they're so easily forgotten. I certainly cannot remember what I bought last Thursday after I stopped by the ATM; all I know is that I found my wallet drained of cash a few days later and had to return for more. This lack of spending visibility escalates as our earning power accelerates, because with meatier paychecks the relative importance of smaller purchases shrinks even more. We grow to the point where we have little concern about withdrawing $20 from the money machine. At the supermarket, meanwhile, the 50-cent-per-pound difference between the boneless chicken and the bone-in brand seems meaningless in the moment. Yet these little costs spread across thousands of purchases in a given year add up to real money.

Few of us ever think about our spending on such a microscopic level, of course, because it's hard to envision these tiny costs in aggregate. Moreover, we hate to deny ourselves a small pleasure or convenience. That bag of chips with our deli sandwich is affordable, tangible, and immediate; the much larger items we might want—be it financial security or a screened-in porch for the house someday—are vague, years in the distance, and can't be bought a half dollar at a time.

Such small expenses, though, are precisely where our budget gets away from us. John, a reader of my Love & Money column in Rhode Island, knew vast amounts of outgoing dollars were draining his and his wife's finances. The couple had basically no money in the bank, despite having what he called "two substantial salaries, a cheap house, no credit card debt and only one fairly low car payment."[1] John is one of those Quicken junkies who, he says, tracks his spending "to a truly insane level of detail." Volumes of data covering a decade show that his family's discretionary spending amounted to more than $10,000 a year, leaving an annual net accumulation of cash of just $3,200, what he saw as a paltry sum, given the family's income.

John had been tracking the family's spending long enough to know he and his wife were wasting oodles of money. "But," he says, "we'd never been able to control the spending. It's easy to set up a budget that gives you N dollars to spend per month. It's much harder to stop spending when N dollars is reached in two weeks."

That's a universal frustration. We work hard for the money we earn, and we all want to enjoy to some degree the pleasures that money can buy. I've had conversations many times with my best friend, Jim, about his inability to save the amounts of money he's capable of saving and that he wants to save. His problem, as he always makes clear, is that "I don't want to live a dull life. I don't want to be a hermit in my home. You have to spend money to enjoy your life."[2] He does that well—buying nice furnishings, topflight electronics, landscpaping for his yard, and other items that give him enjoyment in some form.

At some point, though, you must look honestly at your income and your outflow and wonder why the two reconcile poorly, why you're spending so much, and why you can't save more. What prompts that inquisition could be any number of events, and they're often big, such as the birth of a child, the need to replace a car, the desire to buy a house. Suddenly you want answers.

A friend of mine at work hit that stage one day, a couple of years after the birth of their child and during a period in which she wanted to buy a home. She grew annoyed that she and her husband constantly blew their budget, no matter how hard they tried and despite fat salaries, so she sat down and keyed into a financial management program all their banking and credit card transactions and their earnings. What she found stunned her. Roughly 60 percent of their transactions streamed from one category: cash. "We were grabbing $20 here, $60 there from the ATM. Sometimes it was for items like groceries, but a lot was lunches and books and such." My friend saw that individual restaurant expenses, for instance, were enormous when lumped together. Individually, that $12 budget meal for two at a downscale Indian restaurant seemed cheap. Combine that with a dozen or more similarly cheap and not-so-cheap meals in a month, and all of a sudden their budget was hemorrhaging big dollars.

Equally surprising was where their money was *not* going. "We were spending absolutely nothing on clothes—and our wardrobes showed it," my friend says. "Because our budget was always so tight every month, we were underspending on things we really cared about." They had the money they needed to live the life they wanted. The money just was flowing into all the wrong places.

As an experiment, my friend and her husband agreed to a weekly cash allowance of $50 to cover whatever small, personal wants they might have: lunches, taxis, gifts, magazines. When the cash ran out, my friend says, "that was it until next week." The experiment worked. They stayed within their budget and got a handle on their spending. Knowing they had just the $50 allotment forced them to consider each purchase individually instead of thinking of it as just another small expense easily lost in their income. From this new perspective, they saw that the $10 cab ride home had a far more dramatic impact on their available money than they had previously thought. The smarter choice quickly became the $1.50 subway token.

They've relaxed their rule some, and they still squander cash on discretionary purchases at times, but they're confident the experiment helped them gain control of their budget and their overall spending. More important, their experiment is something everyone can try. For a couple of weeks, allot yourself a set amount of money, in cash, and spend just that amount. Do not hit the ATM if you blow your wad by Wednesday; this is exactly the sort of pain you need to feel to gain a better understanding of discretionary profligacy. You'll quickly realize how fast you throw money away on extraneous purchases and that you really do have choices. This is a simplistic example, but do you really need that Big Gulp when a smaller-sized fountain drink will just as easily quench your thirst? Do you have to be lazy and order takeout tonight when you have plenty of food at home you can prepare with just a modicum of effort? Heck, you probably even have half of last night's takeout still in its Styrofoam box in your fridge.

Playing this game for even a few weeks will help you regain control over your spending and give you a better sense of just where you're hemorrhaging money. That, in turn, will help you see areas where you can easily cut a little financial fat from your daily money diet.

Not all the money we throw away passes from our budgets unseen. Just as often, we're cognizant of the draining cash, but we either make no attempt to stanch the flow or we purposefully choose not to worry about it.

Another colleague of mine knows that because of his habits he tosses away money, but has never mustered the willpower to do anything about it. As an example, he says, he hasn't a clue how much chicken costs, or the price of milk or bread or any other grocery item—and, ironically, he does all the shopping for the family. It's not that he can blow money without a care or that he's cavalier with his finances. It's just that "these are things I'm going to buy anyway, no matter if it's $1.59 or $2.59," he says. "If I'm planning fish for dinner, I'll buy the fish, even if it's expensive that day. I don't pay attention."

Who does? I know I don't, and I do a lot of the shopping in my family. Can you say off the top of your head what the price difference is between the store-brand wheat bread and some upscale brand? What's the difference in price if you buy your milk at the supermarket versus the drugstore when you stop off to pick up a prescription? Yes, I know, these differences are just nickels and dimes, maybe a few quarters. But over time, pocket change really does add up to real money. For the heck of it, spend the next year emptying your pockets into a jar at night. I'll bet after 12 months you will have a couple hundred dollars or more worth of coins.

My friend is not oblivious to his actions in the supermarket. More important, he knows he has paid a high price through the years for his inattention. "Looking back," he says, "I'd have a lot more money right now if I hadn't paid the extra 50 cents over and over again." In part, he says, "the problem was that I never had some big tangible purchase I really wanted, other than paying for my children's education. I never yearned for that really expensive car, that month-long trip, that second home. My goal was more nebulous—financial security. And so I bought that extra newspaper every day, or the fish instead of the chicken, because it was much easier to get my arms around that than some lifestyle I might want in 25 years."

Lou, a reader in New York, shares a more philosophical view of it all: "Life is so fragile, we are tempted not to deny ourselves those small indulgences out of fear everything will end sooner than we planned." Lou looks back on many a fond memory of evenings out with friends spending too heavily on drink and revelry, indulging in too many shows while traveling in London. As a result, his bank account has gone nowhere, he concedes, "But my memories have appreciated all the same. As my late father often said, 'I don't want to die debt-free; it would mean I never lived, and enjoyed life, a bit above my means.' "[3]

Dollars & Sense

Whether you share Lou's view or the view of my frustrated friend who dissected her family's expenses, understanding and controlling discretionary spending is key to financial success. Otherwise, you will always make a hash of your finances, and you'll likely find yourself struggling to live on what is an otherwise adequate income. You'll fear not having enough money for your lifestyle, and you'll lament not having enough money to afford something you really need or want, like a new car or house. Stress will set in.

To curtail discretionary spending, try some financial exercises that will force you to see where you're spending money and make you think more clearly about the value of the purchase. Plugging your expenses into a financial program is a high-resolution way of tracking your spending precisely. Programs like Microsoft Money or Intuit's Quicken are the gold standards of personal finance software. Of course, you don't have to go that route. You can just as easily track your expenses with a computer spreadsheet or the tried-and-true method of pencil and paper.

Whatever path you pursue, tracking your expenses marks the first step in gaining crystal clear insight into where you spend your money and how. *How* is just as important as *how much*. You may see from your accounting that you're using your credit card to spend oodles of money on throwaway purchases like that midmorning, early afternoon, and drive-time latte fix. Switch to a cash-only basis and you'll quickly grow more reluctant to part with your cash, since actually letting go of those dollars is a completely different experience than signing your name to a piece of paper. Paying with cash "keeps us connected to our money," says Denise, my financial counselor friend, because "it connects our behavior (buying) with immediate consequences (less cash)."[4]

My friend's experiment of giving herself and her husband $50 a week is a great way to force yourself to live within self-imposed boundaries; you just have to remain committed to it or you'll be hitting the cash machine the minute your weekly allowance runs dry. If you do that, you've ruined the experiment and accomplished nothing.

I tried a similar experiment, allotting myself a $20 bill every day, including weekends. Each night, I dumped all the change and excess bills into a jar, money that I would put into a savings account at the end of three months. When the finish line arrived, I had accumulated in excess of $400 in my jar. By any stretch, that's not a killing, but the point is that I learned to live happily on much less money than I thought I needed, and I learned to be more judicious in examining whether I really needed what I thought I wanted.

If you just can't kick your credit card habit, or if your use your credit card to collect airline miles or for some other affinity program, then consider the approach of David, a Texan I know who lives in Toronto. When he and his wife are out and about and don't have the cash to cover a purchase, they unleash their credit card. To ensure that they have enough money at the end of the month to cover their bill, they write a check for the amount of the purchase when they return home, deducting the amount from their checkbook register. Then, at the end of each month, David sends to his credit card company 10 or 20 checks to pay off the balance in full. Sure, that's a lot of checks to write and reconcile, but the benefit is that his checkbook immediately feels the pain of every purchase, a surefire way to curtail spending.[5]

Another approach to curb your spending urge: the *moratorium month*. That's how Margaret and her late husband, a couple from California, gained the upper hand in their budget battle when other tactics failed to work. Once each quarter, they designated one month in which they purchased nothing but necessities and otherwise spent money only to pay the bills. With the moratorium in place, Margaret says, "We were not tempted by advertising, and our stress level dropped." They discovered, Margaret says, "that we were pleased with our discipline instead of disgruntled with ourselves for spending foolishly."[6]

Whenever they felt the urge to break the moratorium, they jotted down the enticing item so that they could consider buying it the following month. "We quickly found we seldom needed whatever was on the list," says Margaret, who continues to use the approach.

If nothing else, just admit to yourself you have a discretionary spending problem and learn to manage it by denying yourself some of the smallest purchases you otherwise wouldn't think twice about. Better yet, look for the root cause of your discretionary spending: Do you buy out of boredom? To make yourself happy when you're feeling blue? From habit? Spending may just be a way of medicating some underlying feeling you do not like. If that's the case, you need to seriously analyze your underlying feelings or discuss the matter with a counselor or financial psychologist. Either can help you better understand the triggers that prompt the behavior that is so destructive to your finances and help you reclaim control over your wallet. The Financial Planning Association (www.fpanet.org) and The National Association of Personal Financial Advisors (www.napfa.org) provide web sites that allow you to search for financial professionals in your area. Talk to a few to find out if they can help or if they know of anyone in your area who deals with the psychology of money.

Along with curbing your spending, set up a savings plan in which you pay yourself first. Sign up with your bank or your employer's credit union so that some sliver of your income is pulled out of your salary before your paycheck ever reaches your hands. You'll never miss the money, and your brain will see that you have less to spend, thus helping to stifle your indulgence. This is important: Save something—anything. Just save, regardless of how much it is at the beginning.

Ultimately, how much you save should correspond to how much you need for periodic payments such as car insurance, property taxes, and such; how much you need in your emergency account; and how much you need to invest for the future. Most guidebooks counsel saving 10 percent of your pay. Some suggest more. Maybe you can do that; maybe you feel you can't. Go with what's comfortable for your budget at first, but go with *something,* even if it's just 1 percent. Truthfully, you'll need to save far more than 10 percent a year to build an adequate nest egg, but start with what you can.

Along the way, adjust the savings upward periodically, once a quarter or twice a year, by consciously examining your discretionary spending patterns over the previous several months. Find the items you can live without and increase your automatic savings by that amount. The dollars you save never seem like much, but they grow over time if you just ignore them. Avoid one iced latte each week at $3.50 a pop, and that's $182 a year, or more than $2,000 in a decade, at perhaps 5 percent interest. Find four or five or more such expenses per week that you can ax from the budget, and you're talking about numbers that begin to make a difference in your passbook.

Once you have control of your spending, you'll gain greater insight into how the purchases you choose to make affect your pocketbook.

CHAPTER 4

Emergency Savings

Preparing for the Unexpected Costs of Life

A thousand financial planners can be wrong.

According to conventional wisdom, you should have, stashed away at this very moment, an emergency savings account equal to six months of household expenses—money you can quickly tap during a financial catastrophe, should one happen to befall your family. Six months is the very least; some money pros insist that eight or nine months is an even better cushion.

In the religion of personal finance, this is one of those canons that every planner, columnist, book writer, and TV talk-show host preaches about constantly—one of the thou-shalt rules you're supposed to obey every day.

You might as well call me a heathen.

The funds I've set aside in my official emergency savings account don't even come close to meeting this rule. The emergency account traditionally has equaled roughly three months' worth of our expenses, and that's just for the barest of necessities such as the mortgage, utilities, insurance, food, car notes, and whatnot. In reality, other expenses should be included in the mix, such as gas for the car, replacement clothes, and such.

Still, to me, six months of those expenses—more than $25,000, for us on the bare-bones plan—is simply an irrational sum of money to stuff into an account that yields essentially nothing. To some, though, it's not the yield or rationality that matters; it's the sense of safety.

Divergent views about something as simple as a savings account reflect a fundamental disagreement people often face when it comes to how flexible money needs to be and where their emergency money ultimately should be held. I think you should err on the side of growing your pot of dollars to build the largest safety net possible for the future, when having enough money to live until you run out of air is paramount. For that reason, emergency money in my world should be split so that a smallish portion is readily accessible in a savings account, in case you do need it, while the bulk of it should be invested prudently.

For many other people, prudence means safety. And safety means a more-than-adequate supply of money should be within immediate reach, even if you never need it. Indeed, Amy speaks for that segment of the population when she routinely reminds me that back in our younger days I used to tell her that six months was the rule and that we needed to save that amount to be safe.

She's right. I did say that. I believed it, too. Now I don't. Despite conventional wisdom, this is a rule that was made to be broken.

Every family, without question, needs a rainy-day fund to cover expenses for almost-certain predicaments—such as the morning I walked into the basement to find three inches of water where a dry concrete floor should be. Our relatively new water heater had sprung a leak. Replacing it cost more than $1,000. Then there was the emergency need to replace my beloved Miata, which one morning decided to call it quits after a dozen years and more than 180,000 miles. The savings account covered the down payment for a base-model Jeep.

These are the sorts of unexpected expenses that largely represent why savings accounts exist. Savings keep you from relying heavily on debt. Savings also are the key defense in a major financial crisis, be it the loss of a job, a medical ailment, extensive storm damage to your home, or some such similar calamity.

There's no reason, though, that savings should be the entire defense. By stuffing your savings account with six months or more of expenses, you are essentially self-insuring against the absolute worst-case scenario, even though the absolute worst-case scenario is a fairly rare occurrence for most, though certainly not all, families. In doing so, you're tying up a bundle of cash that could be working much harder to make your life much easier later on, and that isn't so prudent.

Yet prudence, it turns out, isn't the sole determinant in this debate. One of the biggest factors weighing on your savings account is that immeasurable feeling of security. Laura, a friend of mine in New Mexico, found out just how reassuring that feeling can be when her husband's company shut down, necessitating a cross-country move for his new job. They bought a house in the new city before selling their previous home, only to learn that the slump that killed his old job also killed the housing market where they formerly lived. For 15 months they were stuck with two mortgage payments, a burden that would have crushed many families.

"Because we kept that emergency fund available," Laura says, "we were able to cover things without too much pain." A vital lesson she says she learned was that "having an emergency fund is absolutely critical." At the time, she knew other people who also lost jobs but who didn't have a financial backstop for support. "And they were really, really hurting," Laura says. "I spent a pretty miserable 15 months, because I was not able to save anything and we couldn't afford to do things like take a vacation, but at least we didn't have to cash out our retirement accounts or college fund just to eat."[1]

Such self-insurance is precisely the point to many people. Stan, a reader in Colorado, says that setting aside money for life's emergencies "should be considered a very low cost insurance" plan.[2] The downside risk of not setting aside enough money for an emergency "is much greater than the upside of any investment" that allows your capital to grow. Since no one is very good at predicting the future, Stan says, "We really have little choice but to put the appropriate amount of money aside and be satisfied with the security it represents."

That's exactly how Amy feels about what she sees as our underfunded emergency account. She would much prefer that we had the full board covered and then some. "I've always wanted to know we have $30,000 in our savings account," she told me one day after I finished balancing the savings account register and announced to her matter-of-factly that we had exactly $15,401.99. That sum was much too small for her liking, she told me, a comment that blindsided me; until that particular moment, she'd never before uttered any displeasure with the size of our savings. When I asked why she felt that way, she recalled that when we were newlyweds we constantly were "trying so hard to get to $10,000. Every time we hit that mark something would happen and we'd have to cover a big car insurance payment or medical bills, and we kept struggling to stay above the mark. I didn't like that. I want an amount of money that makes me feel secure about our ability to pay for whatever comes up." For her, $30,000 was a number that "in my mind says our account is 'solid and accessible.'"

I don't disagree with her logic or her desire to feel secure financially. Where we differ is in how we achieve that.

Essentially, there are just two places to put your money—assuming you consider a shoebox beneath your mattress a bit impractical. You can stick it in a bank or in an investment of some sort, be it stocks, bonds, Persian rugs, or whatnot.

For Amy, the only security comes in knowing her money is tucked away inside a rock-solid bank. She's always been a savings account girl, likely because her mom works for a credit union and because Amy spent several teenage summers working there as a teller. "We won't lose money in the bank," she insists. "In a bank, it's safe."

Of course it's safe.

It will lose money, though—to inflation.

Inflation, I know, is a nebulous concept for lots of people, since you rarely see the effects on a day-by-day basis. After all, you put a dollar in a savings account today, and, voilà, you get back more than a dollar in the future. Safe and secure. Still, your money loses value because that dollar plus change this year can't buy what that single dollar bought last year. Over the course of the past year, that lost value is pretty meaningless, because, as I write this in mid-2003, inflation is at dramatically low levels. Over many years, though, you can see the damage.

If you'd stuck $100 in the average savings account at the beginning of 1990 and rode it through till the end of 2002, your account would have grown to $138.06, according to some calculations I had Bankrate.com do for me. Not bad; your savings expanded and your money was safe. Yet look at the difference in the cost of living over that same period. The $100 worth of consumer goods you bought in 1990 cost $143.91 at the end of 2002. Sure, that's only a $5 or $6 gap, but multiply that gap over the many thousands of dollars you spend in a given year, and suddenly you're talking about a gulf, not a gap.

Your money lost purchasing power, so you lost money. The big caveat as I write this is the specter of *deflation*, or generally falling prices. Though that risk remains smallish, it remains a risk nonetheless. In such a world, cash is crucial, yet even here the best option is investments, in this case U.S. government bonds maturing far into the future. For those who care about the reasons, I'm going to get technical for a moment. If you don't care, I encourage you to skip down two paragraphs right about now. *Long bonds*, as they're called, pay the highest interest rates, and those rates don't change. In deflationary times, prices for the everyday goods we buy tumble. That's not so bad, but the potential downside is that your income may fall, too—one of the nastier by-products of deflation, arising because employers can't raise prices, so to remain competitive, or alive, they instead cut costs, such as your salary.

In such a world, the relative value of long-bond interest payments increases because they are stable and increasing in worth. Suppose you receive a $1,000 interest check every six months. In one period, that $1,000 might buy exactly $1,000 worth of goods and services that you consume. As prices continue tumbling, the next $1,000 payment might buy goods and services that before would have cost $1,010. The next time around, it might be up to $1,025. Thus, over time, those stable bond payments afford you a better lifestyle. As an added benefit, the price of the bond escalates, since the stream of payments stretching out for many years becomes more valuable to investors who, in a deflationary world, could be looking at interest rates on savings accounts and certificates of deposit languishing somewhere near 0 percent. Now, back to the program. . . .

Whatever the scenario, this philosophy of holding investments versus savings accounts reflects something Dave, a friend of mine in Fort Worth who manages money for a living, once told me. It's something his grandmother instilled in him: A dollar at work is better than a man at work. Putting your money to work where it will lose ground to the cost of living over time certainly won't help meet bigger financial goals you have for yourself and your kids.

All of that, though, is the logical argument. More often, personal finance reflects emotions.

"You're hamburger if you touch it." That's what Carol, a woman I know, told her husband when he complained that the money in their emergency fund was not earning any return. Who cares about the return, Carol replied. "It's earning peace of mind."[3]

Peace of mind generally is at the crux of this debate. I have peace of mind, largely because I know Amy and I could easily cover more than six months of expenses if we had to. Most of the cash we'd need, though, is in an investment account, where the probability of growing our money is substantially greater. Certainly, there's a risk to that approach, and if an emergency ever arises we might have to sell investments at a bad time, taking losses we don't want to take or profits that increase our taxes. I'm willing to take that gamble, though, because the odds are in our favor. To me, three months' worth of expenses is fine in a savings account; the rest we can pull from investments if we ever need to.

Still, Amy doesn't have peace of mind, and she isn't altogether pleased that the biggest chunk of our emergency funds rests on the fate of companies that, as history has shown numerous times, often don't play by the rules themselves. I can appreciate that. While I felt secure with $15,401.99, she didn't.

The only way to address her concern, to set our account so that we both feel okay with our emergency cash, was to work toward some mutually acceptable middle ground. I explained my view, which she understood; she explained her view, which I understood. The only solution we could think of was to systematically increase our savings to $20,000 over several months. That's less than Amy wants and more than I want. We both agreed, though, after looking at our overall investments, that this was a number we could both live with.

Maybe you don't need to break rules, after all. Maybe the truth is that you just bend them to fit everyone's needs.

Dollars & Sense

Before you do anything with your money, you have to differentiate between an emergency expense and a predictable, though irregular, expense. In all honesty, the down payment on my Jeep was not an emergency expense, despite the fact that we had to treat it that way. True, it arose unexpectedly that particular morning, necessitating the emergency, but the reality is that I should have been preparing all along to replace a 12-year-old car with 180,000 miles on the odometer. (This was my beloved Miata, however, and I couldn't fathom anything bad ever befalling her.)

By the same measure, you really should prepare for all those irregular, periodic expenses you know will come up during the year:

- Car and homeowner's insurance
- Property taxes
- Health care deductibles
- Vacations
- Holiday gifts
- Car registration
- New tires
- Any special event you know is in the offing

If you want to be really anal about it, wander around your house making note of the big-ticket items that are aging and likely to require repairs or replacement in the not-too-distant future, like the water heater, air conditioner, carpet or floors, the dishwasher, even the shingles on the roof. Maybe even dying, overgrown, or just plain ugly landscaping you're itching to ax.

I remember when I was really young my grandmother saved money in a Christmas club account at her bank. Your periodic account is no different. Save for these expected costs with every paycheck—because you know they're on the way—and the money you accumulate will keep you from unholstering your credit card when those costs arise.

You should expect that what goes into this account will come out relatively quickly, usually over the course of a year, but possibly longer if you factor into the equation a new car several years out. At the very least, plan for periodic expenses 12 months in advance. That way, your $600 car insurance premium doesn't erupt onto your life as an emergency cost you must scramble to meet.

A true emergency account exists specifically to cover those events you simply cannot predict, such as losing a job or an urgent medical issue. This money goes in, you don't touch it, and you hope you never need to, at least not for an emergency. Basically, it's your security blanket.

Where you save and how much you save are the big issues. No simple answers exist.

Where is based on your own comfort level. You can park all of your emergency savings in a relatively low yielding bank account if you fear the possibility of losing even a penny of it. If you're a heathen like me, you stick a good chunk of it in an investment account (if you're comfortable with a mix of stocks and bonds) that you can easily convert into cash. Most certainly, you don't want any part of an emergency fund locked up in investments that you cannot readily turn into dollars. This would include investments such as art, baseball cards, collectible cars, and whatnot. You could end up having to dump such assets at a fat discount, and it could take months to sell such items—assuming you can find a buyer.

Even stocks and bonds can take at least a day to sell, and you may need money quicker than that, or you may not want to sell just yet. Consequently, some portion of your rainy-day money should be cash that you can tap before you hit up your investments. If you want to take a stab at topping inflation with your cash, or at least running level with it, consider stashing most of your cash in a money market account in cyberspace, at an online bank such as ING Direct or National InterBank. Such virtual banks have substantially lower costs and thus provide plumper interest rates, often several percentage points higher than your local banker pays. These online banks are backed by the same federal guarantees as the neighborhood branch down the street, so they're safe. You can find such banks in large numbers through any search engine. Easier still, try Bankrate.com.

I say "most of your cash" because, like stocks, dollars in these banks can take a couple days to access. In a real emergency, you want money immediately—like, in the next 15 minutes. So keep some portion of your cash in a boring savings account down the street that you can raid via ATM at any time of the day or night, if needed. The return will be paltry, but you can retrieve your money immediately—always a benefit when a true emergency springs up.

How much you save is, again, a function of personal preference. I'm fine with three months of emergency cash; Amy wants many months more. If you're single, six-months of expenses is a sound starting point since you don't have a partner's income to rely on in bad times. Laura, my New Mexico friend with experience in relying on her family's emergency fund, says six months is too conservative for a two-income household "because it presumes you both lose your jobs at the same time," an unlikely occurrence unless you both work for the same employer or are in the same or similar industries—in which case six months remains a good rule of thumb. If you're not in that situation, though, it makes more sense, Laura says, to cover the portion of your mandatory expenses, whatever you determine they are, that otherwise would come from the highest-paid partner's paycheck.

"That way, you know you're covered," Laura says, "but you're not foregoing too much possible future growth."

Whether you're a believer or a heathen, no matter how you view an emergency savings account, you need to look beyond the issues of return and the growth of your dollars. As I learned with Amy, sometimes money isn't about money at all. Sometimes, it's about that comforting sense of security that money brings, the peace of mind in knowing that, come what may, you're capable of fending for yourself and providing for your family.

STAGE TWO

The Early Years

Building a Life Together

"I love you."

Those three words promise to have the most dramatic effect on your personal finances. Whether the impact is ultimately beneficial or detrimental to your financial health is almost irrelevant. Rather, the point is that most of us just never consider money to begin with when it comes to falling in love. That's a problem.

Love never measures any of us by the size of our wallets. Love just happens, regardless of money. Indeed, many of us insist that money plays no part in the decision to follow our heart.

Of course, insisting it's so does not necessarily make it so. For in truth, love and money do mesh—all too well. Money plays a huge role in our lives and in our relationships. It's there every day when we pay the bills, hit the ATM for cash, plan a vacation, buy groceries on credit, pay our kids an allowance, shop for a house, assume debt to buy a car, consider private versus public schooling, eat out at a restaurant, invest for our retirement, plan our kid's birthday party, shop for Christmas presents, purchase gas on a debit card, go online to buy a book, or just balance the checkbook. Many of these seem like simple and mundane money chores—certainly not the sorts of money matters that lead to financial woes. To some degree, they *are* simple and mundane. I guarantee, though, that mundane money matters can—and will—morph into nasty financial flare-ups in your family at some point.

That's Stage Two—recognizing as you build a life together how and where love and money coexist and clash. Unless you've found a perfect clone of yourself, you most assuredly will find that you and your partner frequently do not see money and its uses in the same way. There's nothing necessarily wrong with this. It's just life. We're all different people. The challenges of Stage Two, however, come in understanding that those differences exist, then learning to manage the differences so that the inevitable flare-ups don't rip at the relationship. The patterns established early in this stage play a continuing role in later stages—for better or worse.

It all springs from a basic question: Are we financially compatible?

Few of us stop to consider this question when we hook up with our partners. We're compatible in all the big ways; that's why we're in love. Money is something we can work out along the way.

If only it were so simple. You may see nothing wrong, for instance, with piling purchases onto a credit card every month instead of writing checks or using cash for every expense. Your spouse, however, may flip out over that tactic, concerned that the family's spending is way out of control. After months of seeing the credit card bill hit the mailbox with a fat "amount due," there's a good chance a money fight is going to shake the walls of your home. If you don't deal with the root cause of this concern—a spouse's emotional worry about losing control over the family's spending—the disagreements will soon shake the walls of the relationship.

This notion of compatibility plays out in numerous ways in every relationship, and not everyone experiences the same tensions. Some, though, are nearly universal, such as the debate over whether to open joint financial accounts or to continue to manage your money individually. This is almost always one of the first financial roadblocks couples confront. On the surface, joint versus individual accounts may seem purely a matter of logistics, but lurking just beneath the surface are an abundance of psychological pressure points, not the least of which is fear of relinquishing control over one of the last vestiges of our independence. Successfully managing this debate may take years, as it did with me and Amy, because the underlying fears and emotions typically don't bubble to the surface in the discussions and arguments that arise. Yet these emotions ultimately have far more to do with merging our accounts than logic ever will.

Even then, merging accounts isn't without its flaws. Joint accounts are a breeding ground for one of the sneakiest money cons we perpetrate against one another: the money-laundering gambit. Few of us would consider ourselves money launderers. That's the province of the superwealthy trying to hide dollars offshore. We're guilty of it, too, though, on a more personal, less grand scale. If you've ever written a check at the grocery store for more than the amount of the purchase to retrieve a few extra dollars for your personal wants without your partner knowing, you are a money launderer. Many of us employ tiny deceits like this one and others to boost the cash in our pocket to spend on wants that we know are likely to provoke the disapproval of our partners. At the most basic level, that's stealing, not just from your partner but from the life you're trying to build together. You're also lying to the person you love about the real cost of your life. Sure, it's just a few bucks here and there, but you can't build together the life you ultimately seek if you're both surreptitiously snagging a few bucks here and there, because in the process you're undermining the family's joint goals. When you fail to achieve those goals as hoped for, the frustrations set in.

A more insidious impediment to a relationship is the question of whether a fatter paycheck bestows special privileges on the spouse who earns it. We all like to believe that marriage is a partnership of equals, and that therefore neither partner holds greater financial sway. While most people concede that fact, they don't necessarily practice it. Husbands and wives often assume, even if unconsciously, that a bigger paycheck gives them greater voice in financial decisions or absolves them of household drudgery since they frequently feel they're already giving at the office by providing the most to support the family financially. The result is that pay disparity can become a divisive issue in your personal life, leading to frustrations and feelings of financial subjugation. The biggest problem is that it happens silently, because the lower-paid partner is often reticent to voice his or her concerns for a variety of reasons.

No one can be blamed for overlooking any of these issues. They're difficult to recognize, touchy to deal with once you see them, and often ill explained by the spouse who is feeling shortchanged. The trick comes in recognizing where they exist in your life, or where they have the potential to exist, so that you can effectively address them before they do permanent damage.

We rush headlong into a relationship when we fall in love. In doing so, love blinds us to many things, and money is one of them. Fail to address it, sweep it under the rug, and assume everything will work out in the end— and there's a fair chance money will gnaw at the bonds of your relationship.

Terry, a guy I know in southern California, made the mistake of not considering money when he married his first wife. By nature, he was a saver and she was a spender. Over their five-year marriage they managed to save $20,000, but "it was a Battle Royale all the way," Terry says.[1]

After five years, one daughter, three paid-for cars, a three-bedroom house, not a dime of debt "and numerous money battles, I gave up the fight and divorced her," Terry says. "It wasn't the sex, lack of money, or any of those other things touted as 'marriage breakers.' It was all about the handling of money. I'm not saying either of us was 'right,' only different. Had we looked hard at the differences before marrying in the first place, it could have saved us both a lot of pain."

CHAPTER 5

Speak Now or . . . Forever You'll Regret It

Gauging Financial Compatibility

When I proposed to Amy nearly a dozen years ago in front of a diamond merchant in the Los Angeles jewelry district, the only financial thought on my mind was the cost of the ring on her finger. I had no clue if we were financially compatible. Nor did she. Really, who thinks about that?

Time has proven us lucky. After more than a decade of marriage we've found that we're generally compatible when it comes to money. Without a doubt, numerous financial affairs have cropped up through the years on which we've differed, sometimes vociferously. Even now it's no different. Issues still arise on which we just don't agree. Fortunately, we both share a similar vision for what we seek from our money overall, what we want in life, where we're going, and how we plan to get there. Differences aside, we're both generally diligent at working toward united goals.

That's not always the case when it comes to relationships—often to the surprise of each spouse. Despite good intentions, you might find years into your marriage that you and your spouse just aren't on the same page financially. Big wants and needs diverge. Saving and spending priorities differ. In such instances, compromise can be impossible to find, and what seemed a perfect union suddenly resembles an unbridgeable void that, in time, can turn a relationship into a financial train wreck. Out of frustration, maybe even spite, you both abandon the financial discipline you once lived by and instead seek to fulfill individual wants at the expense of joint priorities. All the while your money woes and worries grow. Frustrations mount. Fights erupt. Once you're consumed in it, it can be impossible to see any way out. Your life degenerates because the financial compatibilities neither of you considered early on have arrived nonetheless to torment your life seemingly every day and seemingly in every way.

While this destruction seems to happen all at once, if you look back across the years you'll usually see that there were warning signs aplenty. Still, the toughest part of it all is that it's all so tough to anticipate at the beginning.

When you decide to partner with a mate, you think you both know each other pretty well at that point. You feel intimately connected because in many ways you are. Maybe love bloomed one night in a cooking class when you both reached for that last éclair after the pastry lecture. Or maybe you found each other in the library checking out similar books on grow-your-own bonsai. Whatever the case, you found a fast fondness that pulled you two together.

As you progressed through your courtship, all the pieces just seemed to fall so naturally into place. You both love Bogart movies and hate tomatoes. Neither of you have a clue what Bob Dylan is really singing, so you just make up the lyrics together. You want many of the same things out of life and you agree on all that big stuff—religion, work, ethics, family, and children. Basically, you're looking at each other and thinking, "Oh, yeah, we're perfect . . . or at least as perfect as we're likely to find."

What, though, of money?

More often than not, we couples are clueless when it comes to knowing whether we mesh financially, or at least we are willing to play blind and hope it all works out in the end. With so much else in common, I mean, really, why worry about money? Everyone knows love and money don't mix, and even if they do just a little, we're certainly not about to let a few dollars or a little debt get in the way of a really good romance.

Glenn, a reader in Rhode Island, says that what saved his marriage—in the early years, at least—was the solid base of assets he had built before the wedding and a constant string of promotions and subsequent pay raises through the years that allowed him and his wife to paper over their differences. Yet they never resolved their underlying stresses.

"When we divorced, for this and other reasons, we divided assets, including all that I had before we ever married," Glenn says.[1] Their problem, he later saw, was that "I was mostly a saver and investor; she was much more 'live for the moment; the future will take care of itself.' "

Glenn's experience is perfect proof that if you and your spouse start off on different tracks when it comes to spending and saving, then soon enough you're miles apart from one another and each chugging in the wrong direction. What's more, even if you *think* you're compatible about money when you marry, that very well may change over time. The people we are at 25 are not the people we become at 35 or 45. As new opportunities and challenges arrive, as our income changes, as children invade our lives, we face new prospects and new hurdles, and we see our life in a different light. You might stumble into an opportunity to work overseas, a possibility you two thought would be a blast when you dreamed about it as newlyweds. You're still game, but suddenly your partner envisions settling down, a little house, the white picket fence, and a dog. A small apartment in Europe holds about as much interest as stubbing a toe.

These changes we all go through ultimately exert pressure on our finances and our relationships, and not always for the better. Indeed, it's these pressures you hear about all the time when you read that money is a leading cause of divorce. Every personal finance magazine ever written has mentioned that at some point. Newspaper articles about personal finance and personal relationships routinely drill this little proverb into our heads. The notion is so common that it's a widely accepted part of American culture, the proof everyone throws around in saying, "See, I told you; love and money don't go together."

Boy, if it were only true. . . .

The fact is, divorce records simply don't track why couples split apart, and academic research refutes what most folks have been taught to believe. A 2001 study by a California State University Sacramento professor concluded that, contrary to popular belief, money troubles are essentially useless predictors of divorce. Instead, finances play a minor role among all the factors that influence any individual divorce—at best just 5 percent of the mix, and more typically 1 percent or less.[2] In fact, rarely does money rank higher than fourth or fifth on the scale of leading causes of divorce. (For the record, incompatibility, sexual problems, lack of emotional support, and abuse typically rank much higher than money when it comes to the rationale for a divorce, according to the study.)

That's not to say money is a nonissue or that financial problems never lead to divorce. Of course they do, on occasion. Less rigorous surveys and popular opinion polls by financial firms and magazines continue to insist that money remains a leading cause of divorce. That's fine, because what these surveys really show is that money most certainly causes friction in a relationship. It may well be that couples are quick to blame money—a convenient bogeyman—because money is a socially acceptable reason to split apart. Moreover, dollars and cents are just easier to fight about because they're tangible, not squishy like all those emotional issues that really underlie the tensions in your relationship.

"My experience has shown me that couples really want to be on the same page and even have similar goals," says Denise, my counselor friend.

The real hurdle, though, is that "many of us are just uncomfortable with looking at our relationships in terms of money," Denise says. "If we don't examine how we relate to our money, we don't have to face ourselves honestly. But there's no freedom in ignorance."[3] That's when you derail.

I know too well this feeling of derailing. At one point, Amy and I moved to Seattle for my job. Up until that move, we felt we were paddling more or less in the same direction, in terms of both our relationship and our finances. We were saving for the same goals and spending on joint priorities. In moving to a new city, she wanted to concentrate on building her nest—painting the interior and exterior of the house we bought, replacing the carpet, buying new furnishings. Before pursuing other expenses, she wanted to make someone else's former home feel like her own so that she could settle in and be comfortable in a new part of the world. That's understandable.

However, I wasn't much interested in nest building and didn't know when I would be. The house was fine by me. I was in this new part of the world, and I wanted to use our money to explore. I came home every night talking up trips to Asia and Alaska and drives through the Pacific Northwest I wanted us to take during long weekends. She talked about color swatches.

Neither of us saw this divide coming when we began planning our life so many years ago. Yet here it was, our fundamental problem: She didn't want what I wanted; I didn't want what she wanted. Frustrated that we didn't share each other's view, we failed at finding the words to talk about any of it. Instead, we papered over the chasm through avoidance. Ultimately, that strain spilled over into other areas of our life. We struggled through a trying period. We fought. We grew apart.

When my friend at work, Michelle, announced her engagement, I asked whether she and her fiancé, Greg, were financially compatible. Granted, this is not a question most folks generally pose to someone getting married, but Michelle is a financial writer as well, so I was curious about whether talking to money pros every day encouraged her to think about financial issues in her own life.

She didn't know the answer. Aside from the cost of the pending wedding, her only financial concern, she said, was "figuring out how to handle our checking accounts." Like most couples, she and Greg hadn't really discussed "the other stuff," she said.[4]

That other stuff, though, sits at the core of so many disputes, given that we're supposedly compatible in the other areas of our life. Indeed, the future seeds of potential financial conflict were already apparent in Michelle's life.

Michelle is a saver; Greg, she says, "would rather spend his money than have it just sitting there." That happens to be the single biggest stress point for couples: A saver hooks up with a spender. Consider this: The Association of Bridal Consultants reported in a 2000 survey that 67 percent of couples say that spending is the most serious conflict to rock their marriage in the first year.[5] That's because we generally know very little about one another's financial habits before marriage, and what we do know we often just label as character traits, and our assumption is that over time we'll grow to accept these little flaws in our mates.

Probably, you won't. More likely, you each just grow increasingly frustrated with the other, even if silently and maybe even unconsciously. In such a situation, spenders feel nagged and hemmed in by demands to keep their wallets closed when they gain so much pleasure out of buying; savers moan about a lack of financial security because they fret that the family's finances are out of control. At some point, the blowup comes.

Maybe the blowup forces you and your partner to pursue the discussions that should have taken place long ago, and maybe those discussions are enough to set you both back on the right track. Then again, maybe the animosity runs so deep that it blows apart your relationship. Maybe much of it could have been avoided if you had both had a better understanding of the way the other views and handles money.

The most obvious source of potential friction between Michelle and Greg is the debt each brings into their relationship. Debt is a huge matter. As a culture, statistics show, we're marrying at an older age—27 on average for men, 25 for women. That means we have more time to accumulate debt before saying I do. For Michelle and Greg, their individual debt loads are roughly equal, yet the nature of the debt is different. Hers consists of student loans; his is credit card debt. The problem: Michelle stresses out about money and, in particular, "doesn't like credit card debt." She pays off her lone credit card in full every month, and the charges rarely exceed a cumulative $1,000. Greg's credit card, however, is larded with consumer debt. What happens, I asked Michelle, once the honeymoon ends and the big credit card statements continue rolling in each month?

"I guess I'll just have to let go of that concern," she says.

Maybe she can do that. However, if she can't, marital strife will likely result. In fact, debt brought into a marriage ranks among the top three problems couples confront during the first five years of the relationship, according to a 2000 survey by the Center for Marriage and Family at Omaha's Creighton University.[6] It's not hard to envision that Michelle's worries about the family's debt burden might beget stress that engenders tension. Worse, if the debt hampers Michelle and Greg's ability to adequately save for the home they both want sooner rather than later, Michelle's frustrations could gnaw at her and spawn resentment, and then it's just a quick slide into anger.

All this can be avoided. The best way to circumvent such potential problems is for Michelle and Greg to talk about his debt and her concerns. Really, it's that simple. Going into the marriage, only Michelle knows what financial issues will raise her hackles; Greg doesn't. By sharing her worries early on, she and Greg can at least begin to design a solution they both can live with instead of waiting for the blowup to happen, only then to work on a resolution at a period of heightened anger and tension. In reaching some sort of agreement, some sort of compromise now, they can address Michelle's worries before getting married. Greg may well continue to rely on his credit card, while systematically paying down the debt so that Michelle can see progress in the shrinking balance. That might be all it takes for Michelle to feel more comfortable about their finances and to give her a sense that she and Greg are pulling in the same direction.

Or they could do nothing. It's so much easier that way, though the problems always catch up with you in the end.

A longtime friend of mine never gave financial compatibility a thought when she and her husband married. Now, more than a decade into their marriage, she looks back and wishes she could change that, because their financial life is in shambles. Despite two above-average salaries, they live paycheck-to-paycheck and, my friend says, "have nothing to show for the money we've earned."

Neither agrees with the other's financial priorities because their individual wants clash so dramatically. With desires that are different—one wants to eat at pricey restaurants and travel, the other wants carpeting for a drafty wood floor and to save for a down payment on a home—compromise is impossible to find. Instead, both spend separately to meet their individual needs. In the end, they spend much more than they should and their finances suffer. Worse, while each knows that common ground exists, they can't see past the friction to create a unified approach to their money.

Looking back through the mess, my friend says she sees the kinds of questions others should at least consider as they're rushing down the aisle: Does your partner want to spend money on travel, or saving for a home, or fixing up the home you have? What feelings are expressed about debt and borrowing? Is saving for tomorrow a priority, or does living a fun lifestyle today seem more important? Do the actions echo those intentions? I mean, if your partner aspires to save for the future, it's not a good sign if all you see is an abundance of spending right now.

"All of these things I didn't think about when I got married," my friend says. "But financial compatibility—financial chemistry—matters just as much in terms of life goals as family, sense of humor, and personality."

Dollars & Sense

First, don't expect to completely mesh financially with your partner. To varying degrees we all harbor divergent views about the way we spend, save, and invest our money. The financial incompatibilities that do exist don't mean we shouldn't be together, and they don't mean misery awaits us years down the line.

Of course, don't go on your merry way thinking that financial incompatibilities are natural and don't mean much or that you'll simply grow to accept them over time. Chances are that if you ignore the differences now, you will instead grow resentful through the years about the way your spouse manages—to you, *mismanages*—money. Glenn, the Rhode Island reader and a self-described saver, says he married a spender who was very much "live for the moment, the future will take care of itself." His savings before marriage and his constant promotions and pay raises through the years allowed the couple to look past their differences, he says. In burying a difficult subject, though, the couple never addressed those differences and, Glenn says, "never resolved the underlying stresses." They ultimately divorced.

A great way to begin a discussion about money is to both order copies of your credit reports and FICO scores, which a majority of lenders use to estimate a consumer's financial risk. A number of Internet sites (e.g., www.myfico.com and www.equifax.com) provide instant access to your credit report and FICO score for a small fee and explain in detail what the numbers mean and how to read the report. Some even offer hints on how to improve your credit rating and FICO score through some very quick, simple fixes. In any event, talk about what each report shows and dissect the blemishes. That will help you each understand one another's financial past.

Interviewing is also a wonderful technique. After all these years together, not until I started writing the Love & Money column did I realize how powerful interviewing a spouse can be. I have to be fair to Amy's views when I write, and, quite honestly, I have not always known what those views are, despite our history together. Indeed, some of her views have come as a complete surprise. Playing the part of an impartial interrogator and listening to her answers and the underlying context have provided on many occasions insight into financial fears and wants and needs that I previously knew nothing about. The success we've had in recent years in improving our financial life stems in large part from asking her questions and understanding her answers.

The trick to interviewing is to remain as detached as possible and to continually ask *why* until you reach a basic, emotional understanding of your partner's position. *Because* is not an answer; it's a wall. It means your partner has either never considered the rationale behind his or her position or, more likely, is uncertain of how to put the thoughts into words. Ask, "What do you feel about _____?" That will help get past the financial and into the emotional. If your partner is leery of spending, for instance, ask "What would you like to do with the money instead, and why?"

Most important, stay neutral and do not rebut your partner's comments. Arguing increases the tension, puts your partner in a defensive mode, and generally ensures that the exercise is doomed to fail. It's fine, though, to play devil's advocate and pose what-if scenarios that might prompt your partner to see a potential downside to some string of logic. By the same token, though, you must acknowledge the flaws in your own rationale that a partner's answers reveal.

If nothing else, interviewing forces you to talk; and getting your thoughts out in the open remains the most productive way to address whatever fears and concerns you each have about money in general or some specific financial matter in particular. If interviewing doesn't work, or if you feel uncomfortable doing that, consider a quiz as a starting point for your discussions. Denise, my financial counselor friend, suggests that partners discuss the following eight statements to assess their financial compatibility:

1. I am aware of my patterns with money and how those patterns affect my well-being.
2. I know my short- and long-term goals.
3. I know what my income is (gross and net).
4. I know where my money goes every month and I feel in control of my expenses.
5. I know my checkbook balance, and it agrees with my bank statement every month.
6. I know how much I owe in debt and the interest costs I'm paying.

7. I know how to communicate to my partner about what I need and want.
8. I know what's on my credit report and my FICO score.

If you have trouble with any of these statements, you need to understand and discuss each other's finances more thoroughly, and possibly you should consider meeting with a financial advisor or counselor who can help you both work toward a better understanding of your soon-to-be joint finances. At the very least, talk about the differences that are apparent in your knowledge of your own and each other's finances.

Your ultimate goal before walking down the aisle should be to map together your financial future over the short, intermediate and long term and to understand what's truly important to each of you over those periods. You each should make a list of your goals. Merge those individual goals onto a single sheet of paper and agree that these are your goals as a couple. No doubt some of your goals will overlap. Some will be miles apart. Some you may never ultimately pursue. No matter; list your individual priorities for your money, regardless of what they are—paying down student debt, erasing credit card debt, buying a new car or a new house, taking a European vacation, saving $10,000 a year for retirement.

This, Denise says, does not mean that each individual goal becomes a "couples" goal. It simply means that as a couple you have agreed on and will support these goals, whether they're shared or individual. Respect each other's list and talk about each item to understand its importance. You'll learn things about your partner you never knew and that puts his or her financial needs in perspective. Your partner learns just as much about you. Such knowledge will allow both of you to more effectively manage each other's financial concerns, not just today but through the years ahead.

Discuss your progress on each goal regularly; examine the list yearly and add new goals that have gained importance in your life. Drop those that no longer mean much to you. Denise and her husband have a ritual they follow every January: They spend a week on California's Sonoma coast "talking about our goals for the year. Being on the same page has helped us to support each other's individual goals as well as our goals as a couple."

To kick-start your relationship, agree on a financial pact that will help you steer through what can be treacherous waters at times. Agreements can be anything that you think is appropriate to your relationship and its specific needs, but here's an idea of what these agreements might look like:

- We agree to sit own each month to create a spending plan.
- We commit to stick to the plan.

- We will decide how to divide up money management tasks like paying bills, comparing insurance quotes, keeping the files organized.
- We will develop a strategy to pay down our debts and not incur additional debt.
- We agree to live within our means, so that our expenses do not exceed our income in any given month.
- We agree to open, honest communication about money and promise not to blame one another, judge each other, or keep secrets about money.

Remember, money isn't the root cause of divorce, but failing to talk about money certainly is a leading cause of financial friction in a marriage. Talk about your money and your goals often and you won't have to worry about money derailing your life.

CHAPTER 6

The Perils of His and Hers Accounts

Merging Your Finances

When you're dating, you try hard to keep money on the sidelines. Dollars aren't part of the chemistry you feel for one another—or, if they are, they're at least not a part you're willing to admit to so you do your best to keep money out of the mix. That philosophy generally works for a while, because both of you willingly discount financial matters for the greater good of a new relationship.

At some point, though, money can't help but surge to the forefront. You do have to pay for life, after all, and you can't just ignore money forever. Often, the first hint of money issues emerge as a couple moves past the get-to-know-you phase and into that comfort stage, when you spend your free time together doing stuff. That's when money suddenly becomes awkward. Your partner calls up and wants to plan a short, romantic weekend. Who pays? Your partner always springs for restaurants you could never afford, but you feel you should pay occasionally, yet you know that doing so would destroy your spending plan for the month. How do you bring this up?

From there, money matters grow progressively more nettlesome as the relationship grows deeper. Just about the time you move in together or return from the honeymoon to begin the rest of your life as one entity, you are struck by a key question: one checkbook or two?

Of course, it's not only checkbooks. Just as easily we could be talking about the savings accounts you contribute to individually or the brokerage accounts you started before you met. Even the separate piles of debt you might be nursing fit in here. The checkbook, however, is the most dramatic symbol of financial couplehood because it's the account into which we generally dump our paychecks and out of which we typically pay for our conjoined life. As such, the checkbook symbolizes our financial coexistence—or independence, as the case may be.

In the early days of our marriage, Amy and I happily pooled our money in a joint checking account. I still remember the brown, plastic checkbook cover from California's now-defunct First Interstate Bank. Picking out a simple check design with Amy marked our first joint financial decision. When those checks arrived, we stared for a while at the first financial instruments to bear both of our names. All in all, a blissful financial union . . . that barely survived three months.

A big problem became apparent very quickly. I never knew before we married that Amy is an all-check girl, keeping mental tabs on her bank balance. She never realized I'm a credit card guy, keeping mental tabs on how much I charge. You can see this disaster brewing: We didn't know who was spending what and how. When our bank and credit card statements arrived, we argued over why our paychecks couldn't cover our bills— a problem we'd never had as singles accustomed to our own ways of accounting and managing money, which we both stubbornly reckoned were the right ways.

The only option: a financial divorce.

That seemed a clean and simple solution. We'd pay family bills from our joint account and pay ourselves an allowance that we could independently manage from individual accounts catering to our own wants. I could pursue my hobbies like beach volleyball or photography; Amy could go shopping for the dresses and shoes she wanted. Yet what seemed clean and simple turned out to be an emotional minefield. A decade into our multiple-account strategy, we realized that perhaps it was time to rethink the one-checkbook marriage.

After all, our parents and grandparents managed their affairs out of a single checkbook. We knew friends who had succeeded at it, too. Frustrated with our own failings in managing dual accounts, we looked at those successes and wondered if personal finance really has become so much more complicated that couples now need multiple accounts to manage a single marriage.

Simply put, family finance is no more challenging today than it was for previous generations. Sure, we have more investment options, and we often lead more expensive lives because of where we live, the times we live in, and a world of new gizmos, gadgets, and doodads on which to toss away our money. But bills are bills and paychecks are paychecks—it's just that some of the income and outflow moves around electronically these days.

If you ask financial psychologists, they blame much of this drift toward separate finances on a cultural shift toward two-income families. Couples have forsaken the lone checkbook because more women are in the workforce and naturally want more direct control over the household money, or at least their fair share of it. Men often are reluctant to relinquish that control. Both sexes come into marriage later in life now, having built up years of managing their own finances; no one wants to give that up.

One of the most common solutions, then, is to share power: You take control of your dollars; your spouse retains domain over his or her dollars. You meet in the middle to pay joint bills, but otherwise you're free to pursue your own financial life independent of your partner's—basically, the college roommate approach to love and money. That approach and the underlying rationale largely explain why individual accounts now are considered a necessary accessory of modern family finance.

"We have separate incomes, why shouldn't we have separate accounts?" asks Hugh, a Love & Money reader in Texas. He and his wife have spent 20 years operating out of separate checking accounts and using separate credit cards. They even have separate telephone lines with separate bills. "Giving each other total autonomy fosters more responsible spending and greater satisfaction," Hugh says. "I have never complained about how much she spends on clothes and other things I consider frivolous, and she has never complained about how much I spend at Office Depot and Home Depot on things she considers silly."[1]

It all sounds logical. In fact, Amy has told me a number of times through the years that in our single-account days, she felt like her financial independence "was being robbed." Not only did marriage mean she suddenly had to share her dollars with me, but, she says, "I also had to answer to someone when I spent them." She just wasn't accustomed to that as a single girl with her own job, her own money, her own desires, and only herself to answer to.

Our joint account also created some odd spending patterns and a weird case of financial competitiveness that worked against our common interests. I'd throw money into a softball bat or some pursuit Amy often saw as frivolous at best and a complete waste of money most of the time. She, in turn, felt the joint account owed her the same amount, so she would spend an equal amount getting her nails done or springing for a massage or shopping for clothes and shoes—lots of clothes and shoes.

The result was that while both of our needs were being met, we grew increasingly annoyed that the other was wasting money on what we silently saw as useless purchases. That money, we both figured privately, was money that we otherwise could be saving for a house or something else in our future.

Still, this explanation that the rise of the two-career household is at the root of this issue seems to me to be a bit misguided. My grandmother began working years before I was born; Amy's mom has worked for several decades. They managed to successfully live out of one checking account with their husbands. Sure, they both grew up and married in a vastly different era, when women often needed a man's permission to obtain a credit card and when the concept of individual accounts for husband and wife was as foreign as a cell phone.

I'm sure the working woman does play a part in the rise of individual accounts, yet I think that explanation is more excuse than reason. If a single account was so torturous and confining all these years, I know both my grandmother and mother-in-law well enough to know they each would have liberated themselves and their dollars long ago. Yet neither did. Nor did they ever harbor such a desire.

Perhaps the better explanation for why we seem to have migrated to dueling accounts has more to do with maturity and commitment to a relationship. The truth may be that many of us are too ashamed to admit that operating out of individual accounts as a couple allows us to continue living as single people financially. We can continue to spend money on whatever we want without notifying the other and without regard for the impact on the family's finances—the bigger picture.

At the core, the issue of merging finances isn't really about money at all; it's about an I-versus-us mentality. Indeed, an old adage holds that couples who separate their accounts separate themselves emotionally. That just might be true.

I know, for instance, that in the past I didn't necessarily want Amy to know that sometimes I would spend $25 on a sushi lunch with Jon, my office buddy. After all, it's my money, why should she care how much raw fish I eat? The truth is that I know she *will* care. Though she might not say anything, she'll give me a look that says I should have used the money on something more practical than a lavish lunch. Because of that, I want to live my financial life outside of her range of vision. If she can't see it, I can't get into trouble.

Amy's the same way, though. She doesn't want me to know when she sometimes shells out upward of $200 on her hair—an expense bound to raise my eyebrows. She'd rather just quietly pay the cost out of her own checkbook, not worry about what I might say, and enjoy it when I admire the results.

For my friend Andrea, the prospect of merging accounts seems entirely impractical and, at worst, confining. She was 35 when her husband proposed, and having built her financial life on her own she didn't cotton to the notion of surrendering her monetary autonomy. Nor did she want to feel she had to live on an allowance in her marriage.

"I've had my own financial freedom throughout my entire adult life, and I'm not ready to let go of that," Andrea says. As a result, she says that she and her fiancé "decided to keep our finances completely separate. And I think it's going to be a long time before we ever merge them."[2]

Andrea's concern isn't just her feeling that she might lose control of her money in marriage; she also doesn't want to impose her financial obligations and expenses on her husband. Andrea knows, for instance, that she one day will need to support her mom, and she wonders if her husband will "really need to know about the minutiae of mom's life, which he would see if the expenses came from a joint account. There is a certain freedom to maintaining your own accounts even in marriage, and for me it would be irritating to know that I can't do something without the knowledge of my husband."

The logic for maintaining separate accounts is understandable and, in some cases, compelling. No matter what, having at least one account in your name, particularly a credit card, is beneficial, since it helps establish your financial history and creditworthiness. Possessing your own credit card is of particular import for women, even if the card is used only rarely. For the sake of financial pragmatism, women often drop their credit cards and sign on as a cardholder on their husband's account. The problem: If a marriage ever falls apart, reestablishing credit and a new financial identity can be a challenge if you have no past—or an exceedingly dated past—to draw upon. To me, it makes sense for a woman to have credit in her name, if only for her own benefit.

Still, after years of operating out of individual accounts myself and living firsthand with the challenges, I look to my friends in Seattle, Jack and Colleen, and see a more effective path to managing money as partners. Jack and Colleen once lived out of separate accounts, divvying up the bills by calculating who owed what based on a percentage of each other's salary. If Jack earned more, then he paid more of the rent or electricity. Neither knew who had how much in their account at any given point. Sometimes a bill arrived that Jack was responsible for, but Colleen paid because it was due soon. Yet asking for reimbursement was awkward; as a married couple it seemed kind of cheap to nickel-and-dime each other.

"The whole setup," Jack says, "just seemed ridiculous. We never knew where each other's money was going, or how much we had left."[3]

The catalyst for change came when Colleen decided to return to law school full time. No longer earning a paycheck, and thus with no income, Colleen saw little reason to maintain her individual checking account. Instead, they consolidated their separate finances into a joint account.

A dozen years later, that single account remains, even though they had the opportunity to return to their dual-account ways when Colleen entered the workforce. Indeed, when Colleen graduated they discussed the possibility of reinstituting separate accounts, yet chose not to because they grew to respect what a single account represents: "Financial honesty," Jack says. With an individual account, it's easy to go about spending as you wish and never worry about the impacts on the family—since you assume there are none because, after all, this is your money, not family money. A joint account, however, "makes you confront all the money in the family's finances directly," Jack says. Colleen, for instance, suffers a weakness for See's Candy, using her debit card to occasionally indulge her vice. Jack sees the expense—$2.23 for five chocolates—when it appears on the monthly statement. Jack jokes with Colleen about her addiction. That's a small expense, no doubt, but to Jack it illustrates a larger point: That merged finances make it impossible to mask the purchases, big or small, that you otherwise could hide in an individual account without worrying about what your spouse will think or say. With a joint account, every expense is visible.

Many people I know, including most of my friends and nearly all my colleagues, find such raw honesty to be precisely the reason you don't join forces financially. "I do *not* want my husband to know about every single thing I buy," says a woman I'm friends with at work. "I make my own money; I should be able spend my own money without him looking over my shoulder or without him lecturing me on how I choose to spend my own money." To be sure, the guys I talk to echo exactly the same sentiments.

Such sentiments, though, miss the point entirely. Joint accounts aren't about limitations. They're about liberation. By seeing all the money flowing through your lives, you gain a more meaningful perspective on your family's real financial picture. More important, knowing that a spouse just might question a purchase likely will prompt you to at least think twice about the necessity of the expense. Maybe you still buy what has caught your fancy, but you certainly won't do it every time, meaning you ultimately become a better steward of the family's money.

Joint accounts also provide a clearer snapshot of your finances. With separate accounts, Jack says, "we never had a true sense of the family income or a true sense of what we really spent each month." Part of their income was flowing into Jack's checkbook; part flowed into Colleen's. Similarly, various amounts flowed back out again each month. At the end of the day, they never knew how much they had together. Without knowing that, arguably the most basic financial information in a couple's life, it's hard to make financial decisions to spend or save with any clarity.

Maybe you can save more money, alleviating a fear of financial insecurity. Maybe in reality you can afford to spend on that major purchase that you otherwise thought you couldn't, like that vacation to Asia or that new refrigerator you want. "You have more money than you think you do," Jack says. "You just don't see it because it's spread across accounts that neither of you have equal access to."

Having a single account thus requires a certain level of trust between people. You need to know that your partner will take your spending seriously, and your partner must know you will honor his or her trust by not raiding the account for selfish wants. Sharing all the family's money creates an intimacy and togetherness that separate accounts rarely can.

Now I should confess: Amy and I didn't just have separate accounts; we had at one point . . . six accounts. This bit of lunacy marked the earliest years of our marriage. Along with a joint savings and checking account, we both had an individual checking account and, to keep monthly services fees at bay, individual savings accounts, too, which of course required a minimum balance. All told, we had several thousand dollars, combined, in our separate checking accounts and a combined $5,000 in our individual savings accounts, money that was simply out of commission.

The arrangement was more cumbersome than it was useful because we constantly had to transfer money around—from joint to individual, individual to joint. That chore was a frequent source of friction between us because I sometimes forgot to transfer money, once resulting in our bank drawing down, by nearly $1,000, our overdraft credit line. I berated myself privately, but was angrier still that I had to sort out the mess just to figure out how much money we really had so that Amy, livid, could pay our son's tuition the next morning.

Not long after that episode, I asked Amy her thoughts on merging our finances again, effectively revisiting the catastrophe we fled shortly after we married. She giggled nervously, yet ultimately agreed. "I'll just learn to mentally relinquish control," she said.

With that, we returned to a single account. The result: Our finances suddenly were substantially less frustrating and we gained greater control over our money, finding out as well that we had more money to control. That's the sort of discovery that boosts your sense of financial security and allows you to do a better job of planning your saving and spending. Combined, those are the financial traits that will go a long way to improving not just your finances, but your relationship.

After all, it's not really about the money. It's about creating another level of intimacy in your relationship and bestowing trust on each other.

Dollars & Sense

Merging your accounts can take time, so don't feel you have to rush it. Remember, this is so much more an emotional issue than it is a money issue, and emotions are not easily swayed. Even though Amy agreed to the merger of our accounts again after so many years, it took her nearly six months to fully commingle her financial life back into mine. With memories of our previous episode still haunting her, she remained leery of the move. She even wanted assurance that if the union failed again she could retrieve from the joint account all the money she was contributing.

Still, she merged—and she's happy she did.

The trick is trust and patience, followed by complete financial honesty. Joint accounts are the quintessential reflection of the trust—or lack thereof—that exists in a relationship. Some people have money secrets they're scared to share or that they find too embarrassing to reveal. Others have been burned so badly in previous relationships that they find it difficult to trust a new partner, no matter how trustworthy. Still others simply want the freedom to spend unfettered.

Couples come to this issue from one of two perspectives: You're either newlyweds debating whether you should merge accounts, or you're both on your second or third or fourth marriage and you're pretty certain you don't want to merge accounts.

The answer is the same for both situations: Just do it. But there's a nuance to understand.

For newlyweds on their first marriage, you've agreed to join your lives, and shared, open finances serve to intensify the intimacy because money is an intimate subject by nature. You're both working toward common goals in your life together—be it a family, a house, a small business—and money plays a key role in all you do. Therefore, your accounts should be as connected as you two are to help solidify your trust in each other.

I'm not talking only about checking or savings accounts. You should merge investment accounts as well . . . and even debt. As I mentioned in Chapter 2, bringing debt into a relationship can be problematic, but if you're comfortable accepting debt into your life along with your new spouse, then you should be comfortable accepting the debt as a joint liability that you work together to eradicate. That will help strengthen the ties because you're pulling together as a unified body to take care of the family—bolstering the financial intimacy.

Blended families, meanwhile, often come together from situations in which trust has a damaged reputation. Trust, or some iteration of trust, often is one of the leading reasons behind a previous divorce. When you jump into a new marriage, you frequently still carry the baggage from your old relationship. As such, you're less willing to merge your financial accounts because they represent your ties to the only person you can trust—yourself.

In working toward joint finances, though, you begin to tear down the walls of distrust that you're displacing onto your new partner. Here's what I mean: My counselor friend, Denise, had a female client who, in her second marriage, went out and set up a trust for herself without telling her husband about it. These were her dollars and she wanted to protect them from her new husband, whom she thought had a laissez-faire attitude toward money.

Denise sent the couple to a series of workshops over the course of a year, and what emerged were indications that the woman was using money as a safety net. Her previous husband had been an alcoholic who destroyed her confidence and self-esteem, and she felt unable to stand up for what she needed financially in that marriage. She unconsciously took it out on her second husband, projecting onto him all of her own insecurities from a failed marriage. By setting up a secret trust, she was attempting to protect herself when the next divorce came along. Basically, the financial trust was proof she had no emotional trust in her relationship.

When she realized these symptoms were reflected in how she handled her finances, she gained a clear perspective of the trust she really had in her new husband—and they merged their accounts.

Ultimately, we form relationships because we share a common bond and common goals with our partner, and a joint account is the single strongest way to demonstrate that bond financially.

In talking to your partner about combining individual accounts into a single account, logic such as "It's all community property anyway" or "We need your money for _____" means precisely nothing. In fact, it could well be the worst thing you say, since it reaffirms the notion that your partner is giving up total say-so over the money and possibly indicates some ulterior motive you have, even if that's not the case. That's certain to quash any hope of establishing a joint account.

A very simple remedy exists, though: unquestioned honesty, open access to all the finances (with a guided tour of where everything is, if necessary) and a promise not to judge each other's spending. By the same token, both partners must understand that they're not just spending their own dollars; they're spending the family's dollars. For that reason, each needs to know the other has the family's best interests at heart and isn't going to do something rash with the money. The first time that trust is broken, don't be surprised if talk of individual accounts resurfaces.

Lots of people feel they're going to lose that sense of independence they feel is essential to their finances. Maybe you don't always want your partner to know how much you're spending on an item, perhaps his or her birthday gift, for example. With creativity, there's a way around this hurdle. You can create a sense of autonomy within a joint account by establishing an "up to" limit: You can each spend up to $100, $500, or any agreed-upon amount without consulting the other and without fear of being reprimanded. That way, each partner retains a certain degree of financial control over his or her own life and spending on undisclosed wants, and neither has to worry about angering the other with relatively small, personal purchases. Anything above the agreed-upon amount, though, should be discussed.

By adhering to such a rule, you and your partner establish trust and keep your spending in check, yet remain free to pursue some of your own individual wants. Equally important, you can still plan your savings and big-ticket purchases together, helping to further strengthen the sense of financial unity.

You don't have to dive headfirst into joint accounts if you still feel unprepared or queasy. Unlike with pregnancy, you *can* go partway. Instead of merging accounts, continue along with individual accounts, but agree to share information on each other's spending. Share your check register with each other when you sit down each month to put together your spending plan. Talk about your finances with one another; share how much you earn and how often you receive bonuses (if you do receive them).

"I'm amazed at how many couples I see that don't have a clue how much the other one earns," says Denise.

Talk about how much you have in your 401(k) or other retirement accounts. Detail how much goes into those accounts with each paycheck.

Certainly divulge your debt, how much you owe, how much you're paying off every month, and what you're doing to keep it in check.

If you feel more comfortable with a professional leading you through the transition, seek out a qualified financial planner who understands the psychology of money or who can steer you toward a counselor who can help in this area. Not all planners and advisors are trained to deal with the emotional components of money, so ask a few questions:

- What background do you have? What workshops have you taken to understand the psychology of money?
- What experience do you have helping people resolve financial conflict in their lives?
- What network of professionals do you have to whom you can refer clients if you don't have this background?

Basically, you want to find a professional who can see past the money and into the mental.

You can find local planners and financial advisors online through web sites run by the Financial Planning Association (www.fpanet.org) or the National Association of Personal Financial Advisors (www.napfa.org). You want a planner who works only for a set fee, not based on a commission from products sold and not based on a percentage of your assets. The Garrett Planning Network (www.garrettplanningnetwork.com) can direct you to planners in your area who operate on an emergency-room model—they charge only for the services rendered, usually on an hourly basis, realizing you might not need a full-blown financial workup, but rather just enough information and impetus to get past some hump.

Ultimately, whatever you do in individual accounts you can do in a joint account if you just talk with your partner about your financial needs and what you both seek from your family's pot of cash.

A joint account is simply proof that you're both in this life together.

CHAPTER 7

Money Laundering

Curtailing Surreptitious Spending

I was a money launderer. So was Amy. Many people we know still are. We certainly never funneled illicit dollars to some offshore bank account in the Caymans. Nor was our laundering considered illegal in the eyes of prosecutors who might frown if we attempted to skip out on our tax obligation. In fact, it might not even seem like a transgression outside of a relationship. What I'm talking about is the practice of laundering personal expenses through your family budget and otherwise hiding money from your partner.

The perfect example of this is Melissa, a woman I know in California who has money laundering down to an art form. At the supermarket, Melissa writes a check for more than the amount of her groceries. That leaves her, she says, "with untraceable cash" to cover costs that might otherwise raise her husband's blood pressure. Those secret outlays include having her nails done, buying shoes and clothes, funding her kids' discretionary wants such as movies, and presents for friends. Oh, and coloring her hair. "An $80 trip to the salon," she says, "is something that a man who tends to spend $7 a cut at the local strip mall cannot understand."

Melissa has laundered money this way for the 27 years she has been married. She says she's "pretty sure I learned it from my mother." As far has her husband knows, she says, "our grocery bill is about $1,400 a month. He accepts this because we do have teenagers in the house—and you know how much they eat." Melissa also has taught her daughter the ins and outs of laundering, and is convinced "that my reality is, in fact, reality for many people."[1]

She's right. Not only do statistics confirm it, but I know that Amy and I have employed similar strategies for washing many personal, discretionary purchases through our budget. Friends and colleagues we know—both male and female—concede that they, too, launder dollars through their family's finances.

So if we're all laundering cash, you have to wonder whether it's bad. Or does broad acceptance of this strategy mean that is has become an accepted, if unconventional, means for partners to live jointly but spend individually?

Many people don't want to believe that money laundering exists because such tactics are unseemly in a partnership supposedly built on respect, mutual trust, and equality. Those sentiments ultimately reflect the right frame of mind. Nonetheless, there's no doubt that such financial chicanery happens all the time in relationships.

A *Redbook* magazine survey showed that 34 percent of the women who responded admitted that they keep a secret stash of money that husbands know nothing about. They amassed their stockpiles the old-fashioned way, by siphoning here and there a few dollars from paychecks and expense checks and household allowances used for groceries and home repairs and such—your basic, run-of-the-mill money laundering.

Men are no different, of course. Zack, a Love & Money reader in Texas, told me that laundering was his principal means of being a closet smoker before he realized the damage he was doing, not just to his lungs but to his family's budget. When grocery shopping, he says, "I would purchase X amount of packs and immediately pocket them, along with the itemized receipt, rather than leave them in the sacks where they could be discovered by my wife and son. Later, at month's end, the amount spent on cigarettes was safely hidden deep within the grocery budget. Thus I was able to launder cash and harbor an addiction at the same time."[2] A reader in Virginia told me he plays a similar laundering game all the time, noting that in his job "I have to expense computer equipment from time to time, and get reimbursed later." That reimbursement check, this Virginian says, "doesn't always make it into the checking account."

On the surface, money laundering would seem to be a quest for financial independence, much like the desire to operate out of individual financial accounts, so that we can individually retain autonomy over some portion of our money. Independence, however, is not the answer, says Denise, my friend who counsels couples about money issues. Laundering often crops up in the relationships she works with, and the issue, she says, grows out of "a lack of responsibility and deeply ingrained money beliefs like 'there's not enough money for me.' "[3] Sometimes, laundering family money is centered on shame and secrecy when one partner is spending on a vice that likely would roil the relationship. You hide the cost any number of ways so that you can pursue an activity you know your partner would not approve of. Instead of talking about it—after all, you are shamed by it yourself—you just sneak the dollars that you need to feed your fix.

You might see in yourself some of the reasons people launder money in their marriages. For some, laundering reflects a desire to secrete assets or build a financial safety net to rely on in the event a marriage crumbles, even if the marriage is happy and its demise remote. You're essentially trying to protect yourself proactively by building a private stash so that you don't have to start all over again if the end does come. If you fit this mold, deconstruct your rationale and ask why this secret reserve is necessary. Does it stem from a previously failed marriage in which you lost everything and so unconsciously don't trust your new partner? Does it come from seeing your parents split apart in your childhood and watching one of them (likely your mom) struggle with little or nothing after the divorce?

For others, laundering is a nonconfrontational way to spend on personal wants that your partner will question or that you feel the family budget doesn't allow because it's too confining or not conducive to equality. By laundering the dollars you desire, you know there's no need to fight over money because you can just clandestinely tap the resources you seek. If this strikes close to home, ask yourself what it is about your relationship that necessitates this strategy. Do you fear your spending patterns will anger your spouse, a budget Nazi? Will your partner berate you for even the basic wants you have that might not benefit the family directly?

Others, meanwhile, use laundering as power over a spouse. By sneaking dollars out of the account, they keep their spouses tethered, unable to spend on items they might otherwise be able to afford. If you recognize this in yourself, you have to ask why you desire such control. Did a previous spouse or a parent wield power over you and you're now doing the same out of displaced anger? Are you silently punishing your partner for some past financial transgression? Has your spouse exerted financial authority over you and this is your means of revenge?

For whatever reasons, folks everywhere employ various backdoor maneuvers to systematically skim money from the family account. By and large, I'm talking about laundering small sums. After all, while you probably can launder enough dollars over time to buy a sports car, you can't just hide a roadster behind the bushes next to the driveway. Instead, what we're really dealing with is pocket money, the dollars we want for relatively small personal purchases that our partners never see and thus never question—a new dress, an expensive golf club, pricey lunches, a manicure every month.

It's not as though laundering is difficult. "Tapping into money is so easy," says Melissa, Amy's longtime best friend in Louisiana. She and her female coworkers sneak the dollars they want for private purchases through their expense checks. You can't easily launder a paycheck these days, what with direct deposit and the fact that a husband probably knows, at least roughly, the amount of his wife's salary. Husbands, however, "have no clue what expenses we've been reimbursed for or when,"[4] Melissa says. Indeed, she relies on this ploy to buy, among other things, several pairs of shoes at a time, evidence of which she further masks by telling the salesperson to keep the boxes, lest they stand out in the trash at home like a crow in a bucket of milk. As long as laundering isn't done to extremes, Melissa says, "I don't think there's anything wrong" with it. Besides, she adds, "it is a cheap thrill to get away with something."

At the root of money laundering is what I'll call the Financial Shadow Realm. Laundering money is so easy because money has always operated in the shadows in our culture and in our psyche. As I said at the beginning of this book, most of us generally are unsure of how to function with any real degree of financial candor, largely because we never learned those skills as kids. We re-create as adults the unconscious messages and beliefs instilled in us in our childhood years by our parents. We do as they did. We learned early on that talking about money is uncouth.

To deal with any money laundering you see—or sense—in your life, then, you have to pull it out of the shadows. "Sunlight," wrote Supreme Court Justice Louis Brandeis, "is said to be the best of disinfectants."[5] In this context that means you need to admit that laundering exists in your life and then openly confront it. Doing so can only restore financial honesty to your relationship. I know because, as I said, I was a money launderer. When I realized the damage I was inadvertently inflicting on my relationship and my finances, I knew the only way to stop it was to admit to it.

My cleanser of choice was always our credit card. If I hit the ATM as frequently as I needed cash, I knew Amy would be all over me like a hound on a scent. She would question my frequent withdrawal of money from the checking account and want to know what I could possibly need with so many dollars during the week—and, I admit, much of that cash tended to be tossed off on lunches and small, irrelevant purchases during the day like snacks and such. All of that would lead to a whole new debate about my extraneous expenses—and probably my diet—and I didn't particularly want to run through those itemizations. Instead, at lunch with colleagues, I'd often put the entire table's tab on my credit card and collect cash from everyone, obstenibly to pay the bill. Then I'd tuck the money into my wallet. Suddenly, I had dollars to last for several days and Amy was none the wiser. The transaction blended seamlessly into our credit card statement, just another restaurant name washing out unnoticed among the many other items on our monthly bill.

Now don't think I'm a lone gunman here. I definitely had an accomplice: Amy. She practiced what she calls "budget shifting." Just as I know she'd question some of my expenses, she knew I likely would raise an eyebrow to some of her acquisitions as well. Amy suffers an inexplicable affliction for the consumer detritus hawked on cable television. Her most famous lapse—the Notorious Ronco Food Dehydrator Incident—has yet to fade in our marriage. She bought this plastic monstrosity just months after our wedding, hell-bent on becoming the doyenne of dried fruit.

Can I tell you I've yet to taste the first banana chip?

For that I tease her all the time. To avoid my sarcastic jabs, she just kept me clueless about many of her questionable purchases, instead shifting the items into an acceptable budget category. One small example of such financial gerrymandering: While shopping at a department store for a birthday present for our son's friend, Amy spent about $25, originally telling me that the money went for "gifts," which she knew would not raise any challenge from me. Only later did she fess up that the birthday present was just $9, and the rest of the money went to a tablecloth, salt and pepper shakers, and stockings she wanted.

I know about Amy's scheme and she knows of my credit card gambit, because we decided to air our laundering—to shine some sunlight on our little tricks because of the effects they were exerting on our finances. One month in particular my lunchtime swindle amounted to $200, and that was for just five lunches. There was no way I could justify that kind of expense. Take away my portion of that bill for the actual food I ate, about $10 a pop, and that means I'd spent about $150 that I couldn't begin to track. This was a large part of the reason our budget never jibed every month—phantom expenses we couldn't see. It doesn't take a math whiz to see that continuing such a charade over time makes it that much harder to meet your financial ambitions.

You can look at money laundering in one of two ways: You can argue, as Amy's coworker Maria does, that laundering money through the family budget or surreptitiously shifting purchases into the wrong category isn't terribly malicious; maybe it's even beneficial to a relationship. The tactic, Maria says, prevents "unnecessary financial squabbles,"[6] because partners always have different spending priorities. Skimming money simply allows each to pursue sundry wants without seeking a consensus or worrying about how a spouse will perceive a purchase. In essence, it keeps the peace while allowing everyone to tend to their individual needs.

Then again, you can argue, as I do, that such laundering is inherently insidious because it destroys the financial honesty and equality that is supposed to cement your relationship. Furtively spending on individual priorities makes it that much harder to attain joint priorities, because you have less to spend as a family. Moreover, such off-the-books transactions mean you lose track of your real finances. You can't very well trim your budget if you don't know what to cut. And how can you know what to cut if you don't have a clue where the dollars are really being spent? It's a nasty little spiral. In reality, those dollars flow right under your nose, an invisible expense that means your joint finances are, at best, a fraud. Worst of all, *laundering* is just another word for lying.

At the heart of money laundering, says MaryAnn, a reader in Wisconsin, "is the lack of self-control and self-discipline needed to sustain a healthy financial relationship with one's spouse."[7] She's right. If you can't put the needs of your partner, your family, and your joint financial goals ahead of your own small wants, then, as MaryAnn says, you're left with a financial system that revolves around yourself and the elevated sense that your desires are more important than your spouse's or the family's common goals.

Whether you see money laundering as beneficial or detrimental, at the end of the day it's clear that laundering robs you and your partner of the money you're both counting on to meet family priorities today or tomorrow. Steal from your spouse—that's what you're doing, no matter how you rationalize it—and you're essentially stealing from your own future to satisfy a small, selfish want right now. There's not much honor in that. I know. . . . I was guilty.

The easy fix for laundering, many readers insist, is for partners to adopt individual accounts or to pay each other an allowance from the family account. "The basic problem," says Mike, a reader in Minnesota, "is that everyone wants to have some money they can call their own, that they get to spend without comments from their spouse."[8] Mike says he and his wife engaged in laundering until they began meeting with a couples counselor. Now they pay themselves an allowance. "This ensures that money is shared equally, that neither party feels that the other is getting more than his or her fair share."

That is one solution. The problem, though, is that if you're not careful you will slip back toward separate finances, at some point possibly necessitating individual accounts once again to manage your allowance money, ultimately masking once again the true extent of your resources.

Moreover, individual accounts don't necessarily erase the need to launder money. It's not too difficult to imagine a scenario where you run out of allowance and you need cash, and you're right back where you started, raiding the joint account either directly through your ATM card or through some backdoor ruse. Or perhaps you're more forthright about it and admit that you need another money fix from the joint account because you spent all yours. Then you're back to feeling you have to justify your spending, and the whole cycle starts again. . . .

The truth is, you need money during any given week. I know I need dollars to pay for lunch or subway fares or a taxi ride or maybe just a magazine I want to read on the train ride home at night. The truth is that Amy is always going to see a pair of stockings or a tablecloth or salt and pepper shakers she thinks will look perfect on the kitchen table. No one should have to curtail every want, or worry about a spouse's potential commentary. Doing so leads to the very sorts of frustrations and conflicts that necessitate money laundering to begin with.

Thus, the change Amy and I made—and the discussion we had—had nothing to do with money or accounts.

It centered on trust.

By keeping our money commingled and by giving one another unfettered access to every penny we possess, we trust we're both striving toward the same goals ultimately. That means we live by an implicit agreement to keep mutual interests in mind and not raid the account for selfish wants. We don't police each other's spending because there's no need to. Knowing your partner is relying on your sense of honor means you police your own purchases. Certainly, individual accounts would abolish any concerns altogether. Yet in keeping your dollars unified instead of splitting them apart, you keep a tighter rein on your finances, a fundamental goal for improving your financial life.

When it comes right down to it, "you've got to be honest about money laundering with yourself and with each other," Amy says. "The first step to recovery is admitting the problem."

Dollars & Sense

Money is not the root cause of this evil, nor is any drive for financial independence. Emotions are the culprit. You might feel that there's never enough money for you in your relationship, so you strive to ensure that there is, even if secretly. Maybe you're ashamed of or embarrassed by what the laundered money is buying, so you keep it in the shadows by sneaking the dollars you need to hide your vice. It's possible you lack the confidence and skills needed to negotiate your wants in your relationship or, conversely, that you're putting your own wants above the family's needs. There's a saying, "We are as sick as our secrets," and that aptly characterizes the emotions behind money laundering.

Money secrets begin innocently enough, but they can grow to such size over time that they damage the core of a relationship. You start off thinking that the $25 you're spending on some private pleasure doesn't mean much and certainly won't be missed. Soon enough, though, laundering becomes an accepted part of your daily affairs, and one day you realize you're expensing $200 for just a few lunches.

You're not just manipulating dollars, you're ultimately monkeying around with trust and respect and a sense of fair play. If you recognize that you are a money launderer, the fix is simple: Just stop. It really is that easy once you admit to yourself that you're not just stealing from your own future, you're lying to your partner. Think about how you'd feel learning right now that your spouse is surreptitiously stealing money from the family's accounts. You'd be angry. Why should your stealing prompt anything other than that response from your partner?

Understand why you are laundering money and address that with your spouse. Laundering is often a symptom of deeper communication problems in a relationship. If, for instance, you feel you have no voice in your family's finances, then you need to speak up for your wants. I realize that's not as simple as just doing so if you've spent years not doing so. You can begin to strengthen your voice by adopting the spending plan discussed in Chapter 1. In creating the plan, you and your partner detail what each of you wants and needs financially during the month. This is the perfect opportunity to bring awareness to your desires and to allocate money to your needs. A spouse must respect the equality of your financial necessities; otherwise, you both should talk with a professional who can help bridge whatever barriers exist.

If you suspect your partner is a launderer, the fix is much trickier. You can't just accuse the love of your life of pilfering dollars on the QT. If you're wrong, you've really breeched the trust in your relationship and demonstrated that you just assume the worst about your partner without giving him or her the benefit of the doubt. That's just never a good thing. Worse, rebuilding damaged trust can take a long while. Conversely, if your partner *is* on the take, then he or she is likely to become defensive and deny your accusations, uncertain of how to rationalize the actions that are in the spotlight. That makes addressing the issue more difficult.

A better approach: Focus on your spending plan. Because a spending plan tracks the dollars as they flow through your life every month, it will expose any laundering that is occurring, because you both have to account for all the dollars that come and go. The spending plan doesn't just shine light on the problem over time, it shows patterns of abusive spending, such as impulse buying.

Never exclaim, "Aha! I knew you were laundering money!" That won't win any love. More likely it will instill anger. Instead, work to revise your spending plan so that it either allows some of the formerly hidden spending to continue within reason or helps your partner curb that need to spend in the first place.

Remember, the fundamental issue driving money laundering is an emotional need to access money on the sly. It might even be a cry for equality. I know a woman who told me all about her money laundering because she felt that her husband would see what she was up to if he read about her shenanigans in print. I asked her how she would feel if he confronted her. "I want him to," she said. "I want him to know."

If you feel an allowance for each partner is the best way to address laundering in your life, then by all means pursue that. Bob, a reader in Iowa, says he and his wife "eliminated this bit of chicanery" by allowing each other a so-called mad-money account, "and we don't ask each other what we use the money for."[9]

That approach generally keeps any financial inquisition at bay. Still, as I noted earlier, my concern is that you may allow that to devolve into "his" and "her" accounts instead of relying on "our" account. When you do that, you begin to live separate lives financially, even if just on the margin. Worse, as a family, you begin to lose sight of your overall financial picture, often a leading cause of those painful moments when you're sitting at the kitchen table, fretting over the bills and arguing with your partner about why you can't afford the vacation you want or why it is you work so hard and have nothing to show for it.

A more interesting approach to that same notion of mad money comes from Charles, a reader in Colorado. He says that while he and his wife early in their marriage didn't necessarily resort to trickery to secretly snatch family dollars, "we did, for some years, disagree pretty mightily on what spending was essential and what wasn't."[10] Such disagreements often presage bouts of money laundering. The Colorado couple finally worked out an approach to personal spending that kept the family's finances fully visible yet allowed each the freedom to pursue independent wants. They negotiated an agreement giving each partner control of a certain percentage of their combined income to spend as he or she wishes, no questions asked.

The benefit of this method is that you don't have to maintain separate accounts; you know the limit to each other's spending every month, so there's no concern of busting the budget through surreptitious expenses, a big setback with laundering; and whatever isn't used continues to accrue in the account for joint uses instead of sitting in a separate account that only one partner has intimate knowledge of. Nothing is hidden in the Financial Shadow Realm; your money life is bathed in sunlight.

"It worked like magic to eliminate the disputes," Charles says, "and to keep our household finances transparent."

CHAPTER 8

Does Money Equal Power in a Marriage?

Balancing the Salary Equation

Except for a couple of years, I generally have earned more money than Amy. That's the way it goes in many relationships; one partner outearns the other—sometimes by a little, sometimes by a lot. The question this raises often has little to do with the actual dollars involved and so much more to do with whether that bigger income brings any special privileges—perhaps a breather when it comes to chores around the house or a greater say in how you spend your paycheck.

Most of us rarely think about or voice our concerns about such issues. In large measure that's because we don't know how. The offending actions play out daily even while the underlying emotions generally remain unspoken on both sides of a relationship. If you are the bigger earner, how do you express without angering your mate the idea that you think you're due some special privilege? You'd be lucky if you didn't get popped on the head for making that assumption.

Equally challenging, though, is being the mate who earns less and trying to explain to a spouse that you feel diminished because of these silent expectations that you must do more around the house or elsewhere in your personal life to make amends for your smaller paycheck.

For me, it took an otherwise innocuous $12 lunch to expose such frustrations brewing in my relationship with my mate and to make me realize I harbored assumptions I never consciously acknowledged. That meal, at an upscale noodle house near my office with friends at work, was no different than any of the relatively small, utilitarian purchases we all make just about every day.

The root of the problem is that Amy generally takes her lunch to work or spends just a couple of dollars for a meal. I generally don't, but she would rather I display a similar frugality when it comes to lunching with officemates. When she chastised me for this particular lunch expense, I replied that because I take on regular freelance work to earn extra money for the family, "I think I can spend $12 on lunch." She glared at me and let it go.

Only later, when talking to a friend about the encounter, did I realize the implication of my comment. Though it wasn't my intent, the words I chose essentially conveyed an unspoken belief that because I made more money, I could decide—unilaterally—how to spend that money. Such a presumption was unfair, since my spending necessarily affects her life. Amy has an understandable interest in protecting her own well-being and thus to question how I spend the family money.

None of that, however, is easy to see in the heat of the moment, and rarely do any of us think about it later. Yet beneath our blithe ignorance lies a question fundamental to the equality that is a cornerstone of any marriage: Does a fatter paycheck imply greater privileges?

The immediate answer almost everyone gives to that question is no. That's because no is the right answer—the answer everyone knows they're supposed to give. "No" says that you and your spouse are financial equals despite any pay disparity. "No" means that how to save or spend the family's income is a joint decision.

Of course, that does not mean "no" is the truthful answer.

Nikki, a reader in Minnesota, says there's no doubt that "there is power in the paychecks."[1] In the beginning stages of her marriage more than two decades ago, her husband was struggling with his new business. Nikki, earning more than $100,000 a year in salary and other benefits, was the breadwinner, keeping the family afloat. When her husband's business took off, she dropped her job to raise the kids. Through the years, his business continued to grow and prosper, and the family was happy.

Still, Nikki says, "to this day, after 15 years at home, I feel that he has the money, he has the power, so I don't spend as freely as he does. I let him make the decisions on stocks and mutual funds. I kind of know what's happening, but defer to him because I don't spend hours talking to people about the options like I did when I went to lunches and dinners. He does everything in his power to make me feel like this is our money, but this woman's old gut says 'Oh, no; it's his money—I didn't get up and go to work today.' "

I've had a number of conversations with friends and colleagues and readers, all sharing stories similar to Nikki's. The clear message: Many husbands and wives assume a bigger paycheck comes with special perks or at least bequeaths greater power in the marriage. Sometimes such sentiments play out as they did in my comment to Amy: I'm free to spend what I earn without much interference; it's my money, after all. Other times, higher-paid spouses believe that because they bring in more money they're already contributing more to the partnership, thereby absolving them of other obligations in the marriage, such as cleaning toilets, cooking, or handling more of the child care duties. The tacit assumption is that a lower-paid spouse must somehow contribute more to the marriage to be considered an equal.

The experience of a longtime friend at the office is the all-too-common anecdote that illustrates this divide. She earns a bit less than her husband, though they work similar jobs and similar hours. When money grows tight, my friend scrambles to drum up freelance work for extra cash. Her husband doesn't seek additional work, feeling that finding added income simply is not his duty.

"It's this unspoken thing with us," she says. "He thinks he already is doing more than his fair share because his paycheck is bigger and therefore it's my responsibility to deal with any money crises. He feels that until I reach his salary, he's doing more than I am. And that drives me crazy."

In large measure, pay disparity splits along gender lines, since men generally still outearn women. Nevertheless, that is changing, and women who earn larger paychecks often face unique challenges because they upend the traditional roles that men and women historically have played in financial relationships. Some men have no trouble with such an arrangement; they don't care because their wife's larger salary simply means a sweeter quality of life for the family overall or greater opportunities to save for the future. Other men freak out when a woman earns more; they resent what they see as a loss of power and feel emasculated because they don't provide the bulk of the family income. These guys don't usually announce their jealousy and resentment outright. Instead, you're more likely to see them wield complete autonomy over their own money, exert influence over their wife's money, or belittle their wife's efforts.

I know a woman who works in the corporate world and earns double the salary of her husband, a plumber. Intimidated by her earning power, her husband, she says, retains the control he feels he has lost by spending money on whatever he likes whenever he wants. His justification, she says, is that "he works hard for his money and he should be able to spend money on what he wants without asking me first." Moreover, he treats her job as all but insignificant, claiming hers is "not a real job" because it's mental, not physical. To further brandish power, he gives his wife a hard time about spending money on herself.

Many married and single women who earn meatier paychecks in their relationships confront a burden men almost never deal with when they bring home bigger salaries. In particular, higher-paid women often feel they must take added care to manage their partner's ego. To keep the peace, female breadwinners typically search out ways to restore tradition, at least on the surface, by taking on added housework or ceding control of their own finances to the man in their life to help nurture his self-worth. Not to be overly sexist, but if you look across generations, it's apparent that women historically have been trained, even if unconsciously, to be caretakers. Money, being the mirror that it is, reflects those same behaviors in a family's finances. Women often diminish their own wants or forsake their own desires in order to put a partner's needs first—and not always with winning results.

Karen, a reader in northern California, bonded with a guy she met shortly after his high-tech enterprise failed. She admired his entrepreneurial zeal, and when he decided to pursue a career in a field where the pay was substantially less, Karen figured it was no big deal.

"I was happy to stand by his decision for a personally rewarding endeavor," she says.[2]

The financial ailments that ultimately would doom their relationship surfaced on the couple's very first date, when what was supposed to be dinner at a midpriced bistro turned into a Dutch-treat affair at a burrito shop. Karen says that night she "resolved privately to put aside any concerns about financial differences and focus on the other riches that were so abundant in this person."

Yet that dinner and her resolve to avoid the money quandary, Karen says, "were emblematic of future problems." A pattern emerged over time in which Karen would propose plans she knew would suit her beau's meager budget and not wound his ego. She frequently bought for him items she knew he needed, such as clothes and even food.

"I was trying to protect him," she says, "from the reality that I could afford things he could not." That carried an underlying cost Karen recognized only later. By keeping the relationship on par financially, she realized she was robbing herself of her own desires, and in time she began to wonder how much she was really willing to compromise her standard of living in order to live down to the size of her boyfriend's wallet. "I harbored resentment," she says, "about making what I considered compromises." Because of her concessions, she had "unspoken expectations of him that he reciprocate in certain ways—doing more chores, cooking, errands." Her boyfriend, meanwhile, felt inadequate, she says, because he was unable to treat Karen the way that he wanted to treat her. Other than a few comments around birthdays and holidays about this regret, Karen says, "he stuffed his frustrations about money."

Such actions and reactions are common, says Denise, my financial counselor friend in California. Women, she says, tend to be "overgivers" and end up silently resenting their own efforts."[3] Resentment and anger are important emotions to be aware of when it comes to money. When you feel such emotions welling up, Denise says, "it's often a sign that a need is not being met in your life, and if that's the case, you need to take responsibility for yourself." Lots of people lack the initiative to do so because these are heavy issues, and talking about money means you're probably going to fight about it, so why bother?

Looking back on the relationship, Karen says that pay disparity became a dominant issue, though neither she nor her boyfriend knew how to address it productively.

"Our mutual failure to discuss money and the feelings around it contributed to the demise of the relationship," she says. Even when the couple parted ways, Karen says, "we never admitted that money was a factor. We just chalked up our split merely to different outlooks on life."

Of course, not everyone works. You might live in a family where one partner is a stay-at-home parent or is out of the workforce for some other reason. Such a situation represents the quintessential divide that can arise: One of you earns all the money; the other earns no money. Who has the greatest say-so over those dollars?

The answer is pretty obvious: You both share in the money equally. It's only fair, because while one spouse is off working, the other is at home, cleaning, taking the kids to school and softball and ballet and piano lessons, and cooking. Although one partner physically brings home the paycheck, both of you earn it, just in different ways.

Such beliefs, however, certainly are not universal. Too often, a working spouse demeans a nonworking spouse for not having a "real job." A woman I know in northern California says that when her first child was born, she and her husband agreed she would become a stay-at-home mom. Still, she says, her husband "castigated me for not bringing home money, and he suggested in subtle and not-so-subtle ways that what I did was worthless unless I got paid." To him, raising kids, cooking, cleaning, laundering, grocery shopping, and transporting kids to and from school and various after-school activities held no value because they didn't generate a paycheck. In her free time, this woman also managed her husband's real-estate investments. Even then, she says, her husband "maintained that I wasn't 'working' " because she did not bring home a paycheck.

She ultimately filed for divorce. The consequence she feels most troubled by, she says, is that her children "did not witness two parents demonstrating maturity, love, trust, and respect" in regard to the family's money. They experienced instead a lack of equality in mom and dad's marriage. As a result, she says, all of her adult children "now have issues with money."

My friends in Seattle, Jack and Colleen, have seen the issue of pay disparity unfold from many different angles. They lived on one income when Colleen was in law school. They earned roughly the same amount when Colleen was working. Then it was back to one income, with Colleen staying home during their daughter's early years.

They agree that Jack's salary belongs to both of them, and they routinely consult one another about major purchases. Yet less money flowing through the family's pocketbook underscores the spending differences that exist between Colleen and Jack. That, at times, gives rise to feelings of entitlement that cause some strife. One small manifestation, Colleen says, is that "we bicker about him going to lunch so often during the week. I make his lunch, and he tosses it out or it just goes to waste."[4] When she has questioned Jack about this, she says he has on occasion responded with, "Hey, I can to go to lunch if I want to." The implication, Colleen says, is that because Jack makes the money he's free to spend some of it as he sees fit. Indeed, Jack concedes that "there are the occasions where I find myself pining for a gadget at the local Home Depot that I'm certain will transform my life, and I admit I feel a tad indignant that I can't just haul off and purchase it without facing the consequences."[5]

Colleen, meanwhile, harbors her own feelings of frustration that highlight what a spouse in her position often deals with. In stepping off the career track, Colleen gave up the financial power she once enjoyed when working as a lawyer. Because she no longer earns any income, Colleen has a tougher time spending as freely on herself as she might like to if she brought in a paycheck. Though they debate this topic on occasion, Colleen says, it remains an issue "that just doesn't get resolved. We just let it go, and nothing changes."

Dollars & Sense

Confronting the question of pay disparity and the feelings it arouses is certainly not easy. So much is often left unsaid that it makes it difficult to talk about the topic or to even see that it's an issue in your life.

If you earn less than your partner, you might feel pangs of guilt at not providing the same financial support, though you work just as hard, either in the workplace or at home. Other times, you might hold your tongue because you don't want to appear ungrateful, given that your partner's beefier paycheck provides you a higher standard of living than you could afford on your own. On the other hand, if you're the partner with the handsome pay, you might feel that you deserve or have earned a certain privilege that you don't express because you know such sentiments aren't necessarily fair. Both of you ultimately bottle those frustrations or resentments or feelings of entitlement and instead avoid the issue.

There is an effective way to manage this situation. Holly, a Love & Money reader in Connecticut, recycles the newspaper in her house and in doing so one day forgot to save the comics for her husband. He took that as a slight and, Holly says, "somehow this led him to comment that I needed a career to start pulling my weight in the household."[6] A comment like that is precisely the sort that prompts a heated exchange in many a relationship. Holly, though, saw that as opportunity not to fight, but rather to educate.

Holly calmly pointed out that "I am the support that keeps you running smoothly." She recited a litany of chores and errands she accomplishes behind the scenes. For instance, she noted that he was wearing clean clothes that she bought and washed and put away; that she had just packed his favorite foods for lunch; that he had just eaten his favorite cereal for breakfast that she bought at the store, brought home, and put into the pantry; that supper, from scratch, is on the table shortly after he walks in the door every evening; that he never has to do the laundry, clean the house, or go shopping for clothes or food; that she makes sure his medications are in stock and that his dentist and doctor appointments are scheduled.

"I said that my 'job' was taking care of him and us," Holly says. Her husband could not help but alter his perspective on the value of his paycheck and the worth of his wife's unpaid work.

That's the fair way of valuing a partner who does not work in a traditional job yet contributes around the home. Imagine the cost of paying a service to clean your house, even if just once a week. Add to that the various costs of having all your clothes laundered, your meals prepared, your cupboard stocked, and your young kids cared for during the day while you're off earning a "real" paycheck. Or consider the expense in time of doing all of that yourself, along with your day job. There's no way to argue that stay-at-home spouses aren't contributing to the family's income— they do so by saving on expenses and handling the daily errands for which you otherwise would have to shell out money. Sure, they're not a profit center for the family; they're a cost savings center, and that can be equally important to a budget.

Denise, my friend who counsels couples about financial issues, says that to more effectively confront pay-disparity frustrations, you should look at the underlying emotions and not the money. Amy wasn't miffed about the 12 bucks I spent; she was miffed because I treated our money like it was mine only. A more effective approach would have been for me to acknowledge Amy's concerns and then try to gain her support by explaining my thoughts honestly—that I'd like to treat myself at times for my added work. Instead of declaring that I deserve a pricey lunch because of my extra workload, a more effective reply would have been to say, "Well, I've been working long hours lately, and going to lunch with friends was a nice way to kick back for an hour. Do you mind if I do that occasionally?" Amy says that had I said something like that, she would have been much more likely to show some sympathy and far more likely to see such a relatively small expense as an acceptable extravagance.

If you see yourself or your partner struggling with issues regarding financial power in your marriage, then you must voice your unhappiness with the way money translates into power in your relationship and press for some measure of equality. Depending on the situation you're in and the ways in which money equates with power, your measure of equality can take many different forms. If your spouse assumes a bigger paycheck is a get-out-of-chores-free card, then maybe he or she could agree to pick up some of the household cleaning duties during the week or perhaps take on the role of family cook on weekends.

My friend at work who earns extra money by freelancing says that when she's forced to find extra work, she has learned to ask her husband to cut spending on the pastimes he enjoys. That way he shares in the pain, too. He agrees to her wishes, and that gives my friend a sense of financial equality.

The biggest problem with pay disparity, she says, is that many of the underlying emotions are based on gut feelings, and gut feelings are tough to change because "some of this stuff is just ingrained in who we are." Nevertheless, that doesn't mean you have to go with your gut.

Ultimately, she says, a relationship of any kind "is not about who makes more or who works harder. It's about whether you both take responsibility for the family finances, sharing the pain of cutting back and spending money on things you both agree on."

STAGE THREE

The Kiddie Years

Big Dollars for Little People

'll never forget the evening Amy walked in from work and, standing there in the living room, looking radiant in the late-day sun, with both arms behind her back, announced with some excitement: "Pick a hand."

I picked the hand nearest to me, and she produced a small, porcelain pink piggy bank. That and the smile on her face announced all that I needed to know. I smartly grunted, "Nuh-uh," and picked the other hand. She produced a small, porcelain blue piggy bank.

With that, I was on the road to parenthood.

Ever since, the journey has been one unending string of financial pay-outs for some expense or another. Kids, I assure you, consume dollars like they're chicken nuggets—if not for medical bills, then for school and snacks and clothes and shoes and way too many school fund-raisers and field trips and day care and Happy Meals (lots of Happy Meals) and toys and collectible trading cards and sports teams and after-school activities and summer camp and. . . . I don't say all of this to be heartless—I adore my son—but simply to make the point that kids cost money. Lots of money. Lots and lots of money. Though, honestly, no one ever wants to admit that because it's somehow impolite to acknowledge the obvious—that children blow through money like tornados through Texas. Soon enough, the reality strikes: Children cost money.

Stage Three of a relationship is confronting that reality when thoughts of populating your life with kids begin to settle in. Money plays an endless variety of roles when it comes to kids, and not just the obvious role of pro-viding the necessities and wants of raising a baby into a very successful lawyer or athlete who will take care of you later in life.

To start with, there is the biggest challenge of all: the debate about whether to have a child in the first place—or another child, as the case may be. Eventually you and your partner come to a point where one of you mentions "baby." When that happens, the other, in a Pavlovian rejoinder, inevitably responds with "budget." This is a big debate among couples, though you'd think families never discuss "money" and "baby" in the same conversation because no one admits to such discussions. This "dirty talk" is best reserved for the bedroom—and with good reason, since tying money to children is routinely regarded as cold.

So call me Iceman. I'm here to state that money most definitely plays a part in this debate. End of discussion. Money simply has to be a part of the formula, because once you and your partner agree to have children, you face a constant demand on your financial resources that begins with decorating the baby's room, ratchets up at birth, and often doesn't cease until your kid is out of college. Even then, you may have to deal with a child who wants to return to the nest because of inadequate finances, or because he or she wasn't able to parlay that art history degree into a lucrative job immediately after graduation and is in need of financial assistance early in a career.

Whatever the case, there's simply no way anyone can argue logically that money plays no part in having a child. After all, as you read in Chapter 9, raising a child ultimately will cost as much as, if not more than, buying a home—and that doesn't include the costs of college.

Thankfully, during this period of hemorrhaging dollars, you'll be sidetracked by all the other challenges of raising a child you simply never anticipated in that early, dewy excitement of building your family. Trust me, the dew evaporates quickly under the heat of reality.

One of those unanticipated moments may arrive like an epiphany when you're looking at a toy store scattered across your den and realize that your child owns enough Super Teenage Power Ninja Mutant Turtle Rangers to invade Canada. In that moment, you will despise the villains who turned cartoons into 30-minute infomercials. You realize just how weary you are of the "Will you buy me a toy" song that plays incessantly when you go to, of all places, an office supply store that, inconceivably, stocks gewgaws for kids. That's the moment you recognize that toys have gotten out of control in your life and that the best way to combat this scourge is to begin paying an allowance, because then, you're convinced, your child will suddenly become a rational, thinking little person who, when given the choice to save or spend the meager pittance you offer each week, will choose the former because, hey, kids are rational that way.

Right.

In reality, an allowance often isn't the cure, but rather part of the disease, largely because we parents rarely employ an allowance correctly. We offer just enough cash to keep our kids living right below the poverty line and, thus, dependent on handouts from Mom and Dad. We're quick to revoke the payout for the typical infractions of childhood, and we force our kids to part with a not-insignificant chunk of their money for charitable contributions, while another portion is earmarked for savings, which, to a child's way of thinking, is a synonym for "seizure." It's no wonder the allowances we parents pay end up creating a consumer rather than a saver. My son figures if he has money he better find a way to spend it fast on something he wants, lest Mom and Dad cook up some notion to reclaim it when he messes up, as he expects to do several times during any given seven-minute stretch. After all, he knows there's more money where that allowance came from.

That's the biggest problem with allowances: parents. We never realize just how demanding an allowance can be on ourselves. It's hard to stick by the allowance, since it's natural to want to help your kids afford the small items their way-too-meager allowance can't cover. Doing so, though, reinforces the idea in a kid that "I can spend this allowance Dad gave me today because I know Mom can afford what I might want tomorrow." At the same time, it's easy to use the allowance as a disciplinary tool, revoking it for various transgressions at home and at school. Both tactics, as Amy and I have learned through trial and much error, are the absolute wrong approaches.

Luckily, parenthood only gets worse, mainly because we think, therefore we talk—and in talking we say the darndest things about money. Through offhand and hyperbolic comments such as, "We're broke," and through simple everyday transactions such as whipping out the credit card to pay for everything, necessary or not, we pass along to our kids unintended messages about savings and credit and spending and debt and a host of other money issues. We think nothing of these words and actions. To us, this is all just normal commerce and conversation. Kids, however, watch us with the scrutiny of an exam proctor, even when it appears they're not. They see money through our eyes, and if this version of money management is good enough for Mom and Dad, then it must be good enough for them.

Without even realizing it, then, we're offering our kids fundamental life lessons in finance that will establish their views about money as adults—and not always for the better. Once you recognize that, you quickly want to change the lesson plan.

Ultimately, what you learn during Stage Three is that when it comes to kids and money, there's often no one right answer—just an endless series of false starts and missteps and options. The great comforter, though, comes in knowing that all of us parents are in the same soup together. Rich or poor, educated or not, we're all screwing up the same things and trying our best to fix the blunders before we send our kids into the world to make the same mistakes we've made. That, of course, is the overriding goal: to turn out adults who are better at managing their finances than we were.

The good news is that you have 18 years to get it right.

The bad news, as you'll read later in this stage, is that only the first 12 years really count.

CHAPTER 9

Having Children

Evaluating the Financial Implications

To be or not to be . . . pregnant.

That may be the single most fundamental dispute you face in a relationship.

At some point, usually a quiet, random moment when you're preoccupied with grander thoughts like what's for dinner, the question of children and how many arises. It's the Inevitable Question.

Whether you and your partner are contemplating the copious decisions inherent in planning your first child, whether you're discussing a second, third, or fourth child, or whether you're just beginning to determine how big a family you want, pregnancy is never an easy topic to talk about in terms of money. Discussing the cost of kids immediately strikes some people as cold and calculating, even shallow. It's almost certain to spark confrontation in your life when it appears. After all, adding a child to the family isn't like buying a new car, so, the argument goes, money should not be an issue. Amy certainly has seen it that way in the long-running debate in our life regarding the possible addition of a second child. She has continually advised me to "just let go of your financial concerns."

For me, doing so would be naive. When I talk about the financial implications of a child, it isn't about whether we go out to dinner once a month or once a week or whether we move to a new house or remain in an old home in need of repairs. Rather, I'm talking about the implications for our family now and in the future. I'm talking about the time we can devote to our son and our wants for him, given that we're a working couple by necessity. I'm talking about the education we can afford and the quality of life we'll have as a family. I'm talking about the goals Amy and I have for our own life today and years into the future.

Overlooking all of this in the emotional tug-of-war that accompanies the question of bringing a baby into your life is really easy, largely because no one wants to concede that money has anything to do with having a child. Truthfully, that's just willful ignorance; in the crudest measure, a kid costs as much as buying a home—and I'm not just being hyperbolic. The 2002 edition of the annual *Expenditures on Children by Families,* compiled by the U.S. Department of Agriculture, estimates that the average family will pay between $169,750 and $338,370, depending on income bracket, to raise a child from birth through age 17.[1] Oh, and here's the sweetest part: Those numbers don't include college costs, which, by the time your toddler hits the campus, will add tens and possibly hundreds of thousands of dollars to the tally.

Just to drive the nail in a bit deeper, a 1996 study by Phoenix Home Life Mutual Insurance Company found that 28 percent of parents expected to provide financial support for their kids after college.[2] There goes another several thousand dollars annually.

Whether you admit it or not, money plays a part in the equation, whether you're talking about your first child or an additional child. Money is there when you weigh the size of this house you might need, the car required to ferry around a larger family, the hours you'll work. Money is there, though not always consciously, when you try to save what you can for retirement and your child's education. Money is there when you decide whether one spouse will stay home or whether you'll need day care if both parents continue to work. Money determines how you'll travel, where you can go, how often you go out to dinner, the restaurants you can afford, the clothes you buy, and the stores in which you shop.

When it comes right down to it, all couples have to make their own, very personal calculations about what they are willing to sacrifice and what they hope to gain from having a child. The fundamental question in all of this isn't whether the decision should be based on financial considerations, but rather, how much of it should.

Opinions abound. Not having any children is selfish, shows a lack of faith in yourself, and, to some people, smites whatever religious beliefs they profess. Not having a second child is a disservice to your current child, not just now but when he or she is older and in need of family support once you're dead and buried. Planning for just one child leads to a self-absorbed, maladjusted child. At the worst, the very idea you'd bring money into this debate is just plain greedy and signals that you have only your wallet's best interest at heart.

These are just a few of the many arguments people have recited to me in making the case that couples should bear a whole brood of rug rats. Taking a single-child stance, or even vowing to go childless as some of my married friends have, is misguided, self-centered, and, to some, a moral affront. It's easy to become lost in those emotional debates, and it's frustrating to feel that maybe your views are wrongheaded.

In large measure the issue of kids and their costs revolves around the question of multiple children—unless, of course, you're inclined to have no children. If so, then this chapter likely won't mean much to you. With the first child, the issue often is just one of timing, though your partner may use money as the foil. That's what I did; every time Amy announced her urge to conceive I earnestly discussed our financial inadequacy. She just rolled her eyes and then showed up one day to declare her pregnant state. I asked who the father was . . . and she hit me. Since then, we've had an on-again, off-again debate about child number two.

That notion of a second child is when the matter of costs really becomes a more concrete affair. You have experience with childhood expenses to draw upon, and you have a better feel for your wants and dreams for your first child and for your family as a whole. Thus armed, deciding to have child number two is often much more difficult than agreeing to number one. Nancy, a reader in Arizona, says she and her husband are "severely undecided about having a second child," and she wonders if her "emphasis on financial security is abnormal."[3]

It's not. Lots of people share similar concerns. The problem is that few folks realize this because discussing such concerns publicly can bathe you in an unflattering light. No one wants to acknowledge such fears or views about this outside of their home. Heck, even inside the home it can spur divisions.

While Nancy's husband is content with their daughter, he nevertheless tells Nancy he wouldn't mind a second child and that, if they do have another, "we'll make do just as everyone else does." Nancy has no doubt that they'll make do, and she says she "does crave another child at times." Yet those cravings, she says, "are strongly stifled by my overall concerns about the trade-offs." Those trade-offs, Nancy points out, have nothing to do with "being unable to feed and clothe two children. It's more about what we are able to provide our daughter and ourselves if there is not another child to make a dent in our cash flow."

You can't deny that kids bring immense benefits to people's lives. I know I would not want a life without my son. His laugh, his hugs, the nicknames he calls me, teaching him to hit a baseball and seeing his wide-eyed joy when he connects—these are the psychic dividends I receive every day from my investment in him. Amy and I also know we may need to rely on him one day when we're too old to care for ourselves or in some other way require his assistance. Having another child ultimately might help us when we're older and possibly could lessen the burden on him. If nothing else, a second child would give him the sibling he may need to lean on himself one day as well. Each of those are valid arguments in this debate, and they deserve serious contemplation.

Still, no matter how you slice it, Nancy is right: Financial trade-offs play a significant role in the decision to have a child in the first place or to give your only child a brother or sister. Many people turn a blind eye to such trade-offs, insisting they either don't matter or are inconsequential, or asserting that "everything has a way of falling into place." It's just not that simple, though. The trade-offs are consequential because the trade-offs have consequences. Moreover, things don't just fall into place. They fall into the only spaces they can, based upon our actions, and we rationalize where we land in life as a result. You don't have five kids and "somehow" find a way to make it work. It's naive to think so. More likely, you have five kids and *out of necessity* spend $1,000 a month on food and clothing and other obligations, and you save a little money only when you can. Years later, when you draw on your savings for that blowout vacation, to replace a car, or to buy a new house, you scale back because you don't have the money to reach for what you really want, or you take on more debt than you feel comfortable with, squeezing your budget in other places and further pinching your current lifestyle and your ability to save for the future.

Those things don't just work themselves out; they are the end results of the conscious decisions you make elsewhere in your life. You may be fine with the result; you may silently resent the result. Whatever the case, you are where you are in life as a direct result of the consequences.

The problem is, even if you recognize all of that, compromise can be intensely difficult when it comes to the inevitable question: to be or not to be . . . pregnant. Not only is it a life-altering decision, there's no practical way to split the difference. It's not like you can get a puppy instead and call it even. The result: If there is disagreement, one spouse gets what he or she wants, and the other must concede. As a result, one of you is going to feel your life is being pushed in a direction you don't necessarily want to go, and there's little you can do about it. Little wonder this topic is often so divisive. Little wonder each spouse is so intensely vested in a personal agenda.

Amy comes from a two-kid family, so she sees life colored in large part by that history. To her, a second child is beneficial to our son because she finds benefits in having a brother. Moreover, she knows another child would bring additional happiness into her life, just as our son has.

I'm an only child, so I see life in that light. I like the idea of having just our son, because it's a more intimate family. I like small. I enjoy the one-on-one relationship of a single child and the truly singular ties that it creates. I've known those ties as both child and adult, and I'm content with our little triangle of love.

Regardless of our childhoods, though, money is clearly an issue as adults. Certainly, we can afford the basics of feeding and clothing a child. Yet a brother or sister necessarily draws away resources that otherwise would benefit our son. For instance, Amy and I strongly prefer to send our son to a parochial school because we feel from our own experience that the quality of education is superior. We want to give him that advantage in life since we saw it as an advantage in our own lives. However, we're not sure we could afford two parochial-school tuitions and still do for both children what we now do for our son. Is it fair, we wonder, to keep one child in a parochial setting if the other isn't? Conversely, is it fair to our son to yank him out of that setting in order to provide equal benefits to the second child?

If you're like most parents, you dream of providing the best that you can for your kid. Maybe you want your child to see the world and get the best college education you can afford. Maybe you want to build a savings account large enough to help your child financially in the future, be it the down payment on a home or to help start a business. Personally, I want to have enough stashed in our nest egg so that Amy and I can live out our retirement without becoming a burden or a financial worry to our one child—or, for that matter, any other kids we might ultimately have. And I want to give our son experiences I've had throughout my life—as well as many I haven't but that I'd like to share with him.

Certainly, there's nothing that says you can't provide all of that to more than one child, but there are costs to consider. Trips "home" to visit family and vacations elsewhere are suddenly 25 percent more expensive. Education is double, and the future costs of college become a potentially impossible hurdle. Even the simple dinner out is pricier. All of those added costs—some big, some small—limit the experiences you can provide your child, or children, and gnaw away at what you ultimately can save for your own future and your own dreams, which, selfish or not, I think should remain important for your peace of mind later in life.

I'm not saying you shouldn't make those sacrifices. I'm just saying that whether you're in the throes of debating your first pregnancy or your fifth, those are the very real financial sacrifices that populate the argument. If you're willing to make those sacrifices, that's fine, as long as you recognize you're doing so consciously. If you aren't sure you want to make such trade-offs, that's fine, too.

The flip side of this argument is that the cost of any child is simply irrelevant.

"One cannot measure the worth of a child; they are valueless," says Rhonda, a reader in Minnesota who comes from a family of three kids. "Nothing can replace the joy I experience raising my two sons and the countless hours spent with their activities and friends. Material possessions pale in comparison to the joy of a full family."[4]

You cannot argue against such sentiments without sounding heartless or uncaring. Still, you must separate emotion from finance and look at both independently. You want a child; that's the emotional side. Can you afford a child? That's the financial side.

Darlene, a reader in Texas, says she and her husband remain torn over the question of having another child. Both have siblings. According to Darlene, "My sister is still my best friend. I want this for my little girl also. What greater gift could you provide for your child than a sibling?"[5] Nevertheless, Darlene says, she and her husband also "realize that a second child will definitely limit" what they can provide their young daughter. They have purposefully chosen to live in a smaller house than they can afford and to drive small, affordable cars so they can save the money their daughter will one day need for college. They want the financial wherewithal to send her to private schools as well, "which is very important to both of us," says Darlene. As an MBA, Darlene knows she could easily chase bigger dollars and make everything possible financially, but that would require moving around the country and sacrificing her proximity to family members and a short commute to work that allows more family time with her husband and daughter.

When it comes right down to it, Darlene says the real question is, "What are you willing to give up" to have a child? Life is about choices, she says, and "you have to choose between dreams" of wanting a child "and what's best for everyone involved in your life now."

There's no doubt that the choice between cost and forgoing a child is a tough one to make. A friend of mine at work with a three-year-old struggled for long hours with the idea of having a second child. Ultimately, she and her husband decided not to give their daughter a sibling. Emotionally, it was a wrenching verdict, because they both have siblings and they know their conclusion means their daughter won't. Implicit in their decision, however, is a range of financial concerns beyond the obvious extra costs of a child.

For instance, they live in New York City and could never afford more than a small two-bedroom apartment. Sure, that's doable—that's what bunk beds are for. Yet neither of them wishes to live in such a cramped fashion, particularly as their kids age. Thus, having a second child would force them into the suburbs, and their family dynamics would change dramatically. My friend and her husband are not in a financial position that would allow either of them to become a stay-at-home parent; thus they both would face long commutes into the city for their jobs. The result: Both children would have to spend long hours in day care, something my friend is adamantly against.

"All of a sudden, the decision to have a second child could mean, for both of us, less time at home with any child," my friend says. "So a second baby would give my daughter a sibling. But she would lose the ready access she has to me now because it's unlikely I could replicate my flexible work situation." In the end, my friend says, "children are wonderful, and they bring lots of joy. But what's best for my child in terms of my time and financial well-being means not having a second child so I can do the best for her in every way."

Dollars & Sense

No single right answer exists when it comes to the question of having a child. You have your own interests that you defend vigorously because you know how you want your life to track and you know how a child likely affects those wants. Your partner, meanwhile, might have other interests to defend, and with equal vigor. Thus, every couple has different concerns to work through when this topic arises—and few of those concerns are simple to deal with.

The simple fact, though, is that kids cost lots of money, and that money should be factored into your decision in some fashion. Consider some of the individual costs of childhood that are broken out in the 2002 U.S. Department of Agriculture report, *Expenditures on Children by Families*. If you're somewhere near the average middle-class family, with annual income of between $40,000 and $67,000, you'll spend nearly $28,000 to just feed your kid until he or she reaches college age. Housing will set you back more than $86,500. Health care and child care combined will surpass

$51,000. Clothes, the cheapest expense, will wring more than $10,500 out of your pocketbook.[6] One cost not included, which many couples overlook: lost pay during the mom-to-be's maternity leave.

As further proof of the impact a child has on family finances, the British office of financial giant American Express released a survey in 2003 bolstering the argument that you must make financial trade-offs to have a baby. Again, I'm not saying those trade-offs aren't worth it; I'm just saying they exist and that you and your partner must address them honestly. The American Express survey reported that 47 percent of parents with kids under the age of five said their first child was more expensive than they had expected, and only 15 percent of the responders said they had budgeted sufficiently.[7] Most folks answering that survey said that the arrival of a child forced lifestyle changes onto the family to accommodate the unexpected costs. The biggest change is the most obvious: New parents curtailed their own entertainment expenses such as restaurant meals and movies. Part of that, no doubt, is just the expected ramification of having a baby and losing much of the free time you had before the baby. Yet additional steps were necessary that cut deep into lifestyle issues: Parents no longer were able to plan foreign holidays, and instead vacationed near home (remember, this is Great Britain, so "near home" means just that); they bought cheaper groceries; they postponed do-it-yourself projects around the house; and, perhaps most important to the family's finances later in life, they reduced their contributions to retirement, investment, and savings accounts. Some even had to downgrade the family car to meet the added costs of a child.[8]

What are those costs? Well, here are several to consider, in no particular order. You might not face them all, but you're certain to face the majority:

- Pregnancy clothes
- Pregnancy toiletries
- Baby furniture
- Decorating the baby's room
- Baby clothes
- Baby shoes
- Obligatory professional photo session
- Diapers (lots of diapers—roughly seven a day for vaguely 30 months)
- Baby food/formula
- Bottles
- Car seat
- Safety products (outlet covers, cabinet locks, security gates)
- Crib and mattress

- Baby linens
- Baby bathtub
- Pacifier (my son, by the way, chose a dog's chew bone in a pet store)
- Eating utensils
- Doctor bills for mom and baby (at least the insurance deductibles)
- Prescriptions for mom and baby (at least the pharmacy co-payments)
- Over-the-counter medications
- Medical procedures, such as tubes to stop ear infections
- Baby's immunizations
- Stroller
- Infant toiletries and hygiene products
- Day care and nursery costs
- Nanny
- Toys
- Baby books
- Swings and other infant exercise equipment
- Additional life insurance on Mom and Dad

This list, of course, continues for a few more days. If you want to play around with some of the basic expenses of adding a kid to your family, you can find a number of calculators on the Internet that project some of the more obvious, major costs over time. The Cost of Raising a Child calculator at Bankrate.com, an online provider of financial data (www.bankrate .com/brm/calculators/manage-money.asp), bases its calculations roughly on the U.S. Department of Agriculture report mentioned previously.

Certainly, a child is more than a budgetary line item. Yet there's no doubting that a child consumes a big chunk of resources, and you simply must be aware of that since the expenses, by necessity, touch your family's wallet. If nothing else, budgeting adequately for the costs by consciously making the trade-offs elsewhere in your spending plan will help the family's balance sheet immensely.

Where opinions differ, it's often too easy to argue about the costs of a baby by flinging a checkbook on the table and exclaiming: "Great, we'll have a kid and just go bankrupt." That never works. Amy and I have talked and talked—and talked some more—about this issue, often heatedly. Though we see the topic from different angles, the most success we've had in dealing with the issue has come in sharing our thoughts in writing. It's far less confrontational and has allowed us more opportunity for intelligent reflection instead of blurting out the first words that come to mind in the heat of a verbal joust (almost always a bad idea). Moreover, it provides each of us the chance to make our case fully, without rushing through our thoughts, trying to get in all our words—and usually forgetting our point—before the inevitable "but" comes flying out of the other person's mouth. Moreover, it gives us each a chance to better understand the other's concerns.

Of course, you don't have to write to communicate. Talk if that works for you and your partner. Maybe you talk over a long dinner away from home. Maybe you get away for the weekend, effectively a couple's retreat. Whatever the approach, the key is to pick a time and place where emotions aren't explosive. The goal is to escape your daily routine and the stresses of worrying about cleaning the dishes, bathing your child, the clothes in the drier, and all the niggling chores that stir frustration and preoccupy our minds.

In the discussions, don't give financial matters short shrift or belittle a spouse's concerns about money. Financial impacts exist and will affect your life, whether you're attuned to them or not. After all, most of us have a limited flow of dollars coming in, and how you spend those dollars affects what you can afford for your children, yourselves, and your future together as a family.

In considering having a child, reflect on your own wants for this child. Innumerable economic models exist for raising kids, but frame the debate, at least in your mind, in terms of approaches that define total opposites. Paula, a financial psychologist I know in Florida, says that many of her friends use the "Buy everything new and at full price" model. Ask yourself these questions:

- Do I want to redecorate a bedroom into a baby's room?
- Better yet, do we need a new and bigger home in a better school district?
- Will we need a bigger car for a bigger family?
- Am I going to shop for clothes at Baby Gap?
- When we save for college, will we save for a state school or will we save for Harvard?
- Do I plan to use the expensive disposable diapers?
- In planning on returning to work, do I expect to hire a nanny?

Then again, maybe you're willing to take the more frugal path. You plan to beg and borrow hand-me-down clothes and used baby furniture from family and friends. Mom will breast-feed, or Mom and Dad will spend part of their weekends mushing, straining, and pureeing peas, carrots, and squash into a week's worth of homemade baby chow. You expect to supply your child's clothing needs from neighborhood garage sales or the discount rack at Wal-Mart and Dollar General. You'll employ cloth diapers and wash them out yourself. One parent plans to stay home to eliminate the cost of child care and will cook nearly every meal to save money. If both parents expect to continue working, you find affordable day care, even if it's not the nice, upscale place to which your friends all send their kids.

Sure, those scenarios are extreme. Yet they show just how many decisions about children have money at the root. More important, they demonstrate how much latitude exists for finding a middle ground you both can live with—because, ultimately, your heart may overrule your wallet. If so, at least know how your wallet will be affected so that you and your spouse can make enlightened decisions that benefit your family.

"In the end, having a child is all about the compromise," says Paula. "What is the baby-wanting person willing to give up in order to have the baby? Trips to Paris? The big house? Private school for the kids they already have? Eating out several times a week? There is a lot of room for compromise."

CHAPTER 10

"All My Friends Have One!"

Managing Kids and Their Material Wants

If I'm right, and if you're reading these words while in the living room, den, kitchen, basement, dining room, family room, home office, guest room, bedroom (yours or your kid's), bathroom, out in the backyard, or maybe even in the car, and if you look to your left or maybe to your right or possibly down at your feet, there's a very good chance you will spy a toy . . . or eight.

Toys are the lint of childhood; they just collect, often in the oddest places. Action figures and cars and dolls and cards and games—they clutter every room in the house. Science may yet prove a genetic link to rabbits, because you leave for dinner one evening and only Barbie is lying on the living-room floor. Yet you return to find she has acquired a town house, a Vette, her own beauty salon, and apparently has invited Ken, Skipper, and the gang over for a plasticine party. How, you wonder, did this mess get here?

I use the word *toy* because most of my direct experiences with this as a parent come from interacting with my young son. But all I need do is look back on my own childhood or pay attention to what readers have to say to know that *toy* carries a meaning much broader than the stuff we buy for a little kid's entertainment. Big kids have toy wants, too; they're just more expensive—the designer jeans, the newest video-game systems with all those pricey cartridges, or shoes that cost as much as a week's worth of groceries. One woman I know recoils when she recalls her 12-year-old niece announcing a desire for a Kate Spade or Prada bag. "It was horrifying," she says. "We're talking about hundreds of dollars."

This desire for luxury items and material possessions is a challenge you face during every stage of your child's development, from the first rattle to the brand-name clothes, the top-of-line surfboard, and the sound system that turns a teenager's bedroom into the neighborhood concert hall. Some of the blame for all of this most assuredly rests with us parents. Really, how many infants do you know who demand an $80 pair of teensy little Air Nike tennis shoes? We start them on the road to possession at an early age, then bewail their wants as teens.

What's going on here isn't just about the gifts, the toys; it's a question of how you control your and your kid's attitude toward material objects. It's all those undercurrents about keeping up with the Joneses when your kids come home tormented that they don't have the latest, greatest whatever that "all the kids in school have."

You can't say yes to it all. Nor can you say no to everything, since a child deserves to share in some of the material items the family's money can buy, just as Mom and Dad do. The challenge comes in figuring out how to maintain a fair balance between providing for what our kids want and teaching them that they can't have everything they see.

Of course, that's a lesson equally applicable to parents, too.

Toys—be it the Barbie for a five-year-old or the new car for a teenager who just earned a learner's permit—represent on some level a kid's psychic need to fit in. The trading cards my young son collects, while he certainly thinks they're cool in their own right, are substantially more significant to him because all of his friends at school collect these cards as well and jabber about them every day on the playground. To simply be one of the guys, he craves experience with these cards, since only with hands-on experience does he gain the ability to talk the talk with authority when his little buddies start discussing the attack and defense power of, say, a Blue-Eyes White Dragon.

Basically, what I'm saying is that our kids' world is bounded by pop culture to a far greater degree than is the world of most adults, and kids are eager to plunge into that world because of their urge to be like everyone they know. Even if your child isn't into television or popular radio stations, his or her proximity at school to other kids who are in tune with the times can't help but influence your child's wants. In the broadest sense, then, toys are a form of currency, status, and even power among kids of all ages. Think back on your own elementary-school days: One kid in the neighborhood always had the coolest toys. In high school, the coolest kids were often the guys or girls who had the cars—the coolest toy for a teen.

Wrapped up in all of this toy talk are a myriad of forces at play. There is the peer pressure kids feel to blend into the clique with which they identify. That might mean your teenage daughter must have the newest low-rise jeans from Old Navy. There are the formative trends that kids so naturally tap into and adopt because they're so malleable in building their identity, easily gliding between one view of themselves and another, often within the same week. The manifestation of that might be that your middle-school-age son must have a ticket to the Avril Lavigne concert or wants you to spend a couple of grand to buy a professional-grade turntable, mixer, and dozens of vinyl albums so that he can rock the school dance as the DJ-for-hire he dreams of becoming—at least for now. There are the beginning stages of class distinction that all kids deal with as they try to rationalize why their family either can or cannot keep up with their friends' families. Maybe that arrives when your child doesn't understand why you can't afford to buy her a designer gown for the prom when all her friends are shopping the pricey boutiques.

The problem with these material possessions we provide our kids is that in succumbing to their wants we continually set the bar ever higher. The portable CD player was fine—for a while. But now, Mom, I really need an Apple iPod so that I can carry around my entire CD collection wherever I go! Soon enough, enough is never enough.

Connie, a reader and grandmother in Florida, has watched her grandchildren growing up for the past decade, living her granddaughters' gift-getting experiences through family videos. Each year, the girls' parents send Connie and her husband a video of Christmas morning. "It's obscene," she says, "with tons of presents for each of the three girls. Big gifts, like a playhouse; bigger gifts, like a white-cedar backyard gym and swing set that cost $4,000."[1] In recent years, she says, the holiday video has become "a real yawn." Kids are knee-deep in wrapping paper "and sometimes they start to open a present, throw it aside, and go for another one, which they barely look at before throwing it aside to go for another one."

The young girls, Connie says, "were not born spoiled. But they have become totally, selfishly addicted to material possessions and expensive pastimes. What hurts me, though, is that a toy should be a special treat. However, with our kids and our grandkids, these gifts have become obligatory."

I realized in similar fashion that toys were a problem in my family's life on an otherwise innocuous, leaden spring morning. My son was five at the time, and I was driving him to school when he announced his hope that the gray day would yield to rain, then sun, "because I'll get to see a rainbow."

For a brief moment, I was warmed by the innocence of his pure love of rainbows. Then reality slammed like a thunderclap; he quickly added, "With all that gold, I could buy every toy in the world."

We are overrun by possessions in our house. We have enough Legos to add on a room, enough Yu-Gi-Oh trading cards to build a house, enough toy cars to open a dealership. My son, I'm pretty sure, is Supreme Allied Commander over a militant wing of Power Rangers plotting against our Siberian husky, who started a war by chewing some body parts off another action figure.

It's not that we can't afford the toys, although the outlays do add up. It's not that I'm against toys—my grandmother certainly gave me all I could want, even on her limited income. Our problem, as I tell Amy time and again, is that our son has too many "things," and I think we often buy them for the wrong reasons. Ultimately, I fear, we are instilling in him misguided expectations that gifts await those who simply do what's expected of them in life. In doing so, we're robbing him of life's little pleasures: those unexpected rewards received for having done something particularly noteworthy and the satisfaction inherent in doing a job just for the psychic value of its completion.

Most parents, I assume, do not want to raise children to have unrealistic expectations about money. We want them to grow up understanding that some tasks are done simply because it's the right thing to do. An appreciation for the value of money and the hard work often necessary to earn it are fundamental precepts we want to instill. Likewise, we want our kids to be practical with money and to realize that just because you have a dollar in your pocket doesn't mean you must spend that dollar on something immediately gratifying. Indeed, those are the rules we apply to our own lives.

Why, then, do we so easily discard them when it comes to our kids and their toys?

Part of the answer lies in the fact that it's not our kids who have the spending problem. It's us parents. The truth is, toddlers to teens will always ask for the possessions they desire—that's just part of their genetic makeup. (In later life, that gene often mutates into a desire for expensive cars or power gadgets in guys and a desire in women to own a horde of black shoes, all practically identical to the naked eye.)

To stop kids from spending is easy—just cut off their source of capital. That's not such a simple solution, though, when that source of capital is you.

"It seems that even when I ran to the local drugstore for a couple of items, I'd walk out with some piece of overpriced plastic for my son," says Gay, in Florida. She was growing increasingly weary of the showdowns with her seven-year-old that preceded the purchases, until she realized one day "that I was just as much a part of the problem—I couldn't say 'no.' "[2]

That is precisely the issue. We parents often can't say no to our children's desire for some possession, blinded by our own desire to make our kids' childhoods memorable. Too, we often project years into the future the melancholy sense of nostalgia we know we'll feel one day when our little boys and baby girls are all grown up and we stumble upon something they used to play with. For a brief moment, we'll be cast back to faded years to briefly relive a part of our lives and their lives forever embedded in our hearts. With emotions such as that tugging at our heart, little wonder we so easily sway ourselves into believing some object is the key to happiness in the moment.

Of course, it's not. We all know that inherently. Yet human nature allows us to delude ourselves into pretending that whatever we just bought will flood our child with immeasurable euphoria. That actually works, too—just long enough for us to continue believing the charade. Though we all know that half a day later, often less, interest in the object begins to wane. Soon, the must-have item is just another future memory collecting dust on a forgotten closet shelf.

The worst part of all of this is that parents aren't always consistent with one another in agreeing on whether to spring for a gift in the first place, one of the big parenting no-nos that moms and dads face the world over. Ashraf, a Love & Money reader and dad living in Bahrain, says his wife constantly is frustrated that she comes off as "the monster who always says no" when their kids want another toy. Ashraf, meanwhile, is the one who generally approves the purchase "and comes off smelling like a rose. She really hates that."[3]

Here's the quandary: Gifts are supposed to be special, but how can that remain the case if you give a gift for any old occasion? At some point, you think, "Wow, you woke up this morning and didn't throw a hissy fit. Well, I think you deserve a big shopping spree at the toy store this afternoon!"

Of course, that's ridiculous. Yet once you've rewarded grades and manners and attitude and eating all the peas and not whining in the grocery store and cleaning up the disaster in the bedroom and getting good grades and brushing teeth and remembering to flush the toilet, what else are you going to reward? Don't think kids aren't going to ask. When you set precedents that benefit them, they don't soon forget. Moreover, when every day or every weekend is potentially a gift day, major holidays and birthdays can't help but lose some of their excitement and luster.

This problem we have with toys starts early. A friend of mine at the office, a mom, began using toys as a tool for behavior modification, if only out of convenience and despite knowing that ultimately it was the wrong approach. In my friend's case, the tactic began when she returned to work after a short stint as a stay-at-home mom. To soothe her daughter's separation anxiety, she started promising, "Mommy will bring you a present." The toys started flowing, and they haven't stopped. She certainly doesn't want her young daughter associating behavior modification or happiness with material gain, but, she says, "Once you start down that path, it's difficult to stop."

A reader once shared with me her frustration at what such an approach often leads to. In presenting her young niece with a present, the woman was told, "I got one of these from my friend at my birthday party. Is this all?" The woman was heartbroken and annoyed. Then again, who wouldn't take issue with that attitude? Meanwhile, her seventh-grade nephew, she says, "is starting to appear condescending when a relative on a fixed income presents something with great love but little cash value." These experiences, she says, make her feel that "there is no pleasure in giving to children for whom receiving gifts is a daily expectation to be met by somebody, anybody."

We are a generation of parents raising our kids to expect a treat for no other reason than "just because."

That seems unacceptable.

In my family, Amy tends to be the parent more likely to indulge our son's material desires. She'll often award what she calls "prizes or treats," toys or gifts priced at less than $5, for satisfactorily completing some task or event, many of which I think are simply expected, such as, say, being good in school or having good manners or doing chores around the house.

To me, a toy is a toy is a toy, no matter the price. It should not be given with such frequency—at least not when the cost comes out of Mom or Dad's wallet. (If kids wants to spend their own money to buy a small toy every day, more power to them, but more on that in Chapter 11.) I'm no stranger to positive reinforcement. I verbally praise my son all the time for his accomplishments, no matter how small. Amy does, too, but she's more inclined to toss in a gewgaw as well. I use gewgaw tossing more sparingly. Once I offered to buy my son two packs of his favorite trading cards if he would hold his breath underwater for two full seconds when he was taking swimming lessons. His instructor hadn't been able to convince him all week to do that, so I offered him a compelling reason to, as he saw it, risk his life in a swimming pool. It worked. Certainly this negotiated bribe sent a message very similar to Amy's—that prizes await you for simply accomplishing a task. The difference, to me, is that I offered a bribe that benefits his life, since knowing how to hold your breath is a necessity of being in the water, whether you're there on purpose or, more important, accidentally. Not acting up in school and not being sassy to your parents are behaviors you learn precisely because they're right.

Aside from that, I'm far more likely to shoot down our son's sometimes-strident demands for new toys. Oddly enough, Amy never received toys in her childhood to the degree she showers them on our son. Oddly enough, I did. Yet I'm the one who thinks we spoil our little boy. And, trust me, I know from spoiled. My grandmother worried constantly about money, yet bought me many of the things I fancied. One Christmas, that meant an overpriced train set that was part of the holiday display at a department store. Another time it was an expensive drum set that I'll bet I banged on fewer than a dozen times. As a high school senior it was a snazzy black sports car that I should never have let her buy.

I look back on all this and see that those toys, while certainly fun, never replaced what I wanted most in my life—my parents. Honestly, I remember just a few baubles from my childhood, and only because of what they represented. The Rock'em Sock'em Robots recall fond memories of my grandfather crawling onto the floor to play with me one Christmas morning. I vividly recollect a plastic boat, four feet long and stacked with tiny cars, that my dad gave me when I was three. And there was that metal Wild West fort filled with cowboys and Indians he bought me at a Toys "R" Us near Los Angeles International Airport when I was five or six and visiting him on the West Coast. (I can still remember sitting in the front seat of his green Dodge Roadrunner as we zipped along Interstate 405 to get there.) These last two memories remain so fresh because they were among the few times in my childhood that I saw my dad. (My parents divorced when I was two years old.) Those toys represented the only memories of him I could hold onto as a kid.

That bit of history explains in part why my grandmother showered me with toys. She sought to paper over as best she could the fact that I didn't have my parents around like all my friends did. She salved my pain the only way she knew how: with possessions. Thus, I can say with some experience and authority that toys never compensate for a larger underlying issue.

Yet I see myself and Amy often doing with our son exactly what my grandmother did with me: overcompensating.

Lots of parents do that. All of our lives are hectic because of our jobs and obligations around the house, and we feel as though we're not spending nearly as much time with our kids as we would like, all the while watching them grow up, knowing that one day, way too soon, they'll be on their own. To hold on a little longer and prove our love, not just to our kids but to ourselves, we buy them whatever they want, be it another set of Legos when they're in first grade or the classic Mustang when they hit driving age. Though those costs are miles apart, the underlying meaning is just the same: Mom and Dad love me because they shower me with things.

I think Amy and I both feel guilty that one of us isn't a stay-at-home parent or, at the very least, that we're not home early enough to allow us to spend several hours together as a family, playing and reading and such, each evening. Certainly, we do all of that with our son, just not for as much time as we'd like. As such, like many parents, I believe we're trying to assuage our guilt by providing happiness through other venues—toys. We know our son will enjoy what we buy, and making him happy makes us happy, and that seems so much more important in the moment than does the relatively minor cost of some random toy, rarely more than a few dollars. Soon enough, however, those small items that cost just a few dollars become the cars and iPods and DJ equipment of the teenage years—and still they don't mean that much.

Lorrie, a reader in South Carolina who has raised three kids, says that "one of the hardest things parents can do is give up the immediate gratification of making their child happy that minute."[4] She knows the temptation of wanting "to give things instead of time when you are feeling guilty, however unconsciously." But she and her husband raised their kids to understand that presents were for Christmas and birthdays.

In looking at the fate of her oldest son and his peers when they graduated from college, Lorrie sees how a constant barrage of material possessions through childhood ultimately shapes expectations in adulthood. Her son, living on his own, took an entry-level job and plans to work his way up like everyone generally must. However, many of his friends are back at home, living off Mom and Dad, "looking for a glamour job," she says. "I sincerely feel that if I had bought him every toy he asked for and gave in to all the demands for brand-name this and that, today he would be back in my home wondering why he couldn't find a job."

Perhaps no parent feels more torn by the need to assuage pangs of guilt than do single parents with demanding full-time jobs, yet who strive to provide as full a life for their children as kids from two-parent families live. The pull is tremendous to supply through spending the happiness you can't provide through time and to make up for the absence of a mom or dad. I know; when I was a small kid living with my mom, I watched her struggle on her thin salary.

Sheila, a Love & Money reader in Washington State, raised two kids on her own. Their dad split when the children were four years old and

10 months old. Through the years, Sheila says, she "watched dear friends face adolescence with their children exerting ever-increasing pressure for the $120 shoes, $75 T-shirts, name-brand this and that, electronic toys, $500 prom dates, and on and on. I saw kids treat their parents with contempt and disrespect when desired objects were not forthcoming. I saw kids who didn't know their own value if they didn't have the latest toy. And these parents were loving, caring people with good values, but they were also people who used their purchasing power as a parenting tool, and I think that was a core mistake."[5]

Sheila says she felt a similar pull herself, wanting to make up for the fact that her husband abandoned the children. Yet she resisted and "rarely gave into the temptation to use 'things' as an apology or replacement for the limits of my time," says Sheila. Part of it, she admits, could have been her lack of funds. Even as her earnings increased, though, reflexively buying a toy to soothe an emotion "was just not in the cards." She used love and affection to reinforce good behavior and used the money that was available for "things we could do together—theater tickets, family trips to the Shakespeare festival, outings to favorite restaurants."

That philosophy, Sheila says, "has paid off in the most important way imaginable—in the lives of my children, who do not find their personal value in their possessions."

Dollars & Sense

Toys are not about toys. They're not necessarily about the money. They are to our kids the exact same thing that the new car stereo is to you (or the new purse, the new power tool, the new car, the new best-seller, the new DVD, the new whatever). They are possessions. Right or wrong, toys are the means by which our kids determine the score in their insular world. "If I have something I want," they think, "then I'm ahead in the game." They see Mom and Dad consume, so that's what they know.

You have to change that game. I'm all for my son having toys; I don't mind buying him a few, usually attached to no particular reason. But I, like most parents I know, want him to appreciate his toys far more than I see that he does. More important, I do not want him associating material gain with intrinsic happiness or the related notion that he deserves material gain for every assigned task he completes or good deed that he does. Check out a book called *Punished by Rewards,* by Alfie Kohn. Basically, he blasts the incentives we parents often rely on when it comes to buying things for our kids—the "Do this and you'll get that" approach to parenting, according to

Kohn. The author is a big proponent of developing in children (as well as in students and workers) intrinsic motivation, encouraging kids to undertake tasks for the satisfaction inherent in the completion. I think back on my own childhood and look at what I most appreciate in my life today, and I see a common thread: I value most those items that I earned for myself—be it my car or my savings account balance. They mean far more to me than what others promise to give me for doing something. It's the internal pride you feel at having accomplished something yourself, at having earned something you want and being able to exclaim to yourself that "This . . . is . . . mine."

That's what I'm talking about.

To ultimately instill that feeling in your kids, as a parent you simply must become more adept at saying no. Alison, a Love & Money reader in Texas, recalls that she once took her daughter and a friend to a movie at the mall. Afterward, her daughter's friend "asked if they could get a Beanie Baby at the mall kiosk," Alison says.[6] "I declined, and during the entire drive home, this little girl went on and on about how her mother buys a toy whenever she wants it and wherever they go. I proceeded to tell her that her mother must be the most wonderful mom in the world, but that she was stuck with me for the day. Tough luck!"

After dropping the girl off at home, Alison explained to her daughter that "we don't buy a toy every chance we get, and my daughter agreed with me and really understood. Just think; you don't want your own child to behave as that little girl did when in the company of others."

No doubt, *no* is one of the hardest words we can say to our children, especially if we have the wherewithal to bring them a little happiness through some purchase, no matter how big or small. Remember, though, that this happiness often is short-lived, and may actually be your kid looking to fill some other void in life—possibly the absence of your attention. Saying no to children gives them freedom to moderate their own wants as they get older, a great trait to possess as an adult.

If we don't rebuff their wants and, instead, continually acquiesce to their demands, then we risk raising children who, as adults, expect the world owes them something—or everything. Kelli, a Love & Money reader and mom in California, worries that her and her husband's philosophy of giving in to their oldest son's wants during his childhood "may have handicapped him." Kelli saw this character trait on display as her son began looking at colleges. When he met with a counselor to discuss financial options so that he could attend the school of his choice and live on campus, Kelli says "he was most distressed to hear about work programs, donating time, and applying for different positions that put more responsibility on him, but would benefit him by maybe letting him live on campus for free." His distaste for such options "became a major source of dissention in our household," Kelli says. "I and my husband created a young individual who believes absolutely that most things should come easy simply because he is a good guy."

How do you stop this from happening?

One way is to provide an allowance, which I'll discuss more completely in Chapter 11. Essentially, in paying an allowance you empower your children financially and allow them to make their own choices about what to do with their money. But let them fritter away their money as they see fit. That's part of the necessary learning curve. At a gas station mini-mart one day, my son wanted to spend $1.50 on a soft, plastic, water-filled ball that he could squeeze into various shapes. Amy told him it was cheap and would probably pop quickly. He didn't believe her, insisted on having it, and, since he had his own money, he bought it. Within 15 minutes, literally, his shirt was drenched. The toy had burst open and sprayed him with water. He was angry that he'd spent a $1.50, which he suddenly wanted back. I'm willing to bet he won't make the mistake again—the lesson was substantially more effective than Amy's words of caution.

The answer all parents seek is how to temper those discretionary wants in the first place. Lori, a mom in Texas, has found one such approach. First, she adheres to an allowance. Whenever her kids want a toy, she makes them cover the cost from their own pocketbook. Then, before they plan a trip to the toy store, each kid must choose one toy they already own and donate it to Goodwill. The idea, Lori says, "is that they learn to help someone else and that the new toy comes with a sacrifice." What Lori discovered, she says, is that her children "are hesitant to sacrifice toys they purchased with their own money, yet the ones I purchase are quite easy to discard." Lori also noticed that her kids are "more careful at the store. Because it's their money on the line, impulse buying at no cost to them has disappeared."[7]

The end result: Fewer toys around the house and, more important, Lori says, her kids "appreciate the toys they've earned."

One of the most important questions to ask yourself when you're contemplating buying for your child the Barbie doll or the hip jeans or the new motor scooter is this: Why do I feel compelled to buy my child a gift today?

Is it because you think your child has earned a treat? Are you trying to help your kid keep up with the Joneses? Are you succumbing to the peer pressure your son or daughter is feeling? Is it out of guilt?

I'm not suggesting that you should never buy what your kid wants. If you think your child has earned some material possession, then that's your call. But I suggest that you don't tie the purchase to some task completed, as a reward earned for doing the expected. Instead, just tell your child that Mom and Dad are buying you this gift because we've saved as a family, so we can afford it and, more important, because you're a member of the family and you deserve to spend some of the family's discretionary money, too.

If you're trying to keep up with other parents or to purge the peer pressure, then you have to stop and realize that the Joneses are always going to have something bigger and better and the peer pressure is just going to continue unabated for years; it might be jeans today, but it's shoes tomorrow and shirts the next day. Give up that fight now and save your money for what really matters in your life.

If it's guilt, then read this: My son did not feel well one day; Amy left work early to pick him up from school and take him to the doctor for a swollen lymph node. She called to tell me that the doctor requested that she take our son to the hospital for some X rays. "Can you meet me there?" my son wanted to know. I was disappointed that I couldn't get out of the city in time to make it to the hospital to ease my son's worry. On the commute home, I decided I would stop at the drugstore to buy him a $4 pack of the collectible trading cards he loves. I knew that would make him happy and show that I cared even though I couldn't be with him at the hospital.

When I reached the drugstore, I stopped just short of the door and realized that my desire to prove my affection through a meaningless gift was just that—meaningless. He knows I love him. What would a pack of trading cards prove? That Daddy has the money to buy your happiness when you're feeling down? That sends all sorts of wrong messages that can only hamper him as an adult. All I really needed to do, I knew, was simply to walk in the front door like I do every evening and give him a hug and spend time with him doing things like we always do, which is exactly what I did. He was just as happy as I'd hoped he would be when I was contemplating his reaction to the trading cards.

That night, just before he bounded up the stairs to put on his jammies, he rushed over and hugged me and said he was glad I was his dad.

In my nostalgic moments many years from now, I may not remember a single toy I ever bought him. But I will never forget that hug.

CHAPTER 11

From Allowances to Summer Jobs

Teaching Kids about Earning Dollars

"Do you have any money?"

If you have kids, you know that sentence well. It rattles around your brain like the malevolent jingle to a bad commercial. It arrives with the precision of a Swiss train every time you step into a store with a child in tow. If you don't yet have kids but are looking forward to their inclusion in your life, this is the sentence you will come to despise, so you should begin hating it now. Answer no, and your child lapses into a funk resulting in the inevitable "I want to go home" chant that kills the rest of your shopping trip. Be honest and answer yes, and suddenly your child wants to buy something, but if you kill that notion, then your child lapses into a funk resulting in the inevitable "I want to go home" chant that kills the rest of your shopping trip.

As a parent, the question "Do you have any money?" and all its associated baggage grows stale so rapidly that you reach a point where you just want your kids to have their own money already and stop hounding you constantly for cash. My son hit that stage near his sixth birthday. He was so accomplished at spending a buck, Amy and I figured it was time to teach him the value of that same buck, the benefits of saving it, the consequences of spending it, and the advantages of delayed—or even denied—gratification.

We figured it was time for an allowance.

However, this thing called an allowance isn't always so clear-cut. Parents have different agendas for the allowance they offer. Some see it as a mechanism to teach kids how to spend money, hopefully wisely. Others see it as a means for teaching children how to save, hopefully without becoming miserly. Still others want their kids to learn to budget and manage money, hopefully without becoming too attached to it. For yet another group, an allowance is all about earning money, either for chores or grades or some other task, hopefully without resorting to trickery to get it. Then there are those, like me, who want it all rolled into one perfect allowance program.

Regardless of your wants, an allowance in the broadest sense is a metaphor for earning money in childhood—the first expression of your kid's inherent desire to generate a paycheck, just as you do. Soon enough, that aspiration will morph into running a lemonade stand on the front sidewalk, babysitting the neighborhood children, cutting lawns, flipping burgers, bagging groceries, and busing tables. You might even be raising a baby Warren Buffett who joins or starts an investment club for teens and is able to parlay several summers' worth of earnings into a few semesters of college costs. Jobs are an important element in a child's road to maturity.

Whatever road your kids ultimately take, the first steps toward their need to earn starts with an allowance. For that reason, an allowance is a challenge. It must have an objective, and it must be given consistently. It can't be so chintzy that its value is useless nor so generous that its value is meaningless. It should help teach children financial fundamentals, but not prompt them to pursue backhanded means of achieving established goals just to obtain a dollar (as our son once did).

Essentially, an allowance demands a level of discipline that parents often find tough to manage, because when it comes to paying an allowance and when it comes to earning money in general in childhood, we parents often expect too much—not of our kids, but of ourselves.

By my last count, parents as a group employ more different allowance schemes than there are pennies in a million dollars (100 million, if you're counting). I admit such hyperbole is stretching reality a bit, but parents inundate me with all sorts of commentary about every conceivable allowance scheme and various iterations thereon.

From the outset, Amy and I opted for a plan that gave our son $1 a week for each year of his age. Basically he started at $6 a week. Depending on your values, that amount may strike you as a fair enough sum or laughably outrageous for a six-year-old. Behind all those thousands of allowance schemes are numerous surveys indicating that either I'm paying my son on par with national norms or I'm much too free with the greenbacks. A Harris Interactive poll conducted in mid-2002 shows that the biggest percentage of parents pay their six- to twelve-year-olds a weekly allowance equivalent to what we pay our son.[1] Various other polls maintain that, depending on what age group you scrutinize, between 30 and 40 percent of parents refuse to pay an allowance at all.

Yet even in families where an allowance doesn't exist overtly, the concept of an allowance—giving kids something of value, even if it's not money, in exchange for housework or grades or some such yardstick—often plays a role. Stacy, a woman I know in Louisiana, doesn't believe in paying her two daughters an allowance. Stacy takes the view that "good grades and helping with household chores are simply expected" of her two girls.[2] Still, Stacy does offer an inducement: permission to participate in extracurricular activities. She keeps mental tabs on school performance and house cleanliness; lag in either category and it's *sayonara* softball or summer camp. She also will spring occasionally for a toy or book as compensation for work well done. Thus, while dispensing a weekly dole isn't part of her philosophy, she nevertheless relies on a form of financial leverage—withholding or offering an item of value—to teach what she wants learned.

Honestly, there's no one right answer, because all parents have different notions about allowances and what they hope to accomplish by paying one—or not. So much depends on the moving parts within each family, not the least of which is your family's income, the age of your kids, your own inclinations and hang-ups about money, and your experiences with receiving or not receiving an allowance when you were a kid. The truth is that as adults most of us will stumble through various iterations of our allowance program before we find one that actually works—and even then we may screw it up out of love. There's no reason to gnash your teeth over how much you pay and why—the first few allowance programs you start are doomed anyway.

At various times through the years, my friend at work vacillated between offering his kids an allowance and not doing so. Most of the time, he didn't pay, mainly because he never could muster the restraint an allowance requires. Offering an allowance, he realized, was a bit useless in his life because he routinely would supplement the payout whenever his kids needed money, thus destroying the purpose of the allowance. Strictly adhering to an allowance, he says, represents "a kind of discipline that I usually don't have with my kids."

Indeed, he never had a problem giving his kids whatever they asked for, which usually wasn't much. Part-time jobs when they hit their teens met their smaller discretionary desires. When they sought big-ticket items, like the occasional concert ticket or a health club membership, "I just gave it to them," he says, "because they never asked for a lot. I knew it would make them happy." Plus, he could easily afford it, and what are a few bucks when those few bucks mean so much to your child?

Reflecting on those years, though, he sees that his kids grew up absent the financial discipline he wishes they would demonstrate, and he blames himself for not adhering to an allowance that would have made them better stewards of their money while at the same time tempering their need to satisfy the small desires they have. "I regret that I didn't give them allowances more when they were younger and stick to the plan," he says.

Many parents I've talked to share similar tales. We all try so hard to abide by the allowances we set, only to fail miserably because of our love for our kids or, in some cases, because we're using money to cover the guilt we often feel for having to work long hours and not spending as much time with our children as we'd like. Amy and I hoped that in starting our son on an allowance program we could begin to provide him a rudimentary financial education, complete with lessons about earning, spending, saving, and managing both your money and your wants. In adopting an allowance, though, we quickly realized that no other outlay of money is burdened by so many expectations, of both our son and ourselves.

Starting about the time a kid can voice a desire for some item in the store is just about the time you need to start teaching about money, even if it's the most rudimentary basics. The good news is that your child is likely to be naturally interested, since money has that effect on people, even youngsters.

The bad news is that it becomes more difficult from that point on. The problem that stumps lots of parents, including me and Amy, is that our families often never had the discretionary dollars to pay an allowance when we were kids. Today, though, lots of parents have plenty of discretionary income. Not only does that make us more likely to offer an allowance, it makes us much more likely to disregard the allowance when our kids want something their savings can't afford. We just cover the cost from our own pockets.

Doling out extra dollars too willingly, though, is rife with wrong messages and mistakenly gives our kids the idea that whatever they want in life they can obtain with little effort—all they have to do is ask someone else. A reader from Connecticut says that when his two daughters were growing up, he and his wife provided an allowance from which the girls were responsible for all discretionary wants—movies with friends, toys, clothes, whatever. By the time they hit high school, that sum was $20 a week. They were also given a quarterly clothing allowance—slightly bigger during the back-to-school period. "They could spend the clothing allowance in one big spree or spread it over the quarter—their choice," he says. The key to the system's success: "Just saying 'no.' The girls learned to plan, and if they didn't have enough saved to buy something in a particular week, they waited until they had saved it."

You have to curb your own urge to open your own wallet to fill those gaps yourself. An allowance seems like the magical tool to do just that—and so much more. With an allowance, you can rein in your inclinations to spend on your child's wants, teach your kids basic math and money management skills, maybe provide an incentive for good grades, and offer encouragement for undertaking a few minor household chores. At the very least, I figured, with a pocketful of his own spending money my son could meet his discretionary wants through his own means.

For the record, aside from teaching math and money management skills and funding discretionary wants, all of those reasons I just stated are bogus reasons for paying your kid an allowance. Take it from me, someone who learned that lesson the hard way.

The problems started when my son fibbed for $1.

Amy knew our little boy was up to something. Standing in the kitchen with a way-too-cool demeanor, his hands were obviously manipulating something behind his back. She saw him surreptitiously slip something into the garbage can, then saunter off.

Adept at spotting the sort of sneakiness all parents master early on, Amy strolled into the kitchen as though on a cleaning mission. She crumbled a piece of paper and opened the trash to toss it. "Hmm," she feigned bewilderment, "what's this?" My son's eyes ballooned. She pulled out an unopened envelope, what turned out to be a note from our son's teacher telling us he'd gotten into trouble that day for horsing around in class. When Amy questioned him, he said he trashed the note "because I didn't want to lose my allowance."

As upset as I was that he tried to hoodwink Mom and Dad, I was more concerned about the system that had a kindergartner so preoccupied with money that he resorted to deception to obtain it. In the months after we began our allowance program, our son had learned to save, to defer some of his gratification, and to weigh the pros and cons of a purchase, no matter how frustrating to choose one toy over another. He even learned to haggle with some independent retailers to get them to cut the price on items he wanted.

Yet here he was, resorting to skulduggery for money.

We had only ourselves to blame. Amy and I had screwed up all of our hard work. Along with using an allowance to teach our son all the good attributes of money management, somewhere along the line we began using it also as carrot and stick—offering it to encourage acceptable behavior at school, threatening to revoke it for sassiness and disrespect at home. That's a big mistake easy to stumble into. You know the allowance means the world to your children because it's the only money they get. Just as your kids learn to manipulate you for money, you learn to manipulate them *with* money. "Keep on acting up and you can say good-bye to your allowance" is so tempting that you succumb to it once out of frustration, and, like a drug, it works so fast the first time that you're addicted, quick to return again and again to the easy fix.

Melissa, Amy's friend in Louisiana, also fell into the allowance-as-behavior-modifier trap. She began to dock her son's pay for acting up at school, not doing his homework in the evening, or failing to help with household chores when asked. Based on two episodes at school, however, Melissa began to see that her son's life revolved "too much around money," she says. "He understands the value of a dollar way too early."[3]

Here's what happened: Her son wanted a $15 set of collectible trading cards. That price, he knew, meant he would have to save his full allowance for three weeks—assuming he didn't blow it in the meantime with temper tantrums or antics at school that resulted in notes going home to Mom and Dad. Three weeks? Kids think in dog years, and in dog years three weeks are just shy of forever. No way he could hold out, so . . . he hatched a plan. During snack break at school each day he headed to the concession stand to buy a box of Gummi Bears for 50 cents. Then, he resold to his classmates the individual pieces of candy, three for a quarter. This was a five-year-old.

Melissa discovered his entrepreneurial plot when she found he had $10 worth of quarters and, with his allowance, enough to buy his card set after little more than one week. Part of her was "kind of proud he was so creative," she admits. "It takes a lot of creativity at his age to come up with this idea. And he executed it well. But a bigger part is really concerned" about his drive for money. In fact, Melissa adds, this candy-selling episode came just a few months after she talked to him about another money-raising scheme: He had been convincing classmates to give him a dollar bill for two quarters.

The boy is so preoccupied with money, Melissa says, that "he'd rather be whipped for doing something bad than have a dollar taken from his allowance."

Melissa and I both hold ourselves at fault. We created these little money monsters by using allowances in the wrong way. Teach a kid to covet a dollar—and you get a kid who covets a dollar. Pretty soon, you've raised the next CEO of Enron.

Personally, I never received an allowance as a kid. Neither did Amy. We both had to rely on the "entrepreneurial kids" method of building wealth: one yard and one Popsicle at a time. Basically, we had to find a job.

For me, that meant that when my friends and I were strong enough to yank a lawn mower to life, we began hawking lawn services around the neighborhood. We bagged groceries and delivered phone books as we got older. On the other side of town, Amy and her younger brother brewed up batches of homemade freezies out of Kool-Aid packets and sold them for a nickel, a dime, and 15 cents to neighborhood kids who stopped by all day long and often into the evening.

The lemonade stand, the lawn mowing, the babysitting—necessary childhood experiences—are a natural outgrowth of your allowance program in that once kids get a taste of how money can improve their lives, they naturally want more. Since Mom and Dad aren't always willing or able to shell out an increased supply, kids realize that they, like you, can work to earn more money for their personal wants. Some people will cringe at the implied consumerism; I simply accept that money is an elemental factor of life for kids as well as adults. As such, the best we can do as parents is to encourage our kids at an early age to use money as you would a hammer or any other tool; you control the power, not the other way around.

Summer jobs, part-time work, and the odd jobs washing cars, raking leaves, or shoveling snow stoke creativity in a kid and spur a desire to excel. Along with generating some spending money, the various jobs of our youth boost self-confidence and self-reliance and help build a strong work ethic and sense of responsibility. They instill discipline and the inner satisfaction of a job well done, and they represent the next step toward maturity. In money terms, such jobs offer self-taught lessons on saving, spending, earning, and the value of a dollar that a parent's words never will. It's also a huge ego boost. Aside from my athletic endeavors, I felt best about myself after sweating all day in the humid heat of a south Louisiana summer, cutting a half-dozen lawns with my buddy Mike, then sitting on the curb outside the Country Corner convenience store, sucking down a Coke Icee and counting the $60 or $70 we earned.

The money was the motivating factor. Jobs allow your kids the opportunity to earn their own money and to freely spend it on what Mom and Dad otherwise can't or won't. Illegal or harmful substances aside, parents should give their kids full authority to dispense with their cash as they wish. No doubt they'll muff it a few times, but they'll learn ultimately what is important to them. And you'll begin to see them save with a purpose, even if that purpose is the latest Playstation video game. The underlying truth that you can't overlook, though, is that in saving for that game, your child practiced self-denial and restraint, giving up small gratifications along the way in order to buy that game—discipline that will go a long way as an adult.

I worked summer jobs and, when I was old enough, after-school jobs as a bag boy at the local Kroger supermarket, largely because my grandparents could not afford to offer me a prescribed allowance, but also because I truly enjoyed the feeling each payday of seeing what I had earned without anyone's assistance. Even today, I still get a little rush seeing my paycheck because of what it represents: that I went out into the great maw of life and made my way successfully. It gives me a bit of pride.

Dollars & Sense

Want of an allowance and, later, a desire to find a job represents your kids' inherent interest in money and providing for themselves financially on some level. As parents, it's up to you to help shepherd both needs.

Let's start with the allowance. Most parents ask two basic questions:

1. When do I begin paying?
2. How much is enough?

There's no single right answer to either of those questions. As I said earlier, when your child begins expressing interest in money, or at least in what money can buy, that's a pretty good time to begin explaining the basics of how dollars and coins work. Even if that means your youngster just learns to differentiate nickels from dimes, that's a start. All the more advanced concepts will begin to flow in time, and your child will naturally ask the relevant questions as the answers become necessary, so don't worry just yet about the need to buy your kid *The Wall Street Journal Guide to Personal Finance.*

As for how much to pay, that depends on a variety of factors. Some parents do as Amy and I do and offer $1 per week for each year of your child's age. Some parents think that's outrageous. The amount you pay should essentially be in line with what your child's peers receive. You don't want your kid feeling like the playground pauper with just two quarters to rub together when everyone else has a couple of dollars. Then again, you don't want your child feeling like the king of the jungle gym with a $20 bill.

Age, obviously, is a big determinant, and so is your locale. The older the child, the bigger the allowance. Again, though, that's a function of local and family standards. A teenager from Wisconsin probably would think a kid in southern Connecticut (a bedroom community of New York City) is overpaid—until the Wisconsin teen spent some time living with the expenses of the Northeast. If you want to review a whole range of money issues when it comes to kids, including allowances, check out www .kidsmoney.com; it's one of the more useful web sites. Sovereign Bank runs www.kidsbank.com, an interactive tutorial to help kids understand money fundamentals and banking.

Also, *First National Bank of Dad,* by David Owen, is a great book to help parents better understand how to institute an allowance program and how to instill in kids the desire to actually save some of their money instead of blowing it all within minutes of touching it.

The most important lesson to learn about an allowance is that if you aim at everything, you ultimately hit nothing. An allowance is just a simple tool to teach kids the simple notions about saving and spending their own money. It's not a tool to reform our kids' behavior. If you do that, kids begin valuing money so highly that they pursue unacceptable paths to obtain it, even at a young age. Just as bad, when you employ money as a behavior modifier, you're essentially telling your child that good behavior is important only as long as they're being paid for acting appropriately, when we should instead be teaching that good behavior is important because . . . well, because it's important, because it's the right thing to do.

Expectations in return for an allowance should be unbearably light. You need to establish just a simple, basic, and uncomplicated goal. The simplest I can think of is this: "Mom and Dad want you to learn the right ways to save and spend money." Nothing more. When you start packaging into a weekly allowance all sorts of hopes and desires for your own and your child's behavior, you're bound to screw up, as we did.

Is it really practical for six-year-olds to save part of their money for college? At that age, college is less real than Scooby Doo. As children age and take on summer jobs or part-time work, then yes, you should encourage your kids to squirrel away a percentage of their paychecks to help pay for some college costs, even if you intend to foot the bill. (I'll talk more about college in Stage Five.)

Lots of parents require youngsters to set aside a portion of their allowance for charitable contributions. That's a wonderful sentiment, but, to me, a bit misguided, particularly for younger kids. What's charitable about being forced to part with money for reasons you don't really grasp— and that's exactly how kids see it. (Does your boss *make* you give to the United Way?) A better approach: Let your child know that you give to charitable causes and explain why you're doing so. Incorporate your youngster's interests into the process. Maybe your daughter has a thing for horses; if so, give a little of your own money, with her assistance, to Habitat for Horses to help abused animals. Over time, your actions will reinforce the message you want to deliver far more effectively than will pressing kids to part with money before they're ready to do so voluntarily. As your children age, you can promote charitable giving as part of an allowance because you will have set the precedent. They'll know it's right, and better yet, they'll want to do it, too.

Nor should you dock your kids for goofing off at school, mouthing off at home, or any other childhood faults. Alex, a friend of mine in New York, gives her fourth-grade daughter an allowance "just because she is a contributing member of the family."[4] That means she doesn't lose her allowance for everyday transgressions. After all, your employer doesn't dock your paycheck if you make a mistake. Instead, Alex punishes misbehavior by taking away privileges such as movies with a friend or some other treat.

Indeed, most psychologists I've talked to about kids and money have told me this is one of those big parental blunders, because at some point children determine they have enough money for what they seek at the moment and no longer care about consequences. When Amy and I realized our son began to disregard our directives if money wasn't involved or if he didn't care about the money at that moment, we altered our allowance scheme, opting to give our son his money with no strings attached. That arrangement worked substantially better. Prior to the change, our son spent his money rapidly, concerned we might confiscate a dollar or two if he smarted off to Mom or Dad. In spending it, he knew he couldn't lose money he didn't have. That concern is no longer a worry, so he's eager to save and contemplate his purchases. He even wanted to open a bank account at age six and half, which he did.

At some point, your son or daughter is going to come to you and want more money. That's the time to say, "Get a job."

I started working for money at eight, when my grandfather let me use the family lawn mower to cut the neighbor's yard for $10. The age you let your child start earning money depends largely on the maturity of the kid. The Family Education Network (www.familyeducation.com) offers a section that explores whether your teenager is ready for a job. Meanwhile, the Department of Labor (www.dol.gov) provides information on the various federal laws that protect kids in the workforce.

There are a variety of ways to help your child find a job:

- *Advertise.* My buddy Mike and I spent the first day of summer break after seventh grade painting a sign on a piece of plywood, announcing

"Lawns Cut. Call . . ." We nailed it to a stake and jammed it into the ground at a red light along a busy highway near our house. We earned some money that summer. You also could pin flyers on the bulletin board that most grocery stores have for local announcements, or hang a pamphlet on doors around the neighborhood to publicize your dog-walking or babysitting business. When Amy and I lived in Texas, one young potential babysitter listed her prices by the hour, highlighted her skills with CPR, and included several references.

- *Use the Internet.* This approach works best for older kids, since local businesses don't often advertise their need for youngsters. They do, however, advertise their need for part-time workers and even interns. Internships.com, for instance, offers information on various internship programs that exist, broken down by region. The list certainly isn't exhaustive, but it's a starting point. Most local newspapers also have online editions, often providing free access to the classified ads.

- *Try word of mouth.* If you shovel your neighbors' snow-shrouded side-walks and driveways, ask them to pass along your name to their friends. If your work is satisfactory and your attitude upbeat, they're generally eager to help out.

Whatever you do as a parent, encourage your child's interest in work. Don't stifle it. A study by the University of North Carolina Greensboro found that six to nine years after high school, seniors who had worked up to 20 hours a week while in school earned 22 percent more than their classmates who hadn't, suggesting that teens who work not only gain workplace skills, they likely build a better understanding of the job market. Another report, this one from the Educational Testing Service, a leader in educational research, showed that high school students working 20 or fewer hours each week actually produced better grades than their non-working peers.

No matter what, when it comes to allowances and money earned on the job, remember this: The dollars are for your child to spend or save. This is not money you can surreptitiously manipulate for some ulterior goal you've established, such as saving for college or giving to charity. If your aim is to teach the basics of money management, then let your children determine how to use their money, no matter how boneheaded it might be. (Admit it, you've done some stupid things yourself with money.) Kids most certainly will rack up a bunch of blunders, but those mistakes will teach them more about the real world of dollars and cents than your admonitions ever will. Certainly you should make your thoughts known and encourage various end uses that will benefit your child and society, particularly when your kid is of an age to absorb your rationale. However, be careful of urging small children to part with money for reasons not completely clear.

Yes, being a parent is difficult when it comes to our kids earning money. We want to help when we can and protect them from the dumb mistakes we see them making.

Sometimes, though, those dumb mistakes are the best lessons kids will ever learn about managing money wisely.

CHAPTER 12

Speaking in Code

Understanding Your Messages about Money

Next time you're in line at the checkout counter somewhere, or maybe strolling through the aisles of a drugstore while the pharmacist fills your prescription, and your child asks the predictable "Can I get a toy?" or "Do you have any money?" pay attention after the fact to the reply you immediately shoot back. I'm betting it's a pet phrase you routinely use, probably out of habit, to bat down those incessant childhood wants.

All of us parents have our succinct one-liners that we toss out whenever blitzed by an attack of the "I wants." We dispatch them liberally because we need any defense that provides logic easily understood and digested by young minds. A prime example: One Saturday morning while running errands, the three of us—Amy, me, and our young son—stopped by a pharmacy to pick up a prescription. When our son asked me if he could buy a pack of trading cards, I replied casually, "Daddy doesn't have any money." His desire faded because he knows that when I announce that, then he's out of luck. Amy's answer would have been similar; had our son instead asked her, she would have replied with her standby, "Mommy can't afford that."

We uncork these phrases with good reason. They're easy, they're mindless, and best of all they work.

Yet there's a problem here bigger than our kids' demands to buy. With these throwaway phrases we so readily deploy, we send the wrong message about money. Those messages, in turn, can have a huge effect on a child's view of finances when it really matters—as adults.

After all, schools rarely teach money skills, other than the adding and subtracting necessary to make change. Thus, the building blocks of money that our kids learn they learn from us parents, and that can create a shaky foundation.

We may be adults, but that doesn't necessarily mean we have grown-up tendencies toward money. All of us have financial hang-ups of one kind or another. Some people are miserly to the point of squeezing the copper from a penny. Others are so freewheeling with their cash that they can't keep a dollar in their wallet for more than a day. Like genes, our words and actions regarding money can't help but transfer to our kids.

Unfortunately, those genes aren't always the best traits to pass along.

Psychologists I've talked to say that our core beliefs about money are formed within the first 12 years of our lives. That means all the things we learn from Mom and Dad—and all the things that our kids, in turn, learn from us—serve as the financial foundation we rely on as adults. That's just peachy. Here we are, vowing never to be like our parents, and it turns out we can't help but mimic them in many ways financially, often without even realizing it. For some of us, that's probably not so bad; for others of us—and I am talking from experience here—impersonating Mom or Dad just can't be good, because those beliefs ingrained in us dictate how we spend and save and, ultimately, the role money plays in our relationships with other people.

I know in my own life I've fought at times *not* to be like my mom. Love her as I do, she just can't manage a dollar. Temptations, nevertheless, arise in me at times that encourage me to follow in her footsteps, to disregard the value of saving, and to pursue some temporary enjoyment by spending foolishly. Thankfully, when those genes kick into gear my dad's genes drown them in prudence—otherwise, Amy and I would be living in a small apartment, but she'd be driving the sports car of her dreams and I'd be watching *Law & Order* on a big, flat-screen, plasma TV . . . in theater-style surround sound, no less.

The experience with my son at the pharmacy that morning, culminating not long afterward in a Mexican eatery, began a chain of events that raised all of these thoughts in my mind. I realized that Amy and I were on the road to turning our son into us financially. That's probably not the worst thing in the world, but it seems to me our job is to make him a better person.

Here's what happened.

Somewhere between the door and my first step into the store, I heard, "Dad, can I get a pack of Yu-Gi-Oh cards?" That would be my son.

"Daddy doesn't have any money, Buddy." That would be me.

That sums up the entire exchange. He said nothing, but was clearly miffed and decided he had no use for the pharmacy. He wanted to go sit in the car with his mom instead of shop with me.

Twenty minutes later, we popped into a nearby Mexican restaurant for lunch and paid the bill with a credit card. At that precise instant, the epiphany hit: Didn't I just tell my son moments ago that Daddy doesn't have any money? If that's the case, how is it that we can afford to pay for these tacos and burritos? How did I purchase those prescriptions at the pharmacy?

I lied to my son.

It wasn't a blatant lie, and certainly our little boy didn't say anything; he was too busy blowing bubbles in his chocolate shake. Honestly, I doubt he even recognized the lie. But the entire episode, starting with his original want in the drugstore and ending with me pulling the MasterCard from my wallet to pay for lunch, sent multiple messages that I'm convinced our son will pick up on subconsciously over time if we continue down this path.

Message number 1: Mommy and Daddy never have enough money, so maybe money is something you hoard.

Message number 2: There's no money for what I want because Mommy and Daddy are always spending it on what they want.

Message number 3: My wants aren't worth wasting family money on.

Message number 4: If you don't have any money, at least you can use that plastic thing to get what you want.

Now, I can assure you that these messages are not accurate, and they're certainly not what we want our son to learn. But how is he supposed to know that when our actions betray our words?

Whenever I talk to friends about the things they say to their children, I constantly hear those mixed messages at work. It's never intentional, and usually not recognized, but the messages are almost always there, hidden in plain view.

Consider some friends of ours, who proudly announce that their son knows he cannot spend more than his weekly allowance. Yet the wife adds that their little boy also knows that if he wants more than his wallet can afford he can always call his grandmother, "because he knows she has a credit card and she'll use it." Our friend jokes that the arrangement "works for me."

Look at the message she's inadvertently sending, though: When money gets tight, someone else will bail you out or foot the bill—even though as a family they certainly do not subscribe to that belief and are actually quite sensible with their money. Such a message, if it does sink in and becomes a part of their son's money conscience, could breed an entitlement mentality—that someone else can always provide what I can't afford for myself. Likewise, her son may determine that whipping out the credit card is a perfectly fine way to sate immediate wants, a philosophy that later in life could lead to spending problems, a struggle managing credit and debt, or an inability to save adequately for his own future.

I'm not saying that's what will happen, and I know it sounds a bit far-fetched when we're talking about a five-year-old. Isn't this what grandmothers are for, after all? Yet when messages like these are hammered into our heads over and over again at an impressionable age, they eventually create some kind of dent.

Marty, a woman I know in Alabama, has seen throwaway comments shape her own child's financial consciousness in unintended ways. As her children were growing up, she always told them, "You're really smart; you better get a scholarship." Though she was only joking about the scholarship, her daughter, she realized too late, had taken Mom's words all too seriously through the years. As her senior year in high school drew to a close, the teenager applied to several schools, including the University of Virginia, where she really wanted to attend. Two schools offered her a full scholarship; Virginia offered her admission but not a free ride. With Mom's words echoing through her head, Marty's daughter decide to turn down Virginia and instead attend a less prestigious school for free. She let her parents know of her decision only well after the fact.

"Years later she leveled with me," Marty says. "She was conscious about the money and felt it was better for the family if she went to a lesser school with the scholarship. I still feel terrible that I sent her the wrong message. You think what you say goes in one ear and out the other, but it doesn't."[1]

Indeed not. We parents have far more power to shape our kids through words and actions than we realize. When you are a kid, some of the things you hear parents say, particularly the frightening stuff, can stick with you for your entire life.

"The way I think about money, even now at the age of 62, was set when I was about eight years old," says Julia, a Love & Money reader in Missouri. "My father was sick with a disease that doctors in the Midwest knew little about in 1948—Parkinson's. My mother didn't have a job, as was the norm at the time, and my father was finding it difficult to work."[2] Finances, Julia says, had always been a struggle for the family; she just never realized how significant that struggle was until she walked into the kitchen one day to find her mother sitting at the table with the checkbook and an anguished expression on her face.

"My father was standing beside her. I overheard her say they had only $28," Julia recalls. "I asked, 'Is that all we have?' I will never forget the look on my mother's face when she looked up at me and simply nodded yes. What was said after that, I don't remember. I just know that one incident was burned into my memory, and I was afraid."

That single instant shaped how Julia still feels about money, and it continues to stoke concerns in her life with her own family. "It has caused me to think of money as security. I am now retired, and even though my husband and I have what we consider healthy savings, I still worry about our financial security." Julia says she fully recognizes that she and her husband have plenty of dollars coming in, with Social Security, pension, 401(k), and IRA income. She knows they've planned well for retirement, with a trust, a living will, great medical insurance, prescription drug coverage, and long-term-care insurance.

"Yet I am still uneasy," she says. All of her fears stem from one sentence her mom uttered half a century ago at the kitchen table, when an eight-year-old happened to be within earshot. "What a parent says to a child, on any subject," Julia says, "can have a real impact on that child's life."

The real difficulty with unintended messages is kicking a habit you don't even see. Until that particular moment in the restaurant, I never paid any mind to the financial phrases Amy and I use. She and I both know that when we exclaim with frustration that "We're broke," it's just our shorthand way of griping about having run through our paychecks so quickly in paying the bills. For us, those are just words with no substance because we both know they're not true. We know we have plenty of money in savings and investments and that we're not literally without any resources, as *broke* implies. But does our young son know that, too? Does he realize that sometimes words mean less than their dictionary definitions?

Honestly, I don't know. At his age, six when this happened, it's hard to distinguish his real concerns, even when I ask, because he's still learning to understand all those confusing emotions he has and to put them into words that actually describe something. He knows we go to the ATM to retrieve cash occasionally, but does he know that the dollars the machine spits out come from our savings account, which is a healthy size? He sees us use our credit card frequently, but does he realize we have to give the credit card company a bunch of money at the end of the month? I know there's no way he can know we pay off the bill in full every month and that we still have money left over for savings and other family needs. He's not an active part of our budgeting and bill paying, so it's likely none of this means anything to him. All he knows is what he sees—that Mom and Dad sometimes have real dollars to spend and sometimes they just use a card that doesn't look like money. Other times they sign a piece of paper and rip it out of a little book. What he sees, though, doesn't always mesh with what he hears. That has to be confusing.

A friend of mine at work recognizes that his words through the years have sent the wrong messages about money to his two kids, both in their late teens now. When they were younger and asked for small items, he routinely said, "Sure, it's only $5 or $10." He wasn't concerned about the expense, when that small outlay could mean so much happiness to his kids. In hindsight, though, he knows that even though those purchases were relatively inexpensive, they were nevertheless costly in terms of their underlying message. He sees in his kids' actions as teens that "they don't think they should deprive themselves of the small items because I essentially taught them that $5 or $10 didn't mean much." In the broader sense of their financial education, he says, "it really wasn't a very good lesson."

It's too early to tell how his kids ultimately will handle money, though my friend does worry that they may grow up not as concerned about saving as they should be.

"Will they be 30 years old, saying, 'I'll buy it; it's only $100'?" he wonders. "I do wish that instead of saying, 'It's only $5 or $10,' I had said, 'No, I'd rather we save that money for *blank*.' I wish I had said that many more times than I did. Because what you say to your kids, if it sinks in, is so hard to take back."

Dollars & Sense

Stop and think for a moment: What casual or inflammatory statements about money routinely echo through your home that your child hears regularly?

Do you and your spouse grouse about being broke? Are you headed for the poorhouse? Do you earnestly or nonchalantly insist, as Amy and I often do, that you just don't have any money for your kid's small want even as you casually rack up the credit card receipts for your own expenses? Are you harsher than that, maybe arguing with your spouse about wasting the family's dollars on this or that? Do you moan in front of your kids about how much either of you spent at the grocery store or the mall, implying that the spending will bust the budget again?

Such commentary can—and does—send messages about money that become ingrained in children's consciousness, even if we think they're not listening. Chances are, they are. Once ingrained, it's only a short synapse to adoption, and all of a sudden you've shaped your child's perceptions about family finance for a lifetime, and you don't even realize it. Indeed, on the way home from an expensive Disney World vacation, Linda, a Love & Money reader, grumbled aloud to her husband, "That's it. We're broke." The next week, her middle-school-aged son came home one afternoon with a form to fill out so that he could receive reduced-cost lunches. Linda was perplexed; her husband has an excellent job and the family is not in dire straits. Turns out Linda simply had forgotten to dump some money into her son's account at school to pay for sundry items such as lunch. When the lunchroom cashier told the boy his account was dry, "he told her his family is broke,"[3] Linda says. Thus the school sent home the note asking whether the family needed to sign up for the reduced-cost lunch program.

The best way to send your kids the correct messages about money is the most straightforward approach: Talk to them directly—and honestly.

You might never have done this because your parents never talked to you about money. That's because their parents never talked to them about money. You can see where I'm going with this: No one ever talks about money, particularly with kids. Apparently, that needs to change. Kids say so. Stein Roe, a mutual fund company, commissioned a study in 2000 that revealed that just 42 percent of eighth- through twelfth-graders said their parents discuss finances with them on a regular basis.[4] Yet in a study by Girls Inc., 79 percent of teens surveyed indicated an interest in knowing how to manage their money.[5]

That's an open invitation for you as parents to begin talking to your kids about money. Take every opportunity you can to explain what you're doing financially and why. If you're at the bank, explain how banking works in terms that are appropriate to your child's age—that a bank is basically a money store where the family stashes its dollars for safekeeping and that the bank pays you a small amount for the use of your money every month. My son was watching the Cartoon Network one day when an ad came on hawking one of those compilation music CDs with all the hottest tunes. He expressed interest in the $24.95 two-disk volume. When we were at the mall several days later I pulled him into a music store and showed him the same CD for $17.99, making the point that if you shop around you generally can find the same item for less, saving a bit of money. (He was no longer interested in the CD—but a Mary Kate and Ashley video, stocked at child height at the checkout counter, grabbed his attention.)

When kids are a little older, say in elementary school, have them do the bills with you as part of a math exercise. Set the stack of bills on the table and explain each one you pay and why you have to pay it: "If we don't pay the cable bill, then you can't watch cartoons every day." Have your child subtract the amount from the register and explain that "these aren't just numbers, but real dollars that are coming out of our bank." For a really dramatic effect, you could do a bit of advance planning by withdrawing from the bank an amount of cash equal to your paycheck. Put the money on the table and as you write the checks, systematically pull out the dollars needed to pay each bill. At the end, you'll have whittled the stack down to a much smaller amount, which you can then explain will go into a savings account to help protect the family in an emergency or into the checking account to pay more bills.

A good resource for parents, kids, and teachers is www.themint.org. The site, backed by the Northwestern Mutual Foundation and the National Council on Economic Education, is designed to teach financial literacy. It offers various activities, ideas, and tips to better understand the role of money and how to spend, save, earn, invest, and track your dollars. There's even a section on using debt wisely.

Along with talking to your kids, you need to rethink the messages you send through your words and actions. My friend at work, the one who knows he sent the wrong messages to his kids when they were younger, now is aiming to undo some of the damage that his words have caused. No longer does he view otherwise affordable expenses, such as a sushi dinner his son might suggest, as just a small cost in the overall happiness of his kids. More often, he's saying no and pointing out when he feels a want or desire is too expensive, even though it wouldn't really hurt his pocketbook. His hope is that his kids see that he considers the costs of even the small things in life. With luck, he says, they'll begin to mimic those actions, too.

Still, he concedes that saying no is not easy after all these years. "Once you set the tone," he says, "it's hard to change it."

Years ago, Dan, a North Carolina reader, realized he needed to change the financial language he used around his two young children. He, too, was unleashing the standard "Daddy doesn't have any money" when his kids wanted something, often followed by a lecture on finances that only increased the tension for everyone involved. A better approach, he has found, is to simply reply that the cost of whatever item your kid requests isn't in the family's budget.

"That type of language," Dan says, "doesn't put a guilt trip on the youngster or the parent. It is a point that the child or young adult can't refute."[6] This is especially true if you've taken the opportunity previously to detail the components of the family's budget and to explain how money flows through the household and which expenses must take priority. With this honest approach, Dan concludes, "the child doesn't feel like he or she has been beaten down. The parents aren't left to wonder, 'Are we bad parents? Are we doing the right thing?' "

Of course, that strategy carries a big caveat: You must be fair. If you're going to rule that your child's desire doesn't fit into the family budget, then you must be prepared to admit when your wants fail that budget test as well, and refrain from constantly spending on your discretionary wants, even if you can afford to. You can't rightly claim "no money" in rejecting your daughter's request for a CD player for her room, then pull into Wal-Mart on the way home to buy for yourself a DVD player on credit. You're sending a powerfully strong, and wrong, message—in this case, that your child's wants are unworthy, among other things, and that because it's your money, not hers, you can spend it freely. Later in life your daughter might unconsciously recall that message in erroneously assuming that her wants are unimportant in the scheme of her own family's spending or that her spouse's income is his alone to spend as he sees fit. In such a case, she's unlikely to speak up for her own wants and needs and may grow increasingly frustrated in her own financial relationships. Or perhaps she'll resort to money laundering (remember that from Stage Two?) to surreptitiously get what she wants. Maybe instead she learns to rely on her credit card, like you do, and racks up so much debt that she must file for bankruptcy. This may not happen because of a single episode, but then again, it very well could—look at Julia, still struggling because of something her mom said in the kitchen more than 50 years ago.

More important, my bet is that such an episode isn't a one-time-only event. These are the messages that you, me, and all of us send every day, out of habit, often without realizing it.

Amy and I set a new tone by forsaking the white lies and being forthright with our son, who most certainly knows we can easily afford the small items he desires. Instead of telling him otherwise, we have decided to consciously rely on the truth—that while Mommy and Daddy can afford to spend a few dollars on the small item he would like to buy, we choose to use the family's money instead on other expenses that are higher priorities for all of us at that particular moment, such as, say, lunch.

So that we don't scare him into thinking money is in tight supply, we also started to include him in the banking process to show him that we do have money, but not always in our wallet. By letting him witness us deposit a portion of our paychecks into the joint savings account and by openly discussing in front of him our account balances and how much money we earn, we hope to instill in him a sense of financial security. Moreover, we want to show him that money is nothing to be afraid of, that money is something you can openly discuss, and, more practically, that you don't have to spend money just because you have money.

Regarding that last point, we opened a bank account for our son a couple of months before his seventh birthday—he actually requested it—so that he could begin to acclimate himself to the ways of banking. We picked a kid-friendly bank on the East Coast, Commerce Bank, because it has a coin-counting machine in the lobby that allows him to dump into it all the change he collects and take the receipt to the teller to deposit in his account. He tracks the deposits in his own little passbook. The biggest benefit I see, though, is that my son is actually excited about banking and about saving some money to put into his account. Although he started off by saving pocket change, he's now saving dollar bills.

Unfortunately, there's no clearinghouse for the kid-friendly banks that exist across the country, so the best bet is to check with the smaller, independent banks in your area and ask if they offer kid-sized savings accounts. An example of what to look for: Woodsville Guaranty Savings Bank in Woodsville, New Hampshire, offers a Young Savers Club that requires a minimum balance of only $1—and the bank *gives* you the dollar. There's no fee, the account earns interest, and your kid gets a biannual newsletter in the mail.

The Young Americans Bank (www.theyoungamericans.org) is the first and only bank catering solely to young people—anyone under the age of 22. Kids can do everything at this bank that grown-ups can do at their banks, including borrowing money and obtaining credit cards, although with ultralow limits, like $100. The average age of the bank's customer base: 11 for savings accounts, 16 for checking accounts. The average balance: $682 in savings, $781 in checking. The average credit card balance: $98.[7] The bank is located in Denver, but has accounts in all 50 states. Your child can open an account easily through the mail.

Changing the messages you send to your kids isn't something you can accomplish overnight. After all, patterns are tough to break. Still, if you expect your kids to view money in a healthy fashion and to appreciate saving a dollar as much as spending one, then you must show your kids that your words don't lie and that your actions speak just as loudly.

STAGE FOUR

The Middle Years

Reevaluating Your Life

This sounds like such a cliché, but it's true: One morning you wake up and you're not the same person you were the night before. The reflection in the mirror looks identical to what you've grown accustomed to seeing, but you can tell inside that you've begun to see your life in different terms.

Things you never cared about suddenly make a little sense. You drive slower in the fast lane. Burgers begin to remind you that your health really does matter. "Saving for the future" has a certain comforting ring to it now.

This middle period of life exists for everyone—couples, singles, one-parent families, dual-income families, blended families, nontraditional families. Everyone. Along with so-called decade birthdays—you know, your thirtieth, fortieth, fiftieth, which seem to encourage reflective moments—our middle years mark the period during which we begin reevaluating the various aspects of our lives, taking stock of what we've accomplished personally and professionally, reviewing what we still want to do, and reconsidering what we've put on hold in order to reach this point.

Now comes the wake-up call. Now comes Stage Four.

During this stage, some fundamental conflicts often surface. Up until now, life has been largely about getting to know one another, building a family together, and trying to raise kids. Stage Four shifts the focus squarely onto us as individuals and what we each want from life. Those wants aren't always connected, and money often gets in the way. I don't mean to imply that Stage Four is all about the money. In truth, it's rarely about the money. Yet money plays a central role now because of what it represents: a resource or hurdle for living the life we've always wanted.

Stage Four starts with one of the most basic questions partners grapple with: One income or two? The notion that you can trade your current life for one altogether different is a revered part of the American experience. At any time the fancy strikes, any of us with the gumption to do it can slough off our current existence and remake our lifestyle. A mechanic can decide to become an archeologist, the archeologist a bookseller, the bookseller a lawyer, the lawyer a mechanic. In the context of Stage Four, that possibility means that you and your partner may decide to try living on one income, or possibly vice versa, depending on your current status. Maybe one of you wants to be a stay-at-home parent; maybe one of you wants to chuck the corporate world to run your own small business out of a spare bedroom or the garage; maybe one of you has stayed at home for years and now longs to pursue a fulfilling career, since many people define who they are in the context of the question, "What do you do?"

Whatever the case, you must pay a price for the choices you make. One income means you scale back your life, possibly dramatically, and likely give up some of the dreams of achieving whatever goals you and your partner have laid out for the family. Two incomes means you forsake some of the freedoms and flexibility your family now has, possibly creating a more hectic lifestyle, yet allowing you a standard of living that you otherwise might not be able to afford. You might be fine paying that price. But is your spouse?

One of the more difficult challenges many people face in this stage stems from job relocations. Transfers are a big deal in the middle years. By this point, some couples seem to have spent their adult lives living out of boxes. For others, the middle years mark the point in their careers where the next move often is into managerial or executive ranks—job titles often packaged with demands to run an office or a division somewhere else. Whether caused by years of a transient lifestyle or the abrupt shock of the first job transfer that severs immediate ties to friends and family, the trials of the trailing spouse frequently are an all-too-silent issue.

These trailing spouses, of which Amy has long been one, often are overlooked in the frenzy of moving and the excitement of a new job and a new city. Their struggles often define who they become in Stage Four, because after flitting from one city to the next, always looking to establish new friends and new jobs and their own sense of self, they've hit the stage where they want to redefine their place in a life unexpected and sometimes unwanted. Trailing spouses might be right in the middle of rewarding careers, only to be uprooted to follow a partner's job opportunity. Perhaps they've followed a leading spouse for so long that they've never had the chance to build the career they wanted for themselves.

In having lost much of their own identity, trailing spouses often emerge in Stage Four in pursuit of themselves once again. They become more vocal about their concerns and more determined to rebuild their identity, sometimes in not-so-obvious ways, as you'll soon read. That can create tension in a relationship, as well as an opportunity to help trailing spouses regain some assurance that this life is about them, too.

Travel can be another source of friction. Of all our pursuits in life, vacations would seem the least likely to create conflict. Vacations are fun. They're relaxing. They take us away from the stress of everyday living. That, though, is precisely the problem. Because of what vacations represent— the chance to decompress—partners sometimes have distinctly different approaches to what they seek from holidays. No one wants to spend thousands of dollars and precious vacation days pursuing things in which they have no interest.

Though this conflict can occur at various points in life, it often arises in Stage Four because it's usually in the years after we've established our lives together that we really begin to focus on vacationing. I know that in the early days of my marriage, Amy and I simply didn't have the resources to take real vacations, so we generally stayed home or took four-day weekends to someplace close, or we just didn't take the time off from work that we were due. As our pay increased and as our individual lives grew more demanding, the desire to travel matured. However, our expectations of that travel did not always coincide, because, like many partners, we had different ideas of what a vacation should look like.

Perhaps the most troubling phase of this stage is the realization that you and your partner aren't financially compatible. In Stage One, you learned why financial compatibility is important in a relationship—it's the tie that binds love and money together and keeps everything running, if not always smoothly, then at least mutually acceptably. If you're not compatible, of course, you can fake it for a while and hope you'll grow into each other's ways. That doesn't usually happen, though, because at some point the reality of two dissimilar financial personalities always surfaces, and generally it's not pretty. When you and a partner derail financially, life is thrown into a tempest, and you can't seem to gain control of anything. You grow increasingly agitated, frustrated, temperamental, worried, anxious, angry, and defensive. Your emotions and your finances suffer, and it's not uncommon for the money woes, serving as a convenient catch-all for every other problem you have, to propel you and your spouse seemingly inextricably toward divorce.

Of course, financial differences don't have to play out that way. While you can consciously try to dodge the differences—substantially easier than confronting the problems in the immediacy of the moment—you also can step back and seek ways to address the divide effectively so that you and your partner can preserve the relationship. Either way, how you and your partner ultimately acknowledge the chasm between yourselves will play a defining role in your ability to retain the love instead of letting money rip your relationship to bits.

Welcome to Stage Four. It's not easy. It's not always fun. Sometimes it's just painful. With effort, though, you can navigate this stage of life with success, build a stronger relationship . . . and maybe even enjoy that vacation together.

CHAPTER 13

One Income or Two?

Making a Choice about Lifestyle

Every day you wake up to face a choice: Do you continue living your current lifestyle or do you pursue a different path?

By *different* I mean that if your family currently lives on a dual income, you may choose instead to live on a single salary. You and your spouse can begin to structure life together so that one of you can quit work and stay home to spend more time with the kids or more time as a family or to start a home-based business you've always dreamed about. Or *different* could mean that you miss your career or are tired of struggling on one income and want to become a two-paycheck family.

Regardless of the path you choose, "One income or two?" is one of those fundamental questions all families face at some point—often right after children arrive or as we move into the middle stages of a marriage, when we're established and begin questioning the direction of our lives. At its core, you're making a financial decision, though on the surface it's often about family values, stay-at-home parenting, career happiness, and such. How you answer the question defines nearly every facet of your life—from where you can afford to live to how much time you can spend together as a family to the length of your commute to the caliber of the car you drive to the number of times you can eat out to what you can save for your future. Not every issue will resonate with everybody—some folks don't care whether they drive a used Honda or a new Porsche. Yet the issue likely will resonate with many of you because it is so fundamental to how we shape our families and achieve our goals.

I'll skip the buildup; the only right answer is the answer that's right for your family. The answer may be found in the life you're living at the moment or that you hope to be living any number of years from now. But the answer isn't the interesting part here. The real challenge comes in evaluating the reasons you live the way you do—or the way you wish to. Because whether you ultimately choose one income or two, arriving at an answer means you must confront the difficult choices of balancing the life you live against the sacrifices you must make.

I wonder about this all the time as Amy and I progress through our life together. Are we making the right decision about the life we pursue—for ourselves individually, for our son, and as a family? I question our reasoning for living on two incomes instead of one and the choices we make in pursuing fulfilling careers.

Ultimately, these thoughts and worries and concerns boil down to a debate between career and family. Both are generally necessities of life. Yet how do you simultaneously value family and career when it would seem at first that choosing the best for one means that you must, by necessity, compromise on the other?

Motives abound for choosing one lifestyle over another, and in many ways the choices that Amy and I confront reflect those that millions of families grapple with constantly. We could pack it in, abandon the life and careers we've built traveling around the country with our jobs (okay, *my* job) and return to our home state, Louisiana, to pursue a different life. I was about to write "a simpler life," a phrase many people are quick to deploy when they talk about this issue, but "simpler" is not necessarily correct. More on that in a moment.

For many reasons, Amy would love to return to Baton Rouge, Louisiana, our hometown, and work only during the hours our son is in school; after all, as she and I both know, we get only one go-round when it comes to raising him. She, like so many people, would like to be closer to family and would like our son to see his dad (i.e., me) more than my four hours a day of commuting allow. Every time this topic arises, Amy wonders why I can't just find a good job in my profession where she wants to live—just as she has found good nursing-related jobs in the cities we've moved to through the years.

You can't dismiss such desires in your spouse; after all, this is her life, too. In some ways I desire some version of Amy's dream myself. However, I see shortcomings in her plan. If you forsake your job to move elsewhere, there are undeniable financial ramifications to the family. You may have to surrender many of the individual and family dreams you seek—the kind of home you'd like to retire to, the kind of schools you want to afford for your kids, the kind of financial security you hope to achieve. On a personal note,

I worry that my son would lose something by having a father who isn't as fulfilled in his job as I am. I know myself well enough to know that discontentment in my professional life always leaks over into my personal life no matter how hard I try to keep intact the barriers separating those worlds.

For better or worse I, like so many people with careers they love, have molded my family around a job not easily replicated. Like many spouses, Amy's choice has been to follow me. Here's the sacrifice we make: Our family must live in a pricey area of the country, requiring two incomes to make our life succeed. My son must attend summer camp and after-school programs because his mom and dad must work. We try to compensate by spending as much time as possible with him when we're at home and on weekends, and we do a lot as a family.

Yet as your kids age, this question of one income or two grows increasingly tormenting. Suddenly, life isn't just about what you seek for yourself, but about what you want for your kids and your family, too. The problem lies in just how different those wants can be.

Most parents, I believe, at some point struggle to a certain extent with career versus family. That's true whether you're the one working 40 hours a week at a wonderful job and can't be there to see your kids get home from school or whether you're the one who loves being home with the kids but thinks wistfully of the challenging career you gave up or the one you didn't have.

Ultimately, the paths we pursue are a matter of personal choice.

Several years ago, a colleague of mine was offered his pick among jobs. One was a low-profile gig on what was then the periphery of the empire. The other option: a high-profile, more lucrative job with a large dollop of international travel on the company's dime. He took the low-profile job.

One day, as we were talking about choices we have to make as parents juggling career and family, he mentioned that he once faced this question. I immediately thought, wow, I would have gone with the international job. But that's me; that's because of the foreign travel and my long-held, unrequited desire to work overseas, a desire that Amy doesn't share. He didn't take that job precisely because of the travel. He was going through a divorce at the time, and he didn't want a job that would keep him away from his two young kids. So he made a choice: "I stepped off the track," he says, opting for flexibility over pay and prestige. In doing so, he made himself more vulnerable to layoffs, and he wondered about the day when the kids would be gone and he was left with a possibly dead-end job.

As it turned out, he enjoyed the job he took a lot more than he imagined. While he says the decision "probably cost me a lot in terms of my career," he remains convinced that it was a "no-brainer. The negatives of the job were vastly outweighed by the benefits to me and my kids."

The point is this: Two people, two situations, two different answers based on two different desires. I saw his opportunity through the lens of my own wants. That's natural, though unfair. Looked at in the context of his life and what he sought at that moment, of course, he made the right decision. Had he not been going through a divorce, or had he and his ex-wife not had kids, then he may have chosen a different direction. Either way, the underlying context—rather than his ultimate decision—means everything to understanding his choice.

To many people, this question of one income or two (or career versus family) is a referendum on stay-at-home parenting. Lots of folks I've talked to through the years are militant about this, insistent that the sacrifices made to live off one income pale in comparison to the benefits of having a parent at home to provide structure and care for a child after school and during the summer months. One woman I know argues that families pursuing a dual income simply justify their lifestyle for their own selfish, usually materialistic wants, whereas those who have opted to live a one-income existence "truly make sacrifices to give our children full-time parenting. God forbid you would ever have to step off the track to realize that."

I'm not going to argue against such a philosophy, because in truth I see merit in it myself. In fact, let me quickly dispense some statistics that show what I think is clear proof that at our core many of us would love to live that archetypal *Leave It to Beaver* lifestyle, where one parent—usually the mom—stays home to tend to the house and family while the other (often the dad) earns the dollars. (Granted, these days the gender roles increasingly are reversed.) Of the 41.8 million kids under the age of 15 who live with both parents, more than a quarter are in situations where Mom is a stay-at-home parent, according to the March 2002 U.S. Census Bureau survey.[1] That marks a 13 percent rise in a little more than a decade. Even the number of stay-at-home dads surged by 18 percent; albeit with just 189,000 such dads, that jump came off a decidedly small base to begin with. Partly driving this overall change: the ripsnorting economy of the late 1990s, which provided millions of families the economic means to pursue happiness on one income. I can appreciate that desire.

Yet imposing in blanket fashion a belief that everyone would be better off in that same pursuit ignores the circumstances and realities particular to individuals and their families. Worse, that mantra ignores statistics that show children often are worse off in households where one parent stays at home. Based on the same census data, researchers at the Annie E. Casey Foundation, a children's advocacy group, found that kids who lived with married, stay-at-home moms tended to be less-well-off economically than those living in two-earner families.[2] That seems intuitive enough, since one-earner families typically earn less income overall. The real trouble the foundation discovered, however, is that 16 percent of those kids lived in poverty, four times the level of kids in families earning two paychecks.

Those are only statistics, though. What really irritates many of the dual-income earners I know are the contemptuous arguments that they're putting careers above family, that they value material possessions above a child's happiness, and that their kids grow up stunted because they're shunted off to nannies and day-care providers instead of being raised by a loving, stay-at-home mom or dad.

Where are the statistics that prove I love my son less because he attends YMCA summer camp every year when school lets out so that Amy and I can earn our salaries? What research shows that all working parents value their new cars more than they do their daughters' happiness? Can someone please provide me with studies showing that all the kids who grow up with one stay-at-home parent are well-balanced, model citizens and those who have a working mom and dad aren't?

The suggestion that any of those notions are true is simply bogus. My financial counselor friend, Denise, says that "actually, there are statistics in psychology that show that kids who grow up with both parents working become more self-reliant and independent.[3] Statistics also show that kids in day care are not less-well-off compared to kids at home with a parent. In fact, there are positive socialization aspects" of the day-care setting that kids with a stay-at-home parent don't always benefit from.

Too often, it seems that my generation battles against the traditions we grew up with, as if all those sitcoms with stay-at-home moms instilled in us some unspoken belief that one parent should stay at home and that doing so is better for the kids, despite the fact that life has changed in many fundamental ways that sometimes preclude such an existence. We simply do not live in that era anymore, as nice as it might be to return to it.

Dual-income parents may both decide to work because they're in jobs they find truly engaging or where they feel they can make a difference in the world, no matter how small. Maybe both work because they have to in order to afford the basics of life. That doesn't mean dual earners aren't as involved in their kids' lives as stay-at-home parents. Many of us arrange our workdays to attend every parent-teacher conference, every play, every lunch shift we're responsible for. We skip or postpone business trips just because our son wants us to be in the stands at his T-ball games.

By the same measure, many stay-at-home parents are angry to be there. Denise says she counsels moms all the time "who can't wait to get back to work." I've heard stay-at-home moms at my son's school whining about missing a tennis lesson because they have to serve pizza to a class of kindergartners. I've seen others miss nearly every one of their kid's soccer games so they can spend the day shopping or tanning. This is somehow better?

A kid's happiness largely depends on a parent's happiness. You can adopt a stay-at-home parenting life, but if your prevailing mood is anger and disdain, then that's what your child will see in you and ultimately learn. Likewise, you and your spouse can both work and enjoy what you do and still provide a loving home for your child, even if that means your son or daughter must attend after-school programs before you get home.

It's a bit like that announcement flight attendants make just before takeoff: Put your own oxygen mask on first, and then help the child seated next to you.

Now, about life being simpler on one income. . .

I bet that's true in some cases, particularly where the working parent earns a fat salary and the family has relatively few money worries. I know that if we could afford for Amy to drop her job it would be much easier around our home. I wouldn't have to worry about getting my son to school, which would allow me to alter my commute, saving at least an hour a day. Amy would have far more time to pursue interests she has and wouldn't fret about staff meetings that occasionally cause her headaches when she's running late to retrieve our son from his after-school program. Our weekends wouldn't be clogged with so much cleaning, and we probably wouldn't eat out so much. Yes, there are numerous changes that would make our life simpler.

Then again, there's reality. Forget about the wealthy one-income family and instead consider the average two-earner family, bringing home a combined income just shy of $60,000, according to the Census Bureau. The change to one paycheck suddenly makes life more challenging financially.

My Seattle friends, Jack and Colleen, chucked the dual-income life when their first daughter arrived in 2000. Colleen stepped away from a law career she enjoyed because she wanted to be a full-time mom when she felt her daughter needed her most. They refinanced their home and pared back discretionary spending and struggled to make it work financially. Looking back on it, Colleen says she wishes they had prepared better for the unexpectedly abrupt shift in their standard of living. She would never give up the time she has had with her two daughters during their early years, but Colleen realizes that "at some point my daughters' needs are not as great as our financial needs as a family."[4]

For Colleen, that means choosing a different path. She expects to abandon her stay-at-home status and return to work. Part of the reason is money: She and Jack still must pay off her law school loans, and they wish to pursue a vision of comfort in their retirement. Part of the reason is idealism: Colleen wants to serve as a role model, to show her daughters that "there's not only value to being a mom, there's value in being a professional woman, too." Part of the reason is the psychic value inherent in a job you love. As a public-interest lawyer, Colleen feels she's contributing to society and "engaging my mind in something I want to be involved in."

That isn't to say that Colleen's view won't change, or that Amy and I won't one day chuck the East Coast for a more Southern pace. Everybody has choices to make about the life they pursue, and those choices play dramatic roles in our relationships with one another.

Maybe loving a career and a job is anathema to you and you'd rather commit all of your time to family. Maybe being without a career is driving you crazy and you want to feel you're making a difference outside of your family. That's the beauty of life—you have the power to change it . . . as long as you're willing to pay the price.

Dollars & Sense

The dying, a famous adage holds, never wish they'd spent more time at the office.

I'm sure that's probably true. Just as I'm sure many people spend their days in a mindless routine, doing the mindless errands of life, never paying attention to what they're missing until it's too late. Yet I'm willing to bet that few people live their lives looking ahead every day to the lamentations they don't want to utter on their deathbeds. From the moment we start our families to the time we check out permanently, we have a niggling little thing called *life* that we have to live. We must find ways to support ourselves and our families, and along the way build up some sort of reserves to support ourselves in old age so that, hopefully, we're not financially dependent on our children or reliant on the state.

Part of the overall balance of life and who we are is our work. You spend 40 hours a week, maybe more, in your job, and you want to feel as fulfilled there as you do in your home life. Me, I'd just as soon take pleasure in what I do all week than wake up every morning dreading the hours I must put in to earn a paycheck. To a large degree, that's one of the reasons Amy and I remain where we are. I love my job and know that it would be very difficult, if not impossible, to replicate it anywhere else. Loving a job, though, does not mean you put your career above your child or your family. Likewise, pursuing a balance doesn't necessarily mean you're a lousy parent or a selfish partner.

Not pursuing that balance, however, certainly can lead to those very complaints, since job dissatisfaction has been linked to disturbed relationships with family and friends as well as increased family violence. When you ignore or take for granted your family while in pursuit of your career, you risk alienating your spouse and your child, and you probably will end up on your deathbed one day moaning about having spent too much time at the office.

Two parents can pursue two incomes and still provide a loving, caring environment for their child, but you do have to work at it. You have to make clear at the office that your child's happiness and your family's well-being rank well above your job. That was hard for me to establish early on because of my concerns that my employer wouldn't care about my personal needs. I shifted my mind-set when I saw in my son's eyes his excitement at seeing Daddy in the audience of his preschool play at midday, when I otherwise would have been at the office. I knew then that my priorities needed to shift, and I found when I began pushing this agenda my bosses gave me great latitude to structure my job around my family. I may work later into the night at times, but it's often from home, well after I spend the evening with Amy and my son, playing, reading, and helping him get ready for bed.

Given that kids must spend the day in school anyway, maybe you can restructure your life so that one parent works part-time, or maybe you can both rearrange your hours to essentially create that effect. If Mom goes to work earlier and Dad is responsible for getting the kids ready for school and then dropping them off, then Mom can leave work early enough to pick up the kids as school lets out in the afternoon. You've engineered stay-at-home parenting in a two-career family.

Talk to your bosses. It certainly can't hurt, and they will at least be more aware of your situation. Employers aren't eager to lose talented workers if there's a way to make everyone happy, or at least partly happy. Workers take time and money to hire and train, so it behooves a company to work with you in some fashion to structure a work schedule more amenable to your family needs. In fact, employers are increasingly creating family-friendly

CHAPTER 14

The Trials of Being the Trailing Spouse

Following Your Dreams

Americans have to be the most mobile people ever. We pick up and pack up and relocate, from one coast to the other, one state to the next, even country to country, all the time. Indeed, 40 million of us boxed up our lives and moved somewhere else between 2000 and 2001, representing about 14.5 percent of the population, according to the most recent census data. Certainly, much of that amounts to folks just moving from one house to another down the block. Yet nearly 8 million of us moved across state lines or international boundaries. That suggests lots of people in any given year are out chasing better jobs.

Often lost in this relocation binge is the *trailing spouse,* the forgotten partner silently resigned to a rootless life trailing a spouse on the move. It's an apropos if unglamorous phrase, trailing spouse, because "trailing" is exactly what happens. A *leading spouse* chases a career, wrapped up in the challenge of a new position and the excitement of yet another move up the corporate ladder. All the while the trailing spouse dutifully trails behind, pushed about like a feather on a breeze, alighting in Atlanta one year only to land in Las Vegas the next, living a life forever blown into tumult, whether or not they want to be wherever it is they wake up and find themselves.

This isn't just about moving from city to city to city, though. This is a story about dreams. For all the while one partner is chasing the dream of a glorious career on the move and on the rise, the other just as often is left to piece together a disjointed life. There's no consistency to their years. No opportunity to set down roots. Friendships are made and then all too quickly forsaken. There's no chance to build a steady work history or a career and, as in Amy's case, a diminished opportunity to build the retirement savings necessary for old age.

policies like telecommuting, job sharing, and other flexibility options that allow workers to better balance home and work life. Employers realize that workers who have greater ability to meet family obligations while performing the duties of work report greater job satisfaction, increased job productivity, higher morale, and greater loyalty to the company.

First put some thought into your plan before you rush into your boss's office and ask to work from home from now on. You need to approach your employer with a thoughtful plan that shows you will accomplish the same tasks, or more, under the new arrangement and that it won't disrupt the office or cost the company more money. Basically, it's up to you to demonstrate why a revised work arrangement makes sense for the company, not just for you.

For many people, it's not a lifestyle change they want, though that can seem the only answer. They're torn because they love their jobs but feel their family lives are out of kilter. There are myriad ways, however, to improve the balance between work and family, more ways than I have room to detail. For women, a host of online sites, such as iVillage.com or BlueSuitMom.com, offer tips for making your life track better at home and at work. For dads, the pickings are a bit slimmer, largely because this is a silent dilemma among men; guys just don't talk about these concerns publicly and rarely among themselves. Still, the Fatherhood Project at the Families and Work Institute in New York City has published a book called *Working Fathers* that offers an effective approach for helping dads—and even moms and managers—better balance the often competing demands of work and family life.

If having a stay-at-home parent in your family is your goal, then maybe you can, in fact, drop down to a single-paycheck household. It can be an ideal arrangement, and you most certainly still can provide the financial security for yourself and your children if you budget right. The money you save on taxes, child care, work clothing, lunches out at the office, commuting expenses, and so on may make the transition easier than you think. Jennifer, in Texas, notes that when her son was born in 2000, she dropped her life as a CPA to become a stay-at-home mom. Her husband, meanwhile, switched to a lower-paying job with substantially less travel. In all, their income fell by 60 percent, necessitating that they eliminate restaurant meals and buying new clothes, new cars, and new furniture.

Yet their savings in those areas still allow them to squirrel away $125 a month for their son's future college costs. They contribute to individual retirement accounts and her husband's 401(k). They vacation occasionally in nice places like Hawaii and, in general, Jennifer says, "still maintain a very nice life. I would go so far as to say that we are happier now than we ever have been."[5]

Using the spending plan discussed in Chapter 1, you can begin to determine how feasible it is for your family to scale back the lifestyle you now live. Examine all your expenses over the course of several months, and categorize them into three columns: fixed expenses (mortgage, car note, life insurance premiums), variable expenses (electricity, groceries, haircuts), and discretionary expenses (movies, restaurants, toys). Scrutinize the costs and pare them back to what you can realistically live on. *Realistically* is the key term. If eating out at restaurants is really important to you, then simply wiping it from your spending plan is useless, because in reality you'll find yourself in restaurants frequently. Compare the costs of your expected life against the income of the sole worker and determine not only whether the math works, but whether you're going to be okay with the lifestyle you've just laid out.

If the math just doesn't work, that doesn't mean the dream is kaput. Can the stay-at-home partner work part-time? Are there opportunities for the stay-at-home spouse to do freelance work or consulting to bring in extra dollars? Is a home-based business feasible?

If life on one income simply isn't possible or is not something you want to pursue, then no worries. In an environment where no job is as safe as you might hope, two paychecks provide greater security for a family.

I had a reader once tell me about a speech comedian Al Franken delivered to Harvard University's graduating class in 2002. In supporting her point of view that a dual-income lifestyle can't properly support a child's developmental needs, she noted that Franken had riffed on the notion of "quality time," that overly ballyhooed concept we parents like to whip out to justify our long hours at work punctuated by short, though intense, bursts of time with our kids when we're home: Franken said, "Being a good parent means spending lots of time with your children. Kids don't want quality time; they want quantity time—big, stinking, lazy, non-productive quantity time."[6]

I went and dug up a transcript of that speech. She was right; those were precisely the words he uttered. However, she conveniently left out the rest of the story. One sentence later the comedian tossed in this tidbit, which casts his comments in a different light: "On the other hand, it's important for every parent to maintain balance in his or her life. Don't be a slave to your child."[7]

Whether you pursue balance on one income or two, don't make the mistake of assuming that either approach is the right or wrong answer for

your child. The only thing that matters is that you lavish on your kids the love and affection they need and deserve, while at the same time pursuing the happiness in life and work that you want to feel.

Family and career aren't mutually exclusive. In choosing what's best for one, you can choose what's best for the other—as long as both share equal value in your life.

We all start off with dreams for our lives—what we want to be, what we want to do, where we want to do it. But in marriage the dreams of two partners collide, and sometimes instead of melding into a single entity, they ricochet in random directions. When that happens, it's generally the case that only one dream can take precedence. Often, that means that one spouse, usually the wife but sometimes the husband, must take up a life living on the coattails of a partner constantly on the move.

Ask these trailing spouses what they forsake when they follow the careers of their partners, and the litany is likely to be long—and most of it has little to do with money.

At the heart of this issue are the conflicts inevitable in a dual-career family. Those conflicts can be relatively small—such as who misses the mandatory staff meeting on the day your son stays home sick. Or they can be much larger—such as this issue of whose career takes the lead when a job offer requires relocation. Managing the small conflicts is challenging, no doubt, but rarely do they alter your dreams. When you've both built careers and a life in one city, and suddenly one of you has the opportunity to push your career in a new direction by moving to another city, well, that's when the dreams come into play, because you now have to navigate one of life's bigger financial crossroads.

A job that requires relocation essentially means you have two choices: The spouse without the job offer either agrees to forsake his or her job and possibly end a career so that the family's fortunes might improve; or the spouse with the offer declines an opportunity to advance to the next salary level, which likely would improve the family's standard of living. Whichever path you pursue, someone is giving up a dream.

Don't move and your life stays the same, but the partner who refuses the offer has either agreed to abandon his or her dreams or to put them on hold indefinitely. Do move, and the partner who agrees to follow behind potentially relinquishes his or her own dreams to become the trailing spouse, a place that my New Mexico friend Laura says can be as lonely as it is isolating. Wrapped up in all the worries about finances and new jobs and severed friendships, says Laura, is the biggest blow of all: the loss of identity.

"For someone who grew up presuming she was going to be self-reliant and financially independent, it's tough when you're forced by circumstances to switch into that traditional role where you're reliant on someone else and having to follow them wherever they go," Laura says.[1]

Before the movers became a fixture in her life, Laura was living her dream, working as a lawyer in Washington, D.C., a year away from making partner in her firm. Then her husband's plant shut down, requiring him to relocate to Colorado to save his job, and shortly thereafter to New Mexico. "Suddenly," Laura says, "his job took on more importance in the family because it went away, and because wherever we go I can get a job, I can always be a lawyer, even if it isn't my dream job—the job I define myself as." (To be fair, many of the same issues affect a trailing spouse who doesn't work and instead focuses on the home and children. In those cases, though, nonworking spouses often structure their lives around the idea of support- ing a partner's career. In allowing that career to flourish, this particular ver- sion of trailing spouse generally is resigned to the notion that relocation is a part of life, even though it's just as challenging to deal with.)

In following her husband, Laura left behind friends and family back East, where she grew up and where she had built through the years her support structure and her own identity. In place of that, she "entered a world where everyone knows me as Marc's wife or Riley's mom," Laura says. "No one here knows me as just Laura. I went from being the star of my own life to a supporting player in someone else's life."

One evening I sat at the kitchen table filling out paperwork so that Amy could enroll in a retirement savings plan at the hospital where she worked. My handing her the documents to sign was a bittersweet moment for her. She was pleased to be saving a few dollars, yet the papers served as just another reminder of the sacrifices she has made for my career through the years. The documents marked the fourth retirement plan she had joined in a dozen years, meaning she has dropped three others to follow me around the country. Each time she enrolled in a new plan, she generally had to wait a year to become eligible for contributions.

The result, as she pointed out that night, is that even though we've both been in the workforce for roughly the same number of years and earned roughly similar salaries, my retirement account is more than double the size of hers. In some sense, that difference is meaningless: Our accounts are community property, and as partners we will share whatever income both of our retirement funds generate when that time arrives. It really shouldn't matter whose account is bigger or smaller.

Except that it does matter. Partners want to feel as though they're equals in every way, including financial. With her diminished account bal- ance as tangible proof of her financial inequality, Amy says she feels "like I don't have any financial consistency or that I'm doing anything to con- tribute to my retirement."

Truthfully, though, the lament isn't about the money, but about what those missing dollars represent. Amy's smaller retirement account is a metaphor for everything leading spouses overlook when our jobs send us from one city to the next. I know; I've been the leading spouse for our entire marriage. We've lived in southern California, Dallas, Seattle, and, most recently, northern New Jersey. During those moves, I admit that I haven't always given Amy's considerations as much thought as they deserve, nor did we talk about her concerns as much as we probably should have. For me, selfishly, a job transfer is the start of a new adventure, something exciting and fresh after so many years seeing the same old sights and driving the same old roads. I love it.

Then again, when you're the leading spouse, you're not giving up your job or salary; in fact, your paycheck usually grows a bit. You're not abandoning your retirement plan or giving up benefits; those follow wherever you roam. You keep many of your friends because you often stay with the same employer. If nothing else, you quickly meet new people in your new locale because you're thrust immediately into the job with employees and clients and customers.

For a trailing spouse, it's all just another headache. You leave behind yet another job and another set of friends to go where nobody knows your name. New bosses don't know your capabilities, and often the flexibility you'd treasured in the old job is nowhere to be found, at least in the early months. Salary, responsibility, and job enjoyment tend to regress, not advance. "It's very stressful," Amy says, "to work to get to a certain level and to a certain salary, and then have to leave a position that you're so invested in personally and financially to start all over again somewhere where no one knows what you're capable of." She sees benefits in our hop-scotches "because I've gained experiences in my jobs that others don't often have, and that makes me better at what I do." Still, after so many moves, Amy has reached a stage that many trailing spouses ultimately reach: "Should I even try to invest in my career anymore?"

We leading spouses don't always pay attention to our partners' struggles or their lost dreams in our excitement at moving one more rung up the ladder. Work is our immediate support system; our identity is in our job; and we dash off to the adrenaline rush of a new life, often forgetting that we've left behind a spouse to wrap up the old life. While we're plunging into our jobs, our partners contend with the drudgery of shutting off phones and utilities in one city and the hassles of hooking them up in another. They pack boxes, shepherd movers, and then unpack and arrange the furniture to make this new house our home. Trailing spouses handle the chores of finding new schools and "reassuring children during a disruptive time in their lives," says Janet, a Chicagoan now living in Minnesota after moving three times to follow her now ex-husband. (The moves, Janet says, helped kill the marriage.)

While relocating has many positive aspects—such as new opportunities, new relationships, and new experiences—the fact is that the first time a relocation comes through "your roots are severed," Janet says, "and you've lost your identity."[2]

What makes it all the more difficult to deal with is that during this stage of life, friendships are tougher to come by. People, wrapped up in their own families, may not be willing to invest excessive energy into building deep friendships with what they may perceive as transient newcomers. They expect you'll leave again, so they protect themselves from getting hurt.

Along with this loneliness is what my friend Laura calls *intellectual seclusion.* "It's the feeling that I'm the only person in the world who is dealing with these things, so no one else understands just how lonely it is when you lose yourself. And so far, I've never found a support group for trailing spouses."

Seeing all of this in terms of gender seems natural, since wives are often the ones who follow their job-hopping husbands. That, however, overlooks an increasingly common situation in which women have moved into management and executive ranks and their husbands agree to forsake careers so that their wives can strive higher. While many of the underlying issues are similar—the challenges of finding new work or building new friendships—male trailing spouses confront several fundamental differences because they are so much rarer.

Mike, a Texas reader now living in California after relocating yet again, has moved four times in a decade, following his wife's career through the financial services industry. The moves started in the early 1990s and have sent the family packing from northern California to Las Vegas to Pittsburgh to Texas to southern California.

Aside from the general challenges any spouse faces in rebuilding a life in yet another new city, Mike says such moves "are difficult for a man who is the family's primary caregiver, because even though this is the 2000s, you still don't fit in with what's normal. Many people are uncomfortable with this arrangement, if not suspicious."[3] Capturing the awkwardness in words "is tough if you haven't lived it," he says. "People don't know what to make of you." The skepticism, he says, is clear even if never uttered: Are you someone to be trusted? Why can't you find a job? Did you fail at your own career and now you're unmotivated and living off your wife's efforts?

It's as though you're defective in some way.

The awkwardness extends into building relationships with other trailing spouses. Because it's still more common for a woman to follow a man, the trailing spouses Mike tends to meet are women married to male managers in his wife's firm—and neither the women nor their husbands are quite certain how to handle the situation "because everyone is used to the reverse," Mike says. Frequently he's invited to gatherings for spouses, and inevitably Mike is the only guy. "I attend these functions and manage to enjoy myself," he says, "but there is always tension. The hosts say they weren't sure how I would take the invite or whether I would even come. Their husbands are suspicious because they're working and you're not and you're interacting with their wives, and they're not sure they want their wives interacting with you. And the women, while they're nice, we just don't talk about the same things. For all the talk of equality, men and women are still different, and I just don't fit in with the things that women talk about when they're together."

More poignant, Mike says, is the realization that the friendships you make ultimately don't mean that much to others. When his wife announced her move to California from Texas, "I heard from no one," he says. "Out of more than 100 people, you might like to hear from at least one person who says 'good luck,' or that they'll miss having you around."

Dollars & Sense

Skipping the trailing spouse issue for a moment, moving is one of the most stressful events you deal with as a couple, supposedly right up there with death and divorce. I don't know how accurate that is, but having moved five times so far in my relationship (that doesn't count intracity moves), I do understand the strains of uprooting everything you both recognize as normal.

You have to find a new home and line up the mortgage, or find a new apartment and come up with the deposit. You have to start new bank accounts and make sure all those direct deposits and automatic withdrawals for investments and insurance and so on are in place to enable the smooth transition of your financial life. Packing and unpacking may well be exactly what people do in hell for all eternity—it's that unpleasant. You must yank your children out of school (assuming you have kids) and place them into a new environment where all of you—parents and kids—are at first nervous.

The leading spouse often is so consumed with the rigors of the new job that he or she may have little or no time to help with moving or resettlement, leaving the trailing spouse to marshal the movers and make sure all the right boxes get to all the right places. All in all, relocation is an unstable situation that leads to tension, frustration, and not a little bit of fighting.

But here's the ultimate truth: You and your spouse have one dependable source of stability when it comes to relocating your life—each other. That's the starting point for addressing the trials of the trailing spouse. The key link is communicating your feelings with one another. This is mandatory. Take it from an authority: We leading spouses aren't always tuned in to our partners' worries or concerns when we're buried in our own little worlds. (I'm not saying that's not selfish; I'm just saying that's how it is.)

Mike, who has moved four times, doesn't regret giving up his career to become a trailing spouse. "What I do regret, though, is that I didn't take a harder look at what my life would be like or talk to my wife about it," he says. "Whether you're a male or female trailing spouse, you have to open the lines of communication. You have to express your feelings. Sit down and really talk about what you're feeling, and what you're concerned about, and what scares you."

I know from experience how very quickly a leading spouse becomes absorbed in a new job and fails to recognize what's happening with a trailing spouse. Still, that's no excuse. A trailing spouse shouldn't feel that they always have to speak up for themselves. A trailing spouse wants to know through your words and actions that you care enough to ask and to show concern for their well-being. As a leading spouse, you must tune in and check in as well. Make it a point at least once a week in the weeks leading up to the move, during the move, and in the first few months after the family has settled in to sit down and talk with your partner about what they're experiencing, what they're feeling, how any job search is progressing, and what you can do to provide some assistance or, at the very least, comfort and support.

Otherwise, Mike says, "you'll be faced with resentment. The trailing spouse will begin to resent the fact that they packed up their life and moved for you, and you're showing more interest in your job than in them."

If a relocation offer comes your way, there are a number of questions you and your spouse need to discuss to determine what's best for the family. Lots of leading spouses mentally check out and start projecting ahead to their new lives, just assuming that's best for their families when, in reality, they're just rationalizing their wants. Here are some topics to consider:

- What would the move mean to both careers?
- How does the would-be trailing spouse feel about giving up a career?
- Is this a permanent move?
- Will there be other moves?
- Is there an opportunity to return to your current life?
- Does living a two-city marriage, even for a while, make sense?
- How soon is the trailing spouse expected to find a job?
- Is finding a job necessary, or will the trailing spouse stay home?
- What if the trailing spouse doesn't like the new city? Is it possible to return?
- Is the added money worth the potential unhappiness?
- How will you both deal with a trailing spouse's loneliness or isolation if those feelings arise?
- How will you help your kids adjust to the move, to being pulled from school and forced to start over with friendships? What if they don't want to go?

My friend Laura struggled for the longest time trying to tell her husband how she felt. She never could get the emotions out, though. Every time she previously had tried to talk to her husband, Marc, about her feelings, "I'd start crying" and be unable to explain everything. Lying awake in bed in the stillness of 3 A.M., she found her answer. She got up and wrote a three-page, single-spaced letter to her husband, "telling him that I just couldn't do this permanently. At some point, I want to be where I'm Laura. I told him when the economy comes around, we move—this time for my job."

When Marc read the letter the next day, he understood what Laura had been unable to say. Without an argument, Marc simply said, "Okay." That became the family plan. "It took me 5,000 words to say what I needed to say," Laura says. "It took him one to make it all right."

One of Amy's closest friends found herself in a miserable situation after moving to the West Coast when her husband found a new job there. Although she was ready for the change, she quickly realized that her husband had traded an easy commute and more family time for a longer commute, more pressure, and less family time. She also discovered that she had left a great job where she had made a name for herself only to find herself in a city where she had no such job lined up.

In talking to her husband about her frustrations with this new life, they both realized the move had been a mistake, and they returned to the state they had left (though a different city). They're happier in the new location, though it's still not what they once had.

If relocation is simply in the cards, then determine whether it's possible to choose your destination, and work with your spouse toward a compromise that's best for everyone's happiness, even if that means ultimately you don't take your first-choice job. Remember, this is still a partnership, and the demands to create a common goal remain.

A colleague at work tried to avoid relocation unhappiness before it ever surfaced by moving to a place where he knew his wife would be more comfortable. Several years ago, he was offered his choice of a number of jobs around the country. All were good jobs, although to him the least desirable locale was New York City. Yet his wife had family in the area, and she wanted to be near them. They compromised: He got to move to advance his career; she got to choose the place. He took the job in New York. "In the end, it made the relocation that much easier," he says. "She had to give up a job that she liked. But she gained so much more by being near her mother and siblings. It was a good trade-off for both of us."

In other situations, the compromise, says Denise, the counselor, "may be that the trailing spouse suffers through the relocations for a couple of years, but then gets to go back to the old life or gets to pursue the old career." In such cases, a leading spouse must realize that a partner has dreams, too. Both spouses have an obligation to help each other strive toward their individual goals in life to the degree that those goals are possible. Is it fair that you get to live your dream and your spouse doesn't?

If you're the trailing spouse, or if you expect to be a trailing spouse one day, then feelings of isolation and loneliness are high on your list of concerns. The feelings, Laura says, are often some of the strongest to emerge, because trailing spouses leave friends and frequently family, and new friendships aren't always fast in coming. The solution, she says, "is coping skills. I realized that in a new place I had to find a new way to define myself as an individual in the absence of all the other things in my life that I used to have, like my job and friends and family." For Laura, coping meant finding a new purpose. That purpose she found in, of all things, the gym.

"The gym provided me an opportunity to try things I'd never done before in my life," she says. Before her series of moves, Laura was not a good skier and couldn't run a mile if she had to. Yet on her thirty-seventh birthday, she skied off "The Ridge" in Taos, New Mexico, an expert-caliber and double-black-diamond run that requires a hike of up to an hour to reach the 12,481-foot jumping-off point atop Kachina Peak. Laura stood on the cornice looking down onto the world for 10 minutes before she could launch herself over the edge into a steep dive down the mountain and, ultimately, into her new life.

"I've never been so proud of myself because I was so terrified," she says. Several months later she ran her first five-kilometer (3.1-mile) course, missing her target time by only four seconds. "I just keep looking for other ways to see myself as a 'success' when the ones I have always measured myself by are kind of on hold for the time being."

In the weeks following the retirement account episode with Amy, I got to thinking about all she has given up to follow my career from one edge of the country to another. In allowing me to be the journalist I've become, Amy has lost sight of the person she always wanted to be. On a couple of occasions, she was headed in that direction and was close to achieving it before my career once again called. That, Amy says, "is the saddest part—that I've had to walk away from such great opportunities."

I realized that, without a doubt, our next move is for Amy. She has allowed me to pursue my life. It's only fair that she gets to pursue hers.

CHAPTER 15

You Take Paris . . . I'll Take Vietnam

When Vacation Desires Diverge

Everybody I know needs a vacation.

Heck, *I* need a vacation, as I routinely remind Amy. She'll often walk into our little home office and catch me fooling around on some Internet travel site, pricing fantasy trips to any number of random spots on the globe. Amy just shakes her head and retreats. Little does she know how truly tempted I am to click on the "Buy now" button and run upstairs to start packing for Morocco or maybe Sapporo. Just driving by the airport with the windows down and the unmistakable aroma of jet fuel in the air is enough to send me into paroxysms of wanderlust.

As Amy's head shaking illustrates, though, travel is not always an easy trip for couples. We all envision different itineraries for our perfect vacation. Many times the components of this idyllic holiday aren't even in the same hemisphere. You're daydreaming about mountains or adventure only to find your spouse all jazzed up for a week on the beach and a big dose of pampering. The perfect amount of rest and relaxation, you figure, is a four-day getaway, after which you're raring to return home. Meanwhile, your partner is still unwinding after three days and insists that a trip isn't a vacation unless it's two weeks long with all the trappings.

As trifling a problem as a vacation might seem in the grand design of life, it's not such an easy impasse to overcome in a relationship. Vacations are important, after all. They are your chance to decompress, to slip away from the same 24-hour routine you live every day, to rejuvenate and reconnect with each other and to kick back and pursue a bit of fun. That makes a vacation a key component of the balance people need in their lives together.

If only picking a spot were just a matter of tossing a dart at a big map and then packing for your days of bliss. Instead, agreeing on a travel destination as a couple is so much more difficult at times because you're not just spending dollars, you're spending limited and valuable vacation days as well. You want to make certain that when you get off the plane or out of the car the place you're at is the place you want to be. After all, you worked hard all year to get here; you deserve vacation happiness.

Of course, your spouse worked equally hard and is thinking the exact same thoughts about their pursuit of vacation pleasure.

Thus it comes to be that what should stand out as one of the more enjoyable chores of couplehood—planning a vacation together—can often feel more daunting than airport check-in.

We travel for all sorts of obvious reasons, but in the end we all travel for one universal pursuit: to gain what we're missing elsewhere in our life.

Me—I seek adventure. I'm a dad and a husband and I have a steady job, and I occasionally want to upset my life just to get the adrenaline pumping again. I can think of nothing more exhilarating than hopping on an airplane and disembarking someplace entirely random or foreign, be it Oshkosh or Tashkent. Travel at its best is slightly unsettling and a bit strenuous, heaving you into unfamiliar locales and leaving you to your devices. I have flown into earthquakes in El Salvador, fallen into a semi-frozen lake in Alaska, had orcas surface just yards from me while swimming in a southern Chilean bay. In eastern Romania, a gypsy family in an open-air market tried to adopt me as a suitor for their bashful daughter; a day later on a train to Bucharest, an 80-year-old former fighter pilot in the Romanian air force shared with me his lunch of dry bread and homemade cheese. Such are the memories good travel is made of.

Such are the nightmares Amy dreads. After working a 40-hour week in her day job, she has the pleasure of strolling into our house and into her second career as full-time mom, wife, and household organizer—an occupation that comes with not a lot of pampering. Thus, when Amy's on holiday, she wants luxury, since the most luxurious moments in her daily life generally come when she has enough free time to amble through a local shopping mall for a few hours, unburdened by child or husband. On vacation, she wants a nice hotel with bathtubs big enough to soak in for long stretches of time. Oversized, comfy beds and ambiance are a must, too. A sunny beach would be nice. Cool ocean breezes, a fruity cocktail with a long straw and a paper umbrella—these speak to the very sort of repose she wants in a holiday away from her daily life.

"People don't come to me and say, 'I went to Iran and it was great,'" Amy says. She mentions Iran because she knows the Middle East is high atop my list of places to see, right up there with Vietnam, Croatia, and Tibet, places that hold no appeal for her. Amy much prefers locales like France and Italy and Tahiti, places that "sound more intriguing because either I've read about them or people I know have been there and say how wonderful it is." Plus, she'd feel safer in Turin than in Tehran.

When I suggest some off-the-beaten-track destination such as the Croatian coast, she doesn't see a vacation, but a hassle. Likewise, when she counters with a beach resort, I generally see a balmy, boring purgatory.

This sort of division is widespread among couples—from newlyweds to lifelong partners. Just look at the challenges that often go into planning a honeymoon, the first trip you take as an official family unit. You debate that trip for months, sometimes fighting about it vehemently. Sure, you probably booked a few vacations when you were dating, but dating trips and married trips are continents apart. When you're dating, you're much more willing to go along to get along. In marriage, you're only going because you want to be there. Indeed, while we were dating I took Amy to Chihuahua, Mexico. She was happy just to travel with me, despite the hot, dusty, and altogether miserable bus ride through the Chihuahuan desert on the road back to El Paso, Texas. If I surprised her with that same trip today, she'd say "*Hasta la vista,* baby. Don't bring anything back I don't want."

Cassandra, a woman I know in California, says that when she and her fiancé began planning their honeymoon, "all of our travel differences really became apparent."[1] Her fiancé figured that hanging out at one of those all-inclusive resorts in the Caribbean would be a perfect way to cap off the wedding. To Cassandra, that sounded about as exciting as watching sand. Something less lazy is what she sought. "The Dalmatian Islands off the coast of Croatia are supposed to be fabulous," she told him. "How about Tunisia? Cyprus? Iceland?" All she heard back was no, no, and no.

Individuality brings a lot to a shared life. That doesn't mean, though, that it brings a lot to a shared vacation. David and Louise have been married nearly four decades, and while the Florida couple has shared short getaways they've rarely shared a vacation together. "I can only walk around museums and historical sites for so long, and Louise will have no part whatsoever of my adventures," David says.[2] So he heads off on solo diving trips while she ventures off to research whatever current writing project she has going. "Friends and family have chastised us for this," David says. "They cannot comprehend that we are not clones of each other."

But David and Louise's predicament raises a question that's not always so easy to answer: Should you give up dreams of ever seeing Hanoi just because your spouse has no interest and would rather visit Hawaii? Then again, should your spouse feel pressured into spending a vacation doing what you want and getting nothing out of it?

Yes, sacrifice is the hallmark of a resilient marriage, and occasionally making such sacrifices for a spouse is an appreciated gesture. Not everyone travels well together, though, and not everyone seeks the same elements from a vacation. At some point, reluctant partners become fed up with the frustrations of vacations they simply don't enjoy, and, instead, revolt.

Let me step back for a moment and look at the bigger picture. Underlying this concept of travel isn't just the vacation itself, but the frequently competing demands we, as couples, place on our discretionary dollars, the limited recreation time we have, and the necessary purchases that go along with it. In some ways this disagreement is natural when it comes to any expenditure of money or time for something that one spouse has a personal interest in and the other finds bewildering. The classic example: weekend golf widows.

Just as easily, though, this could be about the spouse who wants new skis and gear the first time a few flakes waft down from the sky; the spouse who drops thousands of dollars on gardening, maybe even building a greenhouse in the backyard; the partner who becomes infatuated with a really expensive activity such as learning to race cars. (The husband of the couple we bought our house from was a hard-core racing fanatic, spending much of his vacation time racing in Europe and the eastern United States; he even built a separate garage capable of handling automotive projects I can't even imagine and that still houses a couple of racing tires he left behind.) It may even be that one spouse's idea of recreation and relaxation is to simply plop into a La-Z-Boy on the weekends or during a week's vacation, while the other spouse is itching to go somewhere and do anything.

When someone has a hobby or a recreational activity that he or she pursues with an obsession, says a friend at work, "the value of it is so beyond the comprehension of the person who doesn't have the obsession/hobby. It just seems weird. And worse, it seems wasteful because there are so many other things to spend time and money on."

Where I come from in southern Louisiana, LSU football is king of the calendar. From early September through late November, just about every Saturday is structured around an LSU football game, with preparations for tailgating beginning just after sunup and the after-game cocktails winding down sometime after midnight. I know lots of women who, while they tolerate this ritual, are none too pleased by it because their husbands all but abandon the family for the day. Thus, passions and resentment often cloud this issue of recreational time. On one side you have the recreationalist's passion about a pursuit, be it football or golf or even grow-your-own bonsai; on the other side you have the spouse growing marginally more resentful about all the time and dollars that flow into the pursuit.

When you're single, none of this really matters. You can spend freely on any recreational vice you have—maybe fly on the spur of the moment to the Mexican Riviera for the weekend, or pick up a pricey hobby like scuba diving. You have to answer only to your checkbook and your spending plan. However, as half of a couple, personal expenses on recreational activities naturally become subject to broader scrutiny. You're not just spending the family's dollars, you're also spending free time as though it were yours alone. Your spouse might think that just maybe you should be spending that time in pursuit of family pleasures.

Travel just happens to be a high-profile example of how this recreational conflict can play out in a relationship. We all want what we want out of our time away, and that's where the conflict emerges.

In my life, I've typically been the self-anointed vacation planner, and that hasn't always been conducive to mutual enjoyment. The problem stems from my notion—misguided notion, if you ask Amy—that the joy in seeing the world comes in seeing the world, not the inside of some hotel room, where you spend most of your time in the dark anyway. I figure the money we save by staying in less-than-luxurious digs in, say, Dublin can help us later afford a trip along the coast of Maine. I'd much rather experience as many cultures as I can on the cheap than sleep in the finest beds but in fewer locations.

In practice, that generally means I pick off-season vacation spots I think Amy will like, then skimp on the accommodations. Sometimes luck smiles kindly upon my efforts and steers me to hotels that turn out to be wonderful and inexpensive little gems. On a trip to Vancouver one year, Amy all but exploded with pleasure when she walked into a beautiful boutique hotel that she still raves about. In St. Lucia, she loved the hotel built on the side of a mountain and missing the fourth wall; instead, the room just opened wide onto a forest canopy and the ocean below. Both were very good trips for me.

Just as often, though, I book a clunker and our room is more hell than highlight. When I first showed Amy New York I chose a hotel near Central Park for what was a steal of a deal. Some steal. Dirty red-shag carpet greeted us. I had to shoulder-ram the door open every time we returned to the room. The hot water was nonexistent—and this was dead of winter in

January. In one London hotel we walked into a room barely able to contain the double bed; Amy had to roll across the mattress to reach the bathroom. The room had no heat. Again, dead of winter.

To me, and travelers like me whom I have talked with through the years, such inconveniences are trivial. I know, though, that Amy speaks for many people when she calls my cost-saving rationale "nonsense." She's on vacation. Vacations cost money. If you're going to commit to spending the money it costs to take a vacation, then spring for a nice room so that you can enjoy the entire trip, not just the sightseeing and eating. "The hotel," Amy insists, "is a big part of the relaxation, since everything else about a vacation is going here to shop and there to eat and everywhere else to see all the other stuff. I want to come back to the room at the end of the day and not be stressed out because I'm uncomfortable."

The low point of our travels together arrived on a snowy spring afternoon in Montreal. After a scenic, five-hour drive through upstate New York and the Adirondack Mountains one April, Amy, our son, and I arrived late in the afternoon to find the discount hotel I booked near downtown was actually a youth hostel. The discount Internet site made no mention of this not-so-insignificant fact. From what I could tell on my laptop, the hotel looked to be a quaint, bed-and-breakfast built into an old, Gothic-style home dating to the early 1900s. That much was actually true—but only that much.

The room was dilapidated and eerie, the kind of stark, high-ceilinged space you have a vague remembrance of having tried to flee unsuccessfully in one of those dreams where shadowy people are chasing you late at night, possibly through some long-abandoned sanitarium. The heat, controlled by the front desk, was as oppressive as a Dallas summer, and we opened a window in a snowstorm to cool the fevered room. Threadbare linens—and visible mattress stains—so disgusted Amy that she slept in three layers of clothing and made our son sleep in his jeans and hooded sweatshirt rather than his jammies. Amy still recalls the horror of the dark, dank closet passing vaguely for a bathroom, where a narrow, cracked shower stall (no tub) butted up against a leaky sink and a toilet of questionable integrity. Within minutes of digesting this mistake, Amy marched to the front desk and canceled the last of our three nights.

"This is a vacation?" She was not pleased.

Lots of people I know recount similar vacation horrors. They often laugh about it afterward, but at the time anger was the chief emotion. Most of the episodes people share with me happen because one partner inevitably takes the reins when planning the family vacation. Sometimes it works out; sometimes you end up in Montreal.

If nothing else, though, there's a lesson to be learned from any travel nightmare. In our case, on the drive home (a day early) Amy and I devised a new travel treaty we live by: One person picks the city; the other person gets to pick the hotel.

Amy's not about to venture off to Saigon without knowing a comfortable tub awaits.

Dollars & Sense

When it comes to recreation, few couples are always on the same page. You each have different wants from the recreational activities you pursue. Those wants aren't always in conflict, and often a spouse doesn't mind if you pursue your passion, as long as you do so with a healthy restraint, finding time to balance personal pleasures with the wants of the family as a whole.

Then again, many times personal pleasures are, oddly, the source of much tension in couples' lives because both partners spend so much energy fighting for the relaxation they seek. Many of my friends are fans of fishing, for instance. Most of the wives involved are not. Conflict is a part of those relationships.

The reason stems from the fact that fishing is pursued obsessively. It's a nearly every weekend ordeal. Friction, animosity, resentment, and not a little bit of anger are the by-products, because you have a fisherman who can't understand why his wife is so bent out of shape, and a wife who can't understand why her husband doesn't see that he's spending more time chasing a bass than he is recreating with his own family.

The solution is a balancing act. Recreational activities—be it travel or designing jewelry—represent a break from our work lives, a chance to recharge our batteries or use an underexercised part of our personalities for a while. If nothing else, it interjects some enjoyment into our lives. For a spouse who can't understand a recreational obsession or the need to spend money or time on a particular endeavor, you must accept that your partner needs this experience as psychic nourishment. By the same measure, the spouse pursuing a recreational want must realize that it's really easy to get lost in the activity and lose sight of its relative importance. You have to trust your partner's judgment and rein in the obsession if your partner is warning you that it's getting out of hand.

With vacations, you should both seek the pleasure you want from a holiday away from your daily life; otherwise, one of you is going to be resentful taking a trip you have no interest in, because you won't enjoy the time off.

Maybe that means that you and your partner take turns picking the holiday locale. You pick one vacation spot, then your partner picks the next, and you both agree not to complain about each other's choice and to enjoy the itinerary the other has arranged. To add more excitement to such a strategy, the partner in charge of the vacation this time around might keep the destination a secret until you check in at the airport. Just be sure to tell your partner how to pack; showing up in Scotland for a weeklong tour of castles when your partner has only packed a bikini and beachwear isn't terribly practical.

Too often, the recreational divide ends in stalemate, and instead of seeking compromise one spouse just surrenders out of frustration. Golf widows acquiesce because their husbands mope around all day if they have to stay home. A woman I work with always loses the vacation debates in her family because "one of us has to give in, and it's just easier for me not to be the meanie and deprive him of something he really wants, even though what I want I really want, too." When she pushes for Hawaii, he wants Europe. When she'd rather stay in a big, impersonal hotel with lots of amenities, he wants a cozy bed-and-breakfast. He wants wine-country tours; she wants Club Med. "He always wins. He feels a vacation should be all about the culture of a place and about cramming in as much stuff and activity as humanly possible so that we're totally exhausted by the end of the vacation. He doesn't appreciate the simple luxury of a nice tan."

As with spending elsewhere in your life, you have to take a stand for your wants when it comes to family R&R time—be it your desire to pursue some recreational activity or your need for a partner to scale back on one. Once again, it comes down to communication and compromise.

In planning a trip to the Mexican Pacific coast one fall, a buddy of mine at work confronted the quintessential illustration of this recreational divide that separates couples. For him, getting away from work is about travel, and travel is all about "unusual experiences, some of which could even be unpleasant," he says. Thus, he told his girlfriend what he wanted out of a Mexican holiday: driving around nontouristy spots and "possibly staying in some weird, dumpy place in a small town, if it means I can hang out in a seedy bar and get a better feel for what the place is like." He wanted Mexican culture, and no one yet has found it listening to mariachi bands on a beach.

Oddly enough, his girlfriend found that itinerary entirely unpalatable. While she's willing to travel downscale to a certain extent, she had far grander plans for this trip. She told him what she was seeking: A new—and expensive—resort had opened along the coast, and she wanted to stay there. Her reasoning: Why go to the effort and cost of seeing a place if you're not going to experience the best that place has to offer?

They hit a wall. She wasn't willing to tour Mexico on a burrito budget; he would not spend his entire vacation in a sterile resort, "where I probably won't even need to speak Spanish," he griped.

Their solution: Split the middle. He offered to spend half the week in the pricey resort she really wanted to experience, and in exchange she agreed to half a week venturing into remoter corners of the countryside and staying in cheap dives. They both had a blast.

Sometimes, though, even those approaches don't work. I know, for instance, that there's just no conceivable way I could convince Amy to visit someplace like Cambodia, where I really want to go, because she has no interest whatsoever. Similarly, if it's my turn to plan a trip, no matter how upscale I go in setting up an itinerary in Iran or Syria, Amy's just not getting on that plane. Period.

Just as golf widows would not expect their partners to forever abandon an activity they love, spouses shouldn't try to quell a partner's inner drive to pursue some enjoyment alone. Certainly, going solo isn't always ideal, but it may be the fix necessary to keep everyone happy. I'd much rather Amy tag along on all my travels, but just because she has no interest in Poland or Lithuania does not mean I should suppress all of my desires. Moreover, she sees no reason to tolerate my frustrations if allowing me to travel by myself for a few days will quench my needs.

The key to remember is that if you do venture alone to the places you want to see, then your spouse has dibs on selecting the location of your vacation together. That's only fair. Don't try to undermine your partner's choice if it's not the place you'd pick, and don't complain about not enjoying it when you're there. Your spouse has allowed you your happiness; you must give back some of that happiness. By the same measure, says Cassandra, the woman in California who tried to entice her husband to Iceland and Tunisia, a stay-behind spouse "should not make the other spouse feel selfish or guilty for having a more adventurous spirit and having the need to fulfill it." She says she's "working on having my husband realize that I have adventuring of my own to do—and some of it will be done without him."

For years, Ginger, a woman I know in northern California, has traveled without her husband because their vacation wants differ so dramatically. He's a doctor who works long, strenuous hours in a teaching hospital. When the time comes to vacate the operating room, he has little interest in trekking through an arduous or exhausting vacation of the sort Ginger enjoys, which often entails working as a volunteer to help orphans or engaging in other social causes in locales such as Bolivia, Nicaragua, southern India, and Laos. He'd just as soon find a nice hotel at a resort and relax.

Such a schedule holds no appeal for Ginger, who is "loath to spend time—or waste time, as I see it—on the beaches, hammocks, and two-headed showers of the world."[3] Instead, she wants to absorb what a country has to offer without being labeled as a tourist. So, off she goes on her own adventures.

"He says I like to go to countries that 'smell bad,'" Ginger says. Perhaps, but she says that her solo holidays "provide an enrichment to my soul and my memory banks that smells very sweet."

CHAPTER 16

When Financial Incompatibilities Arise

The Art of the Compromise

You come to realize one day that this is how it is: You and the person you've committed to spending your life with just don't see dollars and cents in the same light.

While you certainly are compatible in dozens of ways big and small, you just don't mesh financially, and the resulting strain leaks over into many other areas of your life. Way back at the beginning of your relationship, it was difficult, probably even impossible, to predict that such incompatibilities would happen to you—largely because people don't think about financial compatibility when they marry. We all change over time, though, and as we age we either grow more determined to pursue what we want or more resentful at not having that opportunity because of the life we're living. Either way, when incompatibility strikes, people grow apart and priorities begin to shift, and one of the areas of life where you feel it the most is in your pocketbook. People are acutely aware of money because they need it for just about everything, and they do not want to feel it is being unjustly sucked away by a partner they may be angry with at the moment.

In many ways, these financial incompatibilities are an issue we all grapple with in our relationships. We all have our own views about money—how we make it, how we spend it, how we save it—and conflicts inevitably arise when you want to do something fundamentally different with money than your partner does. How you manage those conflicts ultimately determines how successful you are in preserving the love. Conflict management also determines whether you effectively keep your financial life on track or allow the problems to breed contempt, anger, frustration—maybe even divorce.

Certainly, your life doesn't have to devolve into this. Moreover, not every incompatibility you confront is big. Some are relatively minor, and they're not going to lead to the dissolution of a marriage or a long-term relationship. Nevertheless, even small incompatibilities, if allowed to fester, can amass, like a cancer, into much more malignant troubles. The implications of that can be huge, creating major chasms in your relationship and threatening your financial well-being. Incompatibilities frequently loom so large, and all the peripheral arguments and disagreements seem so suffocating, that seeking a way out can feel like being lost alone in an unnavigable canyon—with the walls closing in.

When you derail financially as a couple, individual desires suddenly take precedence, family goals fade, and you grow increasingly convinced that no compromise exists because the gap between you and your partner's financial priorities seems to be measured in time zones.

What makes it all the more flustering is that because you don't see these differences until they surface, there's no way to deal with them until you're forced to. By then, you're angry, resentful, and disappointed—and left trying to answer one question: What now?

Most people generally recognize financial incompatibilities in the simplest terms: "We're not getting along." If you're struggling through a bout of financial incompatibility, or if you have lived through such a challenge in the past, you'll probably recognize the frequent laments: "We argue about money and I don't know why," or "We just see money differently." On the surface the incompatibility appears to be all about the dollars because it's the dollars you're fighting about. Dig deeper, however, and you find that you're really fighting about the core values you each hold dear.

The experiences of a longtime friend of mine demonstrate how this thinking takes shape. She says that she and her husband have never had a united front when it comes to money; that has been a leading cause of the frustration she often feels in her marriage. Instead of editing her comments, I'm just going to spill her thoughts onto the page as she let them flow. Her stream of consciousness, I think, poignantly captures how your mind works when you feel you and your partner are moving in opposite directions. Moreover, her observations show just how your financial life can spin away from you because you're groping to have your own needs met. Her thoughts indicate how hopeless people can feel in thinking they'll never find a way to reconnect.

For me, for so long, all I wanted was to own a home. That didn't matter much to my husband—he wanted to travel, see the world, eat at nice restaurants, and have fun. So that's what we did. But my goal never changed—I still really, really wanted a house. So when we had to move, I was very willing to make a bad financial decision—cash out some of our retirement account and bear the hefty tax burden—so that we could get the house that we hadn't been able to save for otherwise.

In hindsight, it was a huge mistake. We're overextended, we had a huge tax hit, and we bought at the peak of the market. So my husband's mistake was living an indulgent life short term, and my mistake was getting my home at all costs. The problem with both of us is that neither of us is irresponsible—we're just not on the same page, so we both sort of try to get what we want, and that has been very limiting in the end. I've gotten very depressed about the whole thing.

My husband had no idea that finances and money could stress me out so much, but when I'm worried about money, his life is hell, believe me. I just don't know how two people with very distinct and separate financial priorities and goals can work it out. He spends money on wine; I spend money on new carpet. In the end, we spend twice as much as we should. But where's the compromise? I don't like wine; he doesn't care about carpet. You can't compromise and decide to buy a new sofa instead. There's really no compromise when you have different priorities. Recently, while broke, I wanted that carpet for my living room. We didn't have the money, but cold air was coming up through the floor. I hated my house; it was depressing. He couldn't have cared less. But, see, the house is and always will be my big thing, my priority. I want to build my nest. There really wasn't a compromise option, so I put the carpet on my credit card—another bad financial decision, but I really wanted it, so I prevailed.

We needed to sit down and agree on a plan. We never did that. I talked and he talked but we never solved anything. I wish I had said, "Look, a house is all I care about. I want to put money away for that." I wish we could have come to terms with the fact that we still could have done fun stuff—the travel, the dinners out—but within our means. Talking is not enough, though. You have to push the conversation toward a real, solid plan based on all your various priorities, and you have to agree to stick to it. I think we erred because we haven't really acknowledged our differences and tried to find the trade-offs. You have to be on the same page, and it's very tough to always be on that same page.

A number of problems are going on here. In reading through her words, you can hear the sadness and anger in her voice. You can see that she and her husband, while they have talked, haven't really communicated. She has the house she wants, but their finances are a disaster and they took a huge tax hit. Their retirement account is emaciated. She also has the carpet she wanted, but her debt mounted at a time she really couldn't afford the cost. Certainly, her husband plays a leading role, too, since he generally has pressed for what he wants without acknowledging the importance of what she wants. Basically, there's a lot of rationalizing, a heaping dose of financial immaturity running amuck, and two lives zipping along on different tracks. Compromise is most certainly possible, but it takes two adults willing to sit down and communicate their core money values and work toward an acceptable middle. With apologies to the Rolling Stones, they might not always get what they want, but if they try, they'll find they can get what they need.

My friend's story illustrates exactly what happens when incompatibilities happen in otherwise good marriages: When partners feel that their needs are not being met in the relationship, they set out to meet their needs themselves. That creates animosity, even though it's not always expressed obviously or directly. Resentment bubbles up. Frequently, the outward sign of all the relationship ailments is that you lose control of your finances. Indeed, my friend says, "We both tried to get what we want [individually] and that has been very limiting in the end because we've spent everything we've made." What makes all of this particularly painful, she adds, is that they both know what's wrong: "We don't plan, we don't save, and we make indulgent choices."

Fixing it, though, is the difficult part.

Ultimately, the question you want answered is, "Can our life be put back together again when financial incompatibilities emerge?"

The answer is yes, it can—with real effort.

When incompatibilities arise around money, the reasons typically start and end with the way you and your partner communicate your individual financial needs. My friend noted that she and her husband talked about their money issues but could find no common ground. Yet she also noted that she never made her wants known; she laments never having said, "Look, a house is all I care about." Instead, she allowed his desires to take the lead, pushing her wants to the side until she reached a point where she demanded to be heard. At that point, she didn't care about the repercussions—and look at the effect it had on their finances.

If she and her husband had taken the time through the years to shape their financial life together, to lay out their individual and family goals, and to negotiate the priority of each goal, then they could have trod a much more mutually acceptable path that would have allowed them to pursue what they both wanted.

Though this is precisely what I hope you will avoid, let me share an example of what can happen when the strains of incompatibility grow too taut. The message to take away is this: You cannot succeed at mending any kind of incompatibility when only one of you is trying.

Over the course of a 10-year marriage, Karen, a Love & Money reader, says she "lost track of how many times my husband agreed that we should get out of our tiny apartment and into a house. He also agreed that we should live on one salary, while banking the other toward the down payment." To that end, her husband "religiously put his paycheck into the savings account as promised."[1]

Soon enough, though, Karen realized that her wants and his wants were colliding and that her dreams and his promises meant very little.

Although he was banking his paycheck, he also was making purchases "anytime something appealed to him," Karen says. "Sending him out with only a $20 bill made no difference in his total spending if he had a checkbook, credit card, ATM card, or if he could get into the bank in person to claim he needed cash but had left his ATM card at home. He found that some stores were willing to issue him a store credit card on the spot." Karen once sent her husband to Sears, she says, with exact change for a single item. He returned with a free gift for opening a Sears charge card—on which he had promptly rung up a $500 balance.

"In his mind, he was just spending $5 or $10," she says. "I'd explain it to him again, and again he'd agree that we should save toward buying a house, and after a day or two of watching his spending, he'd again fall off the wagon and start making those irresistible small purchases. After all, in the grand scheme of things, when the goal is to save $30,000, what's a buck or two?" Yet after a year of "diligent" saving, she says, "we actually had less money in the account than we did before we decided to put his whole paycheck in the bank." By the time the marriage died, Karen says, instead of having the down payment for a home, her husband "had run up over $30,000 in credit card debt, and there was only a few hundred dollars left in the savings account."

Though Amy and I generally pull together financially—saving for the same end, nurturing similar dreams, and conscientiously trying to follow our game plan—there are issues between us that represent incompatibilities just as considerable as those that split apart Karen's marriage. One in particular: I want to work overseas as a foreign correspondent, a dream I've had since my first journalism course in college. Amy has no interest in such a life and instead wants to return to our roots in southern Louisiana. These two fundamentally dissimilar views of how to live our life illustrate the very sort of divide that can cleave a relationship when both people want what they want with a real passion. We've argued many times about our dissimilar wants, and often those arguments have been painful if not insanely frustrating. If left unchecked, we both know our separate desires would lead to a much larger conflict. Yet we find détente because in the end our mutual interest is doing what's right for our family in the long run. Agreeing on that philosophy allows us to put incompatibilities in perspective and deal with them constructively.

I know, that's really easy to say, and less easy to put into practice. To some extent, Amy and I are lucky because we have something that obligates us to address our differences: the Love & Money column I write weekly. It forces us to talk about our issues in order for me to write about them. That's precisely the lesson to learn from my experience. We rarely talked about these kinds of issues before. Now we talk about them all the time. Out of necessity has grown a habit. Talking helps immensely because we're compelled to consider solutions—and each other's view—instead of just arguing our points. Arguing, I've learned, is a lot like teaching your dog to whistle—you're just wasting your dog's time and making yourself mad in the process. In the end, you've accomplished nothing.

In talking through an issue, partners must consider each other's questions without simply defending divergent positions. Think of yourself as an outsider trying to help a close friend navigate the exact same situation you're in. You're not there to express anger at your friend for his or her ideas; you're there to brainstorm all available options you can think up that might help your friend address the divide. And who is your spouse if not your best friend?

Here's one example of what I mean: I want to work overseas; Amy wants to live in Louisiana. When I began prattling one day about my desire to work in *The Journal*'s Tokyo or London bureau, Amy asked me at one point if there would be any way I could live in Louisiana as well as work overseas. Now, that certainly seems impossible, and it's one of those questions that, when you're in the heat of an argument, you defend with some snide remark like, "Yes, I can do that . . . just as soon as Honduras annexes New Orleans."

Yet in stopping to think about possible answers, I found what turns out to be a potential solution to our incompatibility. If we lived in Louisiana, which would allow Amy to pursue her career, I would have greater opportunity to pick up and travel overseas doing freelance work or the kinds of stories and photography that I've longed to do. I offered that as a suggestion. Amy said she would be fine with such an arrangement. Suddenly, our incompatibility, while still separating us, is a far less divisive issue. Our individual dreams are still alive. Whether we ultimately pursue that path is a whole different story, but the fact that we both agree on a possible approach at least takes much of the fire out of the debate and allows us to focus on improving other aspects of financial life in the meantime that one day might allow us to better pursue whatever path we choose.

That's not to say our approach is right for every situation. Everyone has a different set of circumstances to deal with in their life, and you have to find a solution that works for you. I have a friend, for instance, who takes an almost laissez-faire approach. He and his wife, he says, are "completely incompatible when it comes to money. We had no idea before we married." It turns out she's a spender: She wants better cars, expensive tile floors, a cleaning service. He's a saver, though only by default. He craves few material items, so he doesn't spend much and instead just lets his cash accumulate in a checking account. Because he has so few wants, however, that makes it easier for him to yield on many of the expenses his wife sees as necessities in her life, though he certainly doesn't yield on everything.

Partly he acquiesces because "it keeps the peace," he says. But he also can't strongly argue his wants against hers. The things she wants, he says, "she so badly wants," like sending their daughter to private school even though the public schools where they live are some of the best in the state. The things he wants—for instance, a beach house someday—"are so far in the future that they're hazy, versus something she wants right now."

To be fair, if he were as passionate about his wants as she is about hers, "it would be a disaster because any compromise would mean she couldn't get some of the things she feels so strongly about." His solution stems from his personality: He doesn't press financial matters because for him money isn't that important, certainly not as important as stability at home.

"There are ways of dealing with incompatibilities," he says. "You just have to work at finding the solution that works for you."

Dollars & Sense

If you're struggling through what you recognize as financial incompatibilities that are separating you and your partner, there's a good chance you can fix the problem. You hooked up with each other in the first place because you both know you're compatible in key ways. Keep that in mind; it's one of the biggest strengths you have in overcoming your financial differences, because if you're still married you must share some common values in your life.

Through the years together, we often lose touch with those shared values and with what's important in our lives, and in drifting away from one another we begin to take for granted what we have because we're so busy chasing what we want next. In doing so, you and your partner may veer off in different directions. When you finally poke your head up to see where you are, you may find yourself looking across a great divide and your partner is nowhere in the vicinity.

Take heart, says Denise, my financial counselor friend, "it doesn't take much work to pull people back together again and get them back on a united path, because underneath it all they're still compatible."

When clashing financial wants have your relationship in a knot, it's easy to think compromise isn't possible because your priorities are so different. That's true—but only from your perspective. You're so wrapped up in the sadness, anger, and animosity of the day-to-day fisticuffs that it's hard to see your life from 40,000 feet. From on high you can see the big picture, but instead you're mired in the daily minutiae. For your troubles to work out, you both have to begin looking at yourselves, your situation, and your behavior in broader terms—and honestly.

A couple of exercises can help you regain a grasp on what's truly important. First, imagine that you have just one year to live. How would you spend those final 12 months? What would you do during that time?

Second, imagine you have all the money you could ever want, an inexhaustible supply. How would you spend your money?

Those two exercises help you examine the same problem from different angles. The answers, though, are connected in an integral way because they reveal your core values. Your answers tell you what's really important in your life and where your passions lie. If I had only a year to live, for instance, I know without question that I'd want to spend it traveling the world with Amy and my son. If I had an unlimited stash of dollars, I'd travel the world and, at some point, build the home of my dreams and settle into a life of writing the books I want to write.

You're basically establishing the values you hold dearest for the life you want to live if given the opportunity. But life *is* your opportunity. If you can see what you want, you can begin to plan the route to reach it.

Once you've established your values, separate out those that you feel really passionate about and those you feel obligated to pursue. Sometimes we get so consumed by our obligations that we inadvertently suck the energy out of our relationships. Here's what I'm talking about: Lots of people feel obligated to care for a parent, for instance, so they direct an abundance of energy and resources into taking care of Mom or Dad or both and, in the process, throw the rest of their lives out of balance. Yes, the obligation is important, but in zooming in on the obligation solely, you're putting your life on pause and living an extreme. You have to get back to a middle ground, and back to what you're passionate about as well, to create a balance in your life. Otherwise, you're shirking your responsibilities to yourself and to your partner.

One way to get back on track together is to reaffirm your goals in life. As I mentioned in Chapter 5 on understanding financial compatibility, before you say "I do," you and your partner should know each other's short-, medium-, and long-term goals. If you slip off track, it's good to go back, draw up a new list of goals, and then compare notes. You'll often find you're still together in many areas, though you don't always see that in the haze of the financial frustrations you're living every day. Knowing you're still together helps rebuild a sense of unity and can help you better plan the road back to one another.

Where you aren't aligned, negotiate and set priorities for individual and family goals, then determine what's needed to achieve them. Neither of you can get—nor should you push for or expect to get—everything you want. Ultimately, though, you're re-creating a financial plan—together—that addresses each of your desires, yet benefits the family overall. For some people, goals are often abstract, such as "I want to be a better steward of our money," or "I want a happy retirement." For others, goals are concrete tasks, such as "I want to see 10 particular sites around the world before I'm 50," or "I want to save enough for a down payment on a new home." Whatever your goals, you need the vision to make them happen. I'm sure you've heard this before, but it's worth repeating: If you can see your dream, then you can live it—as long as you put forth the effort necessary to reach for it. From a financial standpoint, that means working together to create a spending plan (see Chapter 1) so that you remain aware of your resources and how those resources can help you achieve what you seek.

A large part of the success you'll have in hurdling whatever incompatibilities arise is communicating your needs and understanding the feelings you have about money and how money is flowing through your life. I know folks have a problem with this because expressing what you're feeling isn't the easiest chore. Moreover, you're so close to the situation that seeing what options might help you overcome some particular obstacle can be trying. In such a case, you often need a little help.

Most people, Denise says, don't need counselors or therapists, "but instead will do fine with a workshop or reading a book together." Three books to consider are *A Year to Live,* by Stephen Levine; *Creating True Prosperity,* by Shakti Gawain; and *The Way of Real Wealth,* by Mark S. Waldman.

All are good choices for reacquainting yourself with your money in terms of your values and your priorities. "What's important," Denise says, "is that you and your partner are open to what a workshop or a book is teaching, and that you work through the exercises together" to uncover and understand the root of your incompatibility and how you can address it effectively.

Sometimes, though, workshops and books are for naught. One person in a relationship just isn't open to the possibility that the problem can be fixed and may refuse to take a look at his or her role within the struggle. A person might even blame his or her partner for all the troubles that have emerged, asserting accusations like, "You're the problem; not me." That's a sign that two people have been disconnected for so long that antipathy has taken control of the relationship. That's when you need a professional like Denise to step in and hold a mirror up to the relationship so that both partners can see through impartial eyes what's really tearing at the union.

"Ultimately," Denise says, "successfully putting your financial life back on track only happens when you get out of your head and back into your heart—because the answer to what's really important to your life is very different in each of those places."

STAGE FIVE

The Later Years

Planning the Future

"Later years" makes it pretty apparent that Stage Five is all about life many years from now. But don't mistake that to mean you can postpone worrying about this stage of life until many years from now. Truthfully, much of this section could be Stage One, or maybe Stage One and One-Half. The fact is that to prepare for what awaits you in life, you need to be planning and saving through every adult stage—because Stage Five is nothing if not expensive.

Money is fundamental to this stage. So, too, is love. Stage Five centers on some very costly issues—retirement, a child's university education, financing a parent unable to afford life—and lots of folks generally don't want to think about any of that when they're younger. Sure, many of us contribute to retirement savings plans of one flavor or another, but that's almost by rote. We've simply had it drilled into our heads so often that we need to do this that we just do it to say we've done it. We don't put a lot of advance planning into what we're doing, because there's plenty of time to plan later.

The expenses that begin to emerge in Stage Five are so large and the emotional components so challenging that most of us would just rather deal with today and jump off the bridge when we reach that stage later in life.

That's not such a fine plan.

See, the thing is that while you have many choices in life—fish or chicken, cash or credit, paper or plastic—you really don't have many choices in Stage Five. You're going to need lots of money or . . . or you're going to need lots of money. Without the dollars to live the retirement you want, for instance, you'll be stuck with whatever retirement you get, and as you'll see from some of the surveys I cite, you really don't want to live the retirement you get stuck with. The retirees doing that generally are not happy campers—most, in fact, say they're scared and unhappy and uncertain of how they're ever going to pay for their lives.

Retirement might not be quite as certain as death and taxes, since some people never make it to old age. Statistically, though, you have a pretty good chance of reaching retirement and living a long number of years once you're there. So it's best to expect that one day you will retire. If you don't make it that far, no worries; you'll never know about it anyway.

If you do it make it, though, you're going to need a bundle of money to see you through. You'll get Social Security payments, of course, maybe even a bit of a pension if you're one of the lucky ones. But in large measure, your comfort in retirement will depend on your ability to save a few shekels when you're younger. Actually, given that you could live in retirement for 20 or 30 years, you'll need to save a boatload of shekels, several hundred thousand, at least, and more likely more than a million. Even if you retired today, at 65, and lived for the next 25 years on the equivalent of the U.S. poverty level—roughly $11,000 a year for a family of two over the age of 65—you would need a nest egg of $245,000 just to ensure you make it to the end.[1] Social Security will certainly pay some of that, but I just want to make the point that even living like a pauper takes a king's ransom.

Of course, preparing your finances for retirement is just one step. Equally relevant is planning for what you and your partner both want from retirement.

Just because you're married or have been a part of each other's lives for decades doesn't mean you're the same person—and it doesn't mean you know each other inside and out. I'm betting that if you're like most people, you haven't really talked about retirement except in the most general sense of saving for that amorphous event later in life. You both have wants in retirement, and those wants just might differ, possibly dramatically and possibly in ways neither of you recognize. Imagine you're just hitting retirement and eagerly anticipating the warmth of the desert Southwest, only to find your spouse shocked that you don't want to retire in your current home in the apple orchards of Wisconsin.

Wrapped up in what you want, though rarely discussed because the topic is difficult to address, are nagging concerns about health care issues that one day most certainly will arise. Talking about those troubling matters, as well as the lighter side of what you seek in the golden years, is all part of Chapter 18.

Future education costs are another big issue you face in Stage Five, though you must begin planning for these expenses several stages earlier. Unless you're raising the next Tiger Woods or Venus and Serena, the cost of sending your child to college is likely to be enormous. The price of a diploma has escalated at a rate far faster than ordinary inflation in the past few decades, and there's no reason to assume that will abate anytime soon. The result is that by the time a newborn reaches college, your family will have to find a way to cover an expense that easily could run to several hundred thousand dollars overall, depending on what school your kid chooses. Scholarships may pay a part; so might student aid or student loans. But if you plan on helping, you can't wait until the end of high school is in sight to start socking away some greenbacks.

Equally as important as the planning is where to put your savings. Parents and grandparents face an abundance of options in saving for a child's education. Some of those options are better than others, and some have various effects on taxes and, possibly, the family's eligibility for student aid, if that ultimately is needed. Chapter 19 will help you navigate the most popular options—in language that doesn't require an advanced degree.

Perhaps the most difficult challenge of this stage stems from having to finance a parent's old age. Not everyone will deal with this issue, and Chapter 20—which deals with learning how to possibly say no to a parent in need financially—I know will strike some as heartless. After all, we're talking about Mom and Dad, the people who sacrificed to raise you. Yet I know from correspondence with thousands of people around the country that these fears are real and that the number of people angst-ridden by the possibility grows larger every day.

Much as we'd like to wish it weren't so, our parents often find themselves without the means to afford their lifestyles—sometimes out of neglect, sometimes because they never cared, sometimes because they didn't have the opportunities to save, sometimes because of illness or disaster over which they have no control. Whatever the case, the challenge you face as the child is finding a way to deal with Mom or Dad's financial woes without robbing your spouse and children of the resources they need to better their own lives. Sometimes that means learning how to say no to Mom and Dad.

You've made it this far in life. Now all you have to do is successfully plot a course through Stage Five, and you'll win the game . . . however you define that.

CHAPTER 17

Retirement, Part I

Obsessing about Your Future

In my Love & Money column, I frequently write about my obsession with retirement. I plan and prepare for it monthly. I'm constantly saving money for its pending arrival, often wondering if I'll have enough saved when retirement arrives.

Lots of people tell me they feel this is wrong. Friends and readers bombard me with sentiments all the time insisting that I waste far too much mental energy planning and saving for an event still decades away when instead I should be enjoying my money before the ailments of old age set in, when the best you can hope for is a scenic bus ride to your doctor's office. Okay, maybe it won't be that bad, but at my age (late 30s as I write this) I'm constantly told to go out and spend for today and worry about tomorrow later.

"What's the use of having money today if you're not going to live a little," one of my best friends always announces. "Don't worry so much."

I understand the argument—you never know how long you have to live. Still, to me, such an idea is wrongheaded. It's the reason so many retirees today are unhappy. (I'll share some statistical proof of that in a moment.) Worse, it will be the reason so many baby boomers will find their retirement isn't nearly as fulfilling as they might have dreamed.

Think for a minute about what retirement really means in the broadest sense: It's one of only a handful of truly life-altering events we all face, right up there with marriage, having children, and the death of a spouse. Financially, retirement is much more significant than buying a house, typically the single largest transaction any of us ever make. You're talking about financing, possibly over two decades or longer, a need that will cost multiple hundreds of thousands of dollars at the very least, and likely more than a million dollars, depending on how young you are.

Statistically, if you made it to age 65 in the year 2003, you had a 30 percent chance of living another 20 years if you're a man, a 50 percent chance if you're a woman. I know that because I asked a friend at an insurance company, who in turn put me in touch with one of her firm's actuaries. So, those numbers *are* rocket science. Social Security, any pension you might receive, and the pot of cash you squirrel away during your working days are the only paychecks you'll have to live on for many, many years.

Here's how I see it: You essentially face two choices right now—you either begin to shape the retirement you want to live, or your retirement continues to shape the life you ultimately get. Either way, your retirement is taking shape. I choose to be the shaper, because in taking control of my future at a young age, I see the best opportunity for living the retirement I desire.

So let's just agree right now: I'm obsessed with retirement.

And with good reason.

I'm armed with all sorts of statistics and surveys conducted by a variety of financial companies, retirement organizations, and government agencies, all of which show the fears, worries, and finance issues bedeviling millions of folks currently planning for their futures. Possibly the most frightening data comes from an AARP analysis of data in the Federal Reserve's triennial *Survey of Consumer Finances*. From the most recent survey, in 2001, comes this little nightmare: The median net worth of baby boomers who don't own their homes is just $6,720—just about enough to buy one used car, and likely not a very good one at that.[1]

The worst part: Implied in that median number is the realization that half the houseless boomers own even *less*.

Not as dire, though still troubling, is that the median net worth for all boomers is $107,150.[2] That sounds like a pot of cash, and it is if you have to live on it for only one or two years. But life expectancy for a 65-year-old male in 2000 was 16.3 years, for a female 19.2 years, or so says the National Center for Health Statistics.[3] For kicks, I ran that sum of money past a retirement planning calculator operated by T. Rowe Price, a big financial services firm, and here's what it spit out: Stretch that $107,150 across a 20-year retirement, invest your savings prudently between cash, stocks, and bonds, and draw down the money wisely so that you don't deplete the account quickly, and you're talking about monthly income of roughly $525.[4] Just for perspective, the federally defined poverty level for a couple is $920 a month. Sure, you'll get Social Security, but Social Security data show the checks typically cover just 39 percent of total retirement income.[5] Basically, we're talking about a reduced standard of living.

My favorite slice of data has nothing to do with the worries of future retirees. Instead, a 2002 survey conducted for a major financial services firm by Harris Interactive with the help of one of the nation's leading gerontologists polled current retirees about their experiences leading up to retirement and the reality of their lives now that their supposed golden years are here. The numbers should make you rush out to open and fully fund an IRA the moment you finish this chapter. Better yet, go do it now; you can always come back to this when you return. . . .

The results show that the happiest and most contented retirees are those who have planned the longest. That doesn't necessarily mean they accumulated the most cash; rather, it means they spent vastly more years preparing, saving, and giving real thought to the life they wanted to live in retirement and how best to achieve it. Once they reached retirement, they felt immensely better equipped to fund whatever lifestyle they chose. They use phrases such as "extremely satisfied," "perfectly happy with life as it is," and can "travel and spend money freely." These contended retirees say they have freedom and flexibility and are satisfied, fulfilled, and less fearful about retirement. A defining characteristic: They saved for an average of 24 years.[6]

By contrast, today's most disgruntled and anxious retirees generally exerted little effort in planning for retirement when they were younger and did not accumulate the financial resources they one day would need. They represent more than half of all retirees. Many are plagued by worry and regret at having saved so little, and their sad situation, they agree, stems directly from choices made earlier in life. Sentiments that express their experience: "Retirement turned out to be a nightmare," "pessimistic about the future," "simply trying to hang on" and "worried that we're not financially prepared."[7] In essence, this is the retirement they never planned for, and that's just what they got.

In getting to this point, the discontented did exactly what so many people counsel me to do: Live for today. The retirees who did that figured everything would just work out in the end. It hasn't. They're now paying the price.

In other words: You get what you pay for.

I say that not to be callous. It's tragic; I know personally from watching my grandmother cope with few dollars in her retirement, and she's one of the luckier ones because she has a modest pension.

Consider just a few more statistics. (Is this overkill? It's supposed to be.

I want to scare, disturb, or alarm into action all of you who have yet to plan adequately for the day you hang up your lunch pail for good.) All of this information comes from the 2003 *Retirement Confidence Survey* conducted by the Employee Benefits Research Institute, a nonprofit, public policy group.[8]

- Nearly a quarter of workers age 45 and up plan to postpone retirement for financial or economic reasons, up nine percentage points from a year earlier.
- According to the survey, 16 percent of workers say they're "not at all confident" that they'll have saved enough money to finance their retirement, up six percentage points in a year. In 1993, the number was just 6 percent.
- Of the workers who say they *are* confident, many "simply do not know how much money it takes to live comfortably in retirement," the survey concludes. Worse, 61 percent of workers have never tried to figure it out. Possibly even worse than that, many of those who have tried to gauge the potential cost of retirement are relying on a false sense of security at best; their method of calculation: guessing.
- The vast majority of respondents report having spent more time in the previous year planning a vacation than preparing for their futures; 17 percent admit to spending no time at all planning for retirement.
- When asked, 70 percent of today's workers say they plan to work for pay after retiring. Yet today only 28 percent of retirees actually have done so. The implication: While employment trends are likely to change in coming decades, the expectations for future retirees aren't likely to match reality. A number of hurdles, particularly health, are likely to keep many out of the workforce and therefore unable to earn the paychecks they're counting on to live comfortably.
- Finally, half of all workers expect they'll live comfortably in retirement on less than 70 percent of their preretirement income; nearly two in five think they can live as they envision on less than 60 percent of their workaday salary. In reality, financial experts peg the true cost of comfort at between 70 and 80 percent of your current income.

By the way, don't blame the bear market in stocks that began in 2000 for this pessimistic view. The institute points out that its survey, prepared annually since the early 1990s, historically shows that retirement confidence is not tied to Wall Street's ups and downs.

"I watched my parents, who lived in rented housing and saved nothing, spend the final 20 years of their life living very modestly on Social Security," says Michael, a Love & Money reader in Arizona in his early sixties. "I vowed it would never happen to me. People without money are without choices. It's that simple." All it takes, Michael says, "is working, saving, and intelligent investing. The fact that you do those things means that you will almost certainly have a fulfilling and prosperous retirement."[9]

I started saving for retirement in the first week of my first job in 1989. I opened a savings account at a credit union in the tiny northern Louisiana town where I worked and dumped into it all of $15 a week, about 5 percent of my salary, the most I could afford at the time. When I moved to southern California a few months later—bumping up my salary—I increased my weekly savings to $25, recording those tiny deposits in a brown passbook that I still have somewhere. The money certainly wasn't much. Yet it instilled a savings discipline and, along with Amy's savings when we married, served as the nucleus of our nest egg today.

When I became eligible for the company 401(k) retirement savings plan, I contributed enough to at least meet the company match. My friends at the time laughed. We were all in our twenties, a bunch of beach rats, and they thought I was crazy to scrimp on weekend fun or the latest volleyball gear in order to put money into a retirement plan I wouldn't tap for perhaps 40 years.

I looked at it this way: Say you open today's newspaper and see a full-page ad from your local bank announcing that it will pay you 50 cents for every dollar you deposit into a savings account. You'd rush to the nearest branch screaming about free money. Well, what do you think your employer is doing by offering to match all or a portion of every dollar you save?

"Free money," I told my friends.

They still thought I was crazy.

Now in our mid- and late thirties, Amy and I save a combined 23 percent of our gross salary through our company-sponsored retirement plans and in after-tax savings and investment accounts. Even with all that, we have not guaranteed that we'll meet our goal of replacing at least 85 percent of our income. I'm aiming higher than the pros say is necessary to live comfortably, largely because I want to ensure that Amy and I have the wherewithal to pursue whatever we set out to do in retirement. Based on our current savings, our expected future contributions, and the projected growth rates of stocks, bonds, cash, and inflation, we have a 90 percent chance of reaching our financial goal.

I'm not just randomly guessing at that. I've plugged all of our information into a financial web site that uses a sophisticated probability modeling program known as Monte Carlo theory. (For trivia buffs, Monte Carlo, named after the European gambling mecca, was designed for the Manhattan Project.) Much like a weather forecast, the program gauges the chances that you'll reach your goals based on income, current savings, the amount of money you intend to save, and the historical randomness of investment markets and inflation, among other variables.

Not to induce a stupor, but most retirement planning assumes a static, average rate of return over a set number of years—as though investment returns move in a straight line. They most certainly don't. Go tell your average financial planning software that you want to know the value of $100,000 invested in stocks over 20 years at a 9 percent average annual rate of return, in line with historic norms. I'll save you the math: The answer is $560,441.

The Monte Carlo answer is 48.6 percent—meaning you have less than a 50 percent chance that your account will actually reach $560,441. There is, however, a 60 percent chance you will accumulate at least $232,527 . . . and for the dreamers, a 10 percent chance you'll amass more than $53 million.[10] The difference, and the vast spread of possibilities, is a function of how Monte Carlo analysis assesses a portfolio. The program runs through hundreds, thousands, sometimes millions of real-life scenarios that realistically could occur in the stock and bond market and taking inflation into account. The program dishes up a best-case scenario, a worst-case scenario, and a vast continuum of possibilities lying somewhere in between. Then it determines how frequently you'll meet your objective amid the hundreds, thousands, or millions of potential outcomes.

Some years, stocks are up 29 percent; some years they're down 15 percent. Sometimes inflation runs at a torrid pace; sometimes it barely exists. The sequence of returns you get and the sequence of economic environments you live through are the important factors in where your portfolio ends up. Rack up an unlikely, though statistically possible, string of above-average returns and you can retire to your own island. Suffer a bear market close to your retirement date and instead you'll be swinging in a hammock in your own backyard.

To me, a 90 percent chance of hitting your target isn't bad—but that only strengthens my argument. Here I am doing all of this in the hope that Amy and I can live comfortably when we retire, and we *still* have a 10 percent chance of failure. FinancialEngines.com, the web site I used to determine my probability of success, notes that average users, based on their current situations, have only about a 25 percent chance of maintaining in retirement the standard of living they're accustomed to in their working life. In a world where company pensions are no longer the norm and where we're all left to our own devices, are you willing to play Russian roulette with your fate? You literally have a better chance of success betting your retirement on black or red at Caesar's Palace.

Certainly, my family pays a price for this retirement obsession, just like all families pay a price in planning for the future. I drive a base model Jeep instead of the 1966 Mosport green Corvette I've always dreamed of tooling around in. We live in an old home, circa 1911, that, Amy often reminds me, needs help. We live farther away from the city and our son's school than we otherwise could afford; that adds to our daily commute. We could cut our savings to make our life easier, just being content to live for today and worry about tomorrow when tomorrow finally arrives.

The people who are happiest in retirement, though, tell me that's not the path to retirement contentedness. Marilyn, a retiree I know, started saving early, sticking $25 a month into her 401(k) plan in 1985, "a lot of money for me," she says. Instead of buying a fancy new home, she bought older homes and fixed them up. "I traveled and ate out on a budget," she says. "I never bought new cars; I bought reliable used cars, usually in colors I didn't much care for."[11] One of the hallmarks of the happily retired: Marilyn paid herself first, viewing her obligation to fund her retirement savings just as she did her obligation to pay off the monthly electric bill. She retired in 2001 with a pension of $39,000—not exactly a fortune. Her savings, though, supplement that income and allow her to live well.

In saving money, she says, "too many people see deprivation instead of choice. It's not how much money you make; it's how much you keep. Unfortunately, we have very few friends who will ever be able to retire the way I have. I see a whole generation of fifty-somethings who are slowly realizing that freedom in retirement is highly unlikely for them. Their future is part-time jobs as long as their health lasts. However, they have always owned new cars in the colors they wanted."

Dollars & Sense

All I have to do is read through the e-mails I receive at *The Wall Street Journal* to know that planning and saving for the future is the answer to every question about living happily and comfortably in retirement, and not necessarily as a millionaire.

"I am 69-year-old woman," says Margie, a reader in Ohio, "one of those single mothers who never had enough money to feed her four children, let alone put aside enough money for my retirement. I am now five years past retirement, I have barely $10,000 in savings, and I'm still working. My nest egg has been wiped out 50 percent by the stock market, money I could not afford to lose. And although I'm healthy, I have had cancer in the past, and I see a nursing home looming on the horizon for the next 25 years, as my mother died at 95 in that circumstance." Margie knows it's too late for her to make a difference in her life. However, she says, it is not too late for people "who have the good sense to plan for the future and care enough about your spouse and children to insist on it."[12]

Making changes to the way you approach your retirement can make a big difference. The Employee Benefits Research Institute survey I mentioned earlier points out that 40 percent of workers who actually calculated their retirement needs—as opposed to just guessing a number—altered their retirement planning. As a result, 59 percent started saving more. Those savings can add up, even if you just tuck away a tiny bit more.

Consider this: A 40-year-old starting today with nothing could amass nearly $150,000 in 27 years (67 is full retirement age for everyone born in 1960 or later) by saving just $50 a week at a 5 percent average annual return. This is a straight-line average, not Monte Carlo theory, since I'm basically just trying to illustrate the effects of a static fixed-income return that doesn't carry the same sorts of volatility risks that the stock market does. If you draw that money out over, say, 25 years, that sum would mean an extra $540 a month in your retirement income, according to the T. Rowe Price retirement planning calculator. Sure, that's not a princely sum, but it can sweeten whatever Social Security you receive.

Preparing for retirement is as much a mind-set as it is the dollars you stuff into a savings or investment account. Marilyn, my retired friend, says, "The most important thing I learned is that if you reframe your state of mind, saving and planning is not deprivation; it's abundance." That's a concept from Stage One. Adhering to a spending plan is not about depriving yourself. It's about liberating your cash so that you can funnel it to what you really want out of life.

Your goal, I hope, is to begin shaping today the life you want in retirement instead of letting your retirement shape your life. If you're not on board, then I encourage you to skip back several pages and reread those statistics. Do you really want to be miserable for 20 years or more?

If you are on this bus and want to gauge what you need to save for retirement, you must construct some notion of what your life is likely to cost and how much Social Security plus a pension (if any) will cover. Then you can figure out what's on your shoulders and how much you ultimately need to save. Here's a simple way to establish you're objective.

First, determine your cost of life today. Don't guess. Buy one of those financial management software programs, like Quicken or Money, and very nice life. I would go so far as to say that we are happier now than we ever have been."[5]

Using the spending plan discussed in Chapter 1, you can begin to determine how feasible it is for your family to scale back the lifestyle you now live. Examine all your expenses over the course of several months, and categorize them into three columns: fixed expenses (mortgage, car note, life insurance premiums), variable expenses (electricity, groceries, haircuts), and discretionary expenses (movies, restaurants, toys). Scrutinize the costs and pare them back to what you can realistically live on. *Realistically* is the key term. If eating out at restaurants is really important to you, then simply wiping it from your spending plan is useless, because in reality you'll find yourself in restaurants frequently. Compare the costs of your expected life against the income of the sole worker and determine not only whether the math works, but whether you're going to be okay with the lifestyle you've just laid out.

If the math just doesn't work, that doesn't mean the dream is kaput. Can the stay-at-home partner work part-time? Are there opportunities for the stay-at-home spouse to do freelance work or consulting to bring in extra dollars? Is a home-based business feasible?

If life on one income simply isn't possible or is not something you want to pursue, then no worries. In an environment where no job is as safe as you might hope, two paychecks provide greater security for a family.

I had a reader once tell me about a speech comedian Al Franken delivered to Harvard University's graduating class in 2002. In supporting her point of view that a dual-income lifestyle can't properly support a child's developmental needs, she noted that Franken had riffed on the notion of "quality time," that overly ballyhooed concept we parents like to whip out to justify our long hours at work punctuated by short, though intense, bursts of time with our kids when we're home: Franken said, "Being a good parent means spending lots of time with your children. Kids don't want quality time; they want quantity time—big, stinking, lazy, non-productive quantity time."[6]

I went and dug up a transcript of that speech. She was right; those were precisely the words he uttered. However, she conveniently left out the rest of the story. One sentence later the comedian tossed in this tidbit, which casts his comments in a different light: "On the other hand, it's important for every parent to maintain balance in his or her life. Don't be a slave to your child."[7]

Whether you pursue balance on one income or two, don't make the mistake of assuming that either approach is the right or wrong answer for today's dollars, which, as I mentioned way back in Chapter 4, will erode because of inflation. So I have to figure out the 2033 equivalent of $585,000. Any spreadsheet can provide this quickly with the future-value function. I'm using an inflation rate of 3 percent, the historic norm, even though inflation is substantially lower as I pen this. Ultimately, the answer is that for me and Amy to live in retirement on today's equivalent of $60,000 a year, we must have in place a stash amounting to $1.42 million when we hit age 67. That's a big chunk of money. Luckily, though, we have three decades for our investments and monthly savings to get us there.

Since I'm a bit conservative when it comes to financial expectations, I assume our investments will return about 8 percent a year, a bit below historic norms. All told, that means if Amy and I started from scratch, we'd need to save $952 a month for the next 30 years to reach our goal. This is a straight-line, average-annual-return approach, but by running the results through a Monte Carlo–based simulator like the one at FinancialEngines.com you can determine whether the projected savings will be enough. In my case, there's strong likelihood our expected savings will see us through.

Thankfully, we've been saving since our first jobs, so our hurdle is much smaller. Still, the point is that you should regularly save for retirement, kind of like paying a monthly mortgage or car note. This, basically, is your retirement payment. Fund it and you live happily ever after. Don't and you won't.

If you can't afford the entire expense, at least save as painful a slice as you can muster. Whatever you manage to set aside from here on out will make a dramatic difference in retirement, possibly even the difference between volunteering your time to do something you love or working menial jobs just to live.

If you're having trouble getting yourself moving in the right direction toward retirement, then follow these seven steps:

1. Start saving now. Commit to saving any amount you can. Remember, the happiest retirees saved longest. The little bits you save now will grow much larger in time and will instill in you a savings ethic.
2. Invest some time to determine logically what your life likely will cost in retirement. Don't just guess. Follow the steps outlined earlier in this chapter. It's pretty easy.
3. If you don't have a Social Security benefits statement, contact the Social Security Administration (www.ssa.gov) and get a copy of yours. From there you can begin to figure out how much you'll still need to reach the goal established in step 2.

other flexibility options that
life. Employers realize that
obligations while perform-
tion, increased job produc-
ompany.

you rush into your boss's
n. You need to approach
s you will accomplish the
and that it won't disrupt
asically, it's up to you to
akes sense for the com-

y want, though that can
love their jobs but feel
riad ways, however, to
nore ways than I have
such as iVillage.com or
track better at home
er, largely because this
about these concerns
nerhood Project at the
ablished a book called
r helping dads—and
competing demands

ur goal, then maybe
sehold. It can be an
rovide the financial
ght. The money you
he office, commut-
er than you think.
2000, she dropped
r husband, mean-
less travel. In all,
minate restaurant
are.
irrel away $125 a
ute to individual
tion occasionally
"still maintain a

4. Contribute to your 401(k) plan if you don't already. Contribute at least 1 percent of your salary or, if you can, up to the company match. Remember, this is free money. If you can, save even more. Either way, increase the amount you save by 1 percent periodically, either semiannually or yearly. Each time you get a raise, increase your 401(k) contribution by an amount equal to half the raise. That way, your standard of living benefits from the extra cash, but you also save more without feeling any pain.

5. Routinely check in with an online retirement planning calculator to ensure you're still on track. The one I mentioned at T. Rowe Price is free and is pretty good. The one run by FinancialEngines.com is more advanced, but unless your company pays for the service, and some companies do, then you'll have to pay either $150 or $300 a year, depending on the service you want.

6. Don't rely on straight-line average annual projections, and don't let a financial planner convince you of their usefulness. There's a great likelihood you will be disappointed in the end. I know a couple in the Midwest who several years ago paid a bunch of money to a planner who produced all sorts of nifty charts in sober colors explaining how, if they'd just stay the course, the average annual return in their portfolio would produce a nest egg plenty large enough to provide annual income of $50,000. Their plan did not work out, and now they don't expect to retire as planned.

7. Think in terms of your future, not just your present. Live within your means so that you can systematically save the money you'll one day need to support yourself when it matters most—when you're retired and the only paycheck you have is the one you generate for yourself.

For those moments when you question your commitment to funding your retirement, when you'd rather dump $10,000 into a flat-panel television to hang on your wall, reflect on Marilyn's parting words: "My feeling of freedom in retirement is the most wonderful present I could ever give myself. It is absolutely beyond description—and even better than I thought it would be."

CHAPTER 18

Retirement, Part II

Making Sure Your Dreams Are in Sync

What do you want from retirement?

I ask that to make a point. We—all of us—toss around the word *retirement* constantly. At the office we talk to our friends about our 401(k) plans or our pensions. At home we occasionally talk to our partner about saving for those golden years we see way off in the ether. During tax season, we contemplate individual retirement accounts and Roth IRAs. Here's my point: With all this talk of retirement, do you know what you're saving for? The answer I'm looking for isn't the word *retirement*.

Chapter 17 detailed the absolute necessity of planning for retirement because of the sheer financial significance of that life event. This chapter isn't so much about the financial as it is the temporal. If you're like most people, you're diligently, maybe even mindlessly, setting aside money from your paycheck each month to bankroll retirement.

But what does that really mean? Do you know what you expect your money to pay for one day? Do you have any notion of your spouse's expectations?

For all the effort that each of us puts into this notion of "saving for retirement," few people I know have ever taken the time to consider what retirement might look like, or what they want and need from retirement, or what their partners want and need from retirement. Couples rushing through life together have grown so comfortable just knowing that they're saving that they never stop to measure whether their desires mesh.

If you think about it, that's like driving without a map to a location you've never seen—you have a vague indication you're heading somewhere, but you're not sure if you'll end up in the right place.

There are so many things you need to be prepared for: the activities you want to pursue, the house you'd like to retire to, the health care costs you most certainly will have, travel, education, a vacation home, helping your kids and grandchildren, establishing an estate you hope to leave behind. You don't need to begin planning for everything all at once; some of that stuff you can worry about when the time arrives. What you do need to know, though, is how your and your partner's wants fit together as they relate to the retirement dreams you each have.

After all, if you're on the road to retirement together, doesn't it make sense to know you're both driving toward the same destination?

I know exactly how it goes. . . . You get busy in life; you have to get up early enough each morning to get yourself and the kids ready; you rush home after work to carpool them all over town for birthday parties and after-school activities; in the middle there's shopping for groceries, paying the bills, and putting dinner on the table to worry about; you've got bathing and homework to accomplish so you can get the kids in bed in time to prevent grouchiness in the morning. Somewhere in all of this you'd like to spend a few minutes alone with your partner. Really, there's just no good moment in your day to sit down and reflect on what you'll need 30 years from now when all you want at the moment is a 30-second breather. I'm living it with you every day.

Even when you try, it's easy to brush aside the conversation when the inevitable differences crop up. Jack, in South Carolina, says he and his wife, Tammy, have had many discussions about what they want from retirement. Yet while saving for retirement has been a priority, "there still is no plan in place for when it gets here," Jack says. "We talk about RV-ing across America, boating up and down the Intracoastal Waterway, and seeing things we haven't had the time or the funds to see. We talk about visiting our kids and grandchildren wherever they may end up when they start making their own choices and lives. This is yet another variable that is difficult to quantify. It seems whenever we have these discussions we stumble over where we want to live, in addition to what our financial and health circumstances may be. Consequently, it's not uncommon for the topic to get shelved until something causes us to think about it again."[1] Part of the problem, too, Jack concedes: "It's difficult to grasp that the sunset of my working life is close enough to ponder all of this seriously."

Yet as Jack recognizes, determining how you want to live in retirement is an important exercise, because if you can foresee what you want and then plan for it, you can be relatively certain you won't wake up one morning as a retiree disappointed that you're living a life you never sought. As my financial planner friend, Linda, says: "A goal without a plan is just a wish."

She admits she snagged that off a bumper sticker, "but it really is the truth. You have to take the blinders off. You can't just wish for something and then go about your life. You have to stop and look at where you're going, and plan for what you want, so that you can figure out how to get there."[2] Otherwise, you just end up someplace you may or may not want to be.

Imagine going to the airport with your sight and sound temporarily suspended. You hand a note to a ticket agent that simply says "sun and sand!" You're guided onto an airplane, excited that you'll soon be landing on a Caribbean beach where the ocean will restore your senses. How disappointed are you to open your eyes and find you're in a waterless desert? You got your wish, though certainly not as you'd envisioned. Slightly more planning, and you're resting under the balmy shade of a beachfront palm.

This is where a list comes in really handy. You might recall that in Chapter 5, on understanding financial compatibility before you get married, I mentioned the benefit of listing your short-, intermediate-, and long-terms goals when you go into a marriage so that you both can plan for the future you see together. Well, the same idea applies here. Lists provide clarity and serve as concrete reminders of what you're striving to attain. I know a couple with a dream home in mind, and when they find in magazines and advertisements examples of what they want a particular room to look like, they clip it out and tape it to the refrigerator. They're making a visual "list," building on the doors of their fridge a room-by-room blueprint of their dream home, a vivid reminder every time they grab a snack of exactly what is relevant in their financial life. These sorts of visual cues keep us moving in the direction we want to go together, and that's important because the road to retirement isn't so much an uninterrupted freeway as it is the Atlantic City boardwalk; its entirety is lined with a never-ending array of shops and booths where we can gleefully lighten our wallets and waste a little time.

Here's what I did as it relates to making a retirement list: I knew Amy and I had never had any discussions about what we each seek from retirement, so one weekend morning, when all was still unexpectedly calm, I handed her a piece of scrap paper and a pencil and asked her to just jot down in no particular order her thoughts about what she sees in her life decades from now. Basically, I asked her to catalog the dreams, wishes, wants, necessities, and expectations she envisions for her retirement. While she was thinking and scribbling, I did the same on my own piece of paper. A couple minutes later, we compared notes.

These were some of the items:

- See the running of the bulls in Pamplona and the Indianapolis 500 car race (those were Amy's, by the way)

- Build a retirement home of our dreams
- Have no mortgage
- Go back to school, maybe be a chef
- Cover our health care costs
- Help our son financially, if he needs it
- Help any grandchildren we have pay for college
- Own a 1966 Mosport green Corvette (that's the year I was born and my all-time favorite car)
- Run a small business, maybe a restaurant
- Have the money to visit our son frequently, wherever he lives
- Travel as a volunteer to help children in developing nations
- Don't have to worry about money

Your retirement list could be just about anything, and it's certain to be different from mine or Amy's or your neighbor's or your coworker's. No doubt you'll find that you and your spouse have some unexpectedly similar goals. Amy and I learned that we both want to own a little vacation loft in Vancouver, British Columbia, a city both of us are drawn to and where we know we want to spend months at a time when we're retired. In other areas, you could easily be a continent apart from your partner. In fact, our lists were different in several areas, the biggest split being that Amy wants to retire to Louisiana, while I'm more in tune with the climates and seasons along the Oregon coast, or maybe some small New England town. Such similarities and, particularly, differences are precisely the point. The aim of this exercise is to gauge your views and your spouse's views on where you're both going—that way, neither of you is surprised to find that when you arrive at where you're headed, the other has no interest in being where you are.

I know that sitting down to contemplate the sunset of your life is not what a lot of people want to do on a Saturday morning—or any other day of the week. Then again, I don't necessarily want to suffer through a proctology exam, but if it's going to ward off my premature death from colon cancer then it probably makes sense to tough it out for a few minutes once a year. In some ways that analogy is more on the mark than you might imagine. As you hopefully recall from Chapter 17, lots of folks who have made it to retirement without preparing essentially say it's all one big pain in the . . .

A little discomfort now will help ward off greater pain later in life.

There is, of course, an entirely different way of looking at life. As long as the world can surprise us with disease, war, terrorism, violence, and random acts of nature, we're all vulnerable. Why bother with any of it? Failing to consider that something might run amok with your perfect plan, says Hillery, a reader in central Florida, "is like having your total portfolio invested in tech stocks—and getting blindsided by the market."[3] In other words, a premature death or disability or unexpected health problems can destroy the life you've been planning for all along.

Longevity and fiscal prudence are in Hillery's family; her dad lived well into his nineties, grew up in the Depression era, and worked in the financial services industry. "Medical care improves all the time, and as a woman I get an extra 15 years just because," she says. Everything in her background, Hillery says, "warned me to save, save, save" because her life looked like it would be long.

Cancer was not a part of her background and not a part of her plan. Still, it arrived.

"When the laughter, tears, and anguished discussions were finished, I had learned this: 'Certainty' is a comfortable illusion we create for ourselves to ward off fear. Fear would paralyze us, so our survival mechanism leads us to create 'certainty' and 'future projections.' It is, indeed, a lovely thing to feel that I Save, Therefore I Control My Destiny." Hillery says that the paradigm most people, me included, have for retirement is something akin to Aesop's fable about the busy ant, who worked all summer to prepare for winter, and the lazy grasshopper, who played and prepared not.

The truth, she says, is that "the grasshopper fiddled all summer, the ant worked hard, a human came along and killed the ant, and the grasshopper did indeed starve. They all ended up dead—but at least the grasshopper had a nice life."

I'm sure that rings true for lots of people. Tragedy does strike all the time and is a graphic reminder of just how fragile we really are. If you've got only one go-round in life, you might as well make it a party. I know plenty of people who feel that way and thus spend that way.

People like to say, "You don't know if you're going to step off the curb tomorrow and get hit by a bus." You're right; no one knows that. Then again, you might wake up tomorrow and realize you're 72 and out of money and fearful of where your next meal will come from. The best any of us can do is plan our life based on physiological expectations. For people like me, in their late thirties, that means the expectation of living another 43 years, according to the Centers for Disease Control.[4]

Really, it comes to this: You can gamble that you *won't* live long and spend your money to enjoy life today, or your can gamble that you *will* live long and conserve some of your capital to pay for a better retirement—namely, health care and a quality of life that doesn't leave you wishing you were dead. (Notice, I said *some* of your capital. That means it's perfectly fine to enjoy life today as well. Like a healthy diet, though, your spending should be in moderation.) If you're wrong with the first gamble, you live miserably when you're old because you haven't the resources to pay for life. If you're wrong with the second gamble, you've missed some of the fun while you're young—but then again, you're dead and clueless. It would seem to me that it makes more sense to gamble on a long life and plan accordingly.

Many of the items on the retirement wish list that Amy and I drew up—and I shared only a few of them—are material in nature. Some of that is wishful thinking, little more than what kids dispatch to Santa every Christmas. What the list doesn't show is what both of us ranked as our primary goal: Affording the cost of health care in the future.

As much as people don't plan for retirement, they plan even less for future health care. No one wants to contemplate the ailments of aging and all the associated dollars it will cost for doctor visits and surgeries and prescriptions and more prescriptions. "I have insurance," you might be thinking, "so at least that's covered."

You hope. Today is today; tomorrow is something all together different. Consider these sobering little tidbits:

- In 1993, about 40 percent of large employers offered health care coverage to their retirees, according to Mercer Human Resources Consulting. By 2001, the rate had dropped to 23 percent. For those employers still offering health care coverage, many are shifting an increasing share of the costs onto their retirees.[5]
- Only 5 percent of small firms, those with fewer than 200 workers, offer retirees coverage.[6]
- Among large companies, only 29 percent offer coverage to early retirees, those under 65 years old.[7]
- Retirees are expected to be responsible for 90 percent of their total medical costs in 2031, according to a survey by Watson Wyatt Worldwide, a human-capital consulting firm.[8]

Basically, by the time you make it to retirement, you may find that you have minimal coverage, no coverage, or are responsible for shouldering a huge portion of your annual health care premiums. You're probably going to have to come up with the money necessary to pay for your insurance policy—and at that stage in life, insurance promises to be expensive.

Look, I know no one wants to think about this kind of stuff, but this is a real part of life. These are the real financial issues that families have to deal with as they're progressing through their days. You either handle them before the day arrives or after the fact, when it will be substantially more expensive or difficult or maybe even impossible. Yes, it's so much easier to just go about your life, blocking out the uncomfortable issues that aren't pressing upon you, but soon enough they will. And the question is, will you be prepared?

Here's my single biggest fear for retirement: Nursing homes. I don't fear dying early; I fear living a long time and with inadequate care. I walked the halls of a nursing home with my grandfather in his last days, and I dread the thought of incompetent, inattentive care when I'm old. I fear not being powerful enough to fend for myself and being at the mercy of health care workers who show little compassion and, often, too little competence. I don't mean that as an indictment against all health care workers, but I've been inside nursing homes, and Amy has been inside hospitals her entire adult life, and we both know that compassion and competence often are conspicuous by their absence.

As I've told Amy many times, "I don't want to be alone in an institution like my grandfather was." Nor do I want to be separated from her, even if we get too old to care for ourselves. Basically, I want to know that our money will afford us in-home care and see us through to the end—together.

Those are huge costs. AARP, the big retiree association, reports that in 2002 the average hourly rate for bringing a licensed practical nurse into your home to care for you or your spouse or your mom or dad averages about $37 an hour. Depending on where you are in the country, that could fluctuate from $23 to $75 an hour.[9] A home health aide averages $18 an hour (ranging between $13 and $27). Do a little multiplication. If you need assistance for, say, four hours a day, you'll be paying anywhere from $19,000 a year on the low end to well over $100,000 on the high end.

Nursing homes are no different. The national average cost for one month in a nursing home was $4,654 in early 2003, or nearly $56,000 a year, according to an AARP study.[10] Meanwhile, a 1999 study by the American Council of Life Insurance projects that one year in a nursing home will cost $190,000 in 2030.[11]

Most people think Medicare, Medicaid, and Medigap (a private insurance supplement to Medicare) will cover their in-home and nursing home costs. That's not likely. Private insurance and Medicare generally don't cover extended nursing home stays. Medigap nursing home benefits end after 100 days, and while Medicaid will cover some of the costs, it's only for people who meet very specific medical and financial criteria. (Basically,

CHAPTER 14

The Trials of Being the Trailing Spouse

Following Your Dreams

Americans have to be the most mobile people ever. We pick up and pack up and relocate, from one coast to the other, one state to the next, even country to country, all the time. Indeed, 40 million of us boxed up our lives and moved somewhere else between 2000 and 2001, representing about 14.5 percent of the population, according to the most recent census data. Certainly, much of that amounts to folks just moving from one house to another down the block. Yet nearly 8 million of us moved across state lines or international boundaries. That suggests lots of people in any given year are out chasing better jobs.

Often lost in this relocation binge is the *trailing spouse,* the forgotten partner silently resigned to a rootless life trailing a spouse on the move. It's an apropos if unglamorous phrase, trailing spouse, because "trailing" is exactly what happens. A *leading spouse* chases a career, wrapped up in the challenge of a new position and the excitement of yet another move up the corporate ladder. All the while the trailing spouse dutifully trails behind, pushed about like a feather on a breeze, alighting in Atlanta one year only to land in Las Vegas the next, living a life forever blown into tumult, whether or not they want to be wherever it is they wake up and find themselves.

This isn't just about moving from city to city to city, though. This is a story about dreams. For all the while one partner is chasing the dream of a glorious career on the move and on the rise, the other just as often is left to piece together a disjointed life. There's no consistency to their years. No opportunity to set down roots. Friendships are made and then all too quickly forsaken. There's no chance to build a steady work history or a career and, as in Amy's case, a diminished opportunity to build the retirement savings necessary for old age.

your child. The only thing that matters is that you lavish on your kids the love and affection they need and deserve, while at the same time pursuing the happiness in life and work that you want to feel.

Family and career aren't mutually exclusive. In choosing what's best for one, you can choose what's best for the other—as long as both share equal value in your life.

you have to be poor and have few assets.) Nursing home and in-home care are instead the province of long-term-care policies. More on that in a moment.

There are so many ways to prepare for the financial burden of medical care in old age that it would take another couple books to detail. Everyone has their own specific needs and circumstances that must be addressed when searching for a plan. Personally, I've looked at long-term-care insurance, reverse mortgages, and a relatively new financial planning tool known as *life settlements* (essentially, selling your life insurance policy for cash when you're old). I'll explain a bit more about those options in the upcoming Dollars & Sense section.

My first line of defense will always be the nest egg that Amy and I manage to amass before we retire. Ultimately, Amy may never see the running of the bulls. I may never become a chef or drive the classic Vette I'd really love to have. We may never build the retirement home we foresee. As long as we have the funds to pay for our health, neither one of us cares.

In the end, is knowing all of this and planning for health concerns 30 years before the fact really that useful? I realize that in some ways, making a list of your retirement wants is little more than daydreaming. Amy and I probably won't pursue all these dreams, constrained ultimately by either time or money or maybe health. Clearly, many of our desires are predicated on a string of what-ifs that may never arrive. Moreover, we're both well aware that as we get older our dreams no doubt will change, making some items on our list pointless and raising others to must-have status.

However, for me, failing to prepare means preparing to fail. If nothing else, each of us has a clear understanding of what the other expects of our retirement together. Better yet, we know where our wants overlap and diverge and where we must find compromises in our plan. We know some of our fears are similar. Most important, we know we're steering in pretty much the same direction. We've both begun to think more about how we're going to foot our health care costs years into the future. We still have plenty of time to do something about it, and we're exploring the options we have so that we can be prepared. We may be early, but so be it. The price for being late is steep.

Daydreamer or not, this knowledge provides comfort to me: Instead of saving for some nebulous notion of "retirement," our list of wants, needs, and dreams, and our early preparations for health matters, gives us specific targets we can work toward. To that end, not long after our little exercise, we opened a special joint savings account into which we funnel a little money every month.

It's specifically earmarked for that loft in Vancouver.

Dollars & Sense

Planning for what you want out of retirement is second only to planning for retirement. It's like a road trip across the country. You've saved enough resources to make the trip fun, but you have only one shot at doing what you want. A plan would help greatly. While you're dying to spend time seeing the world's Largest Ball of Twine (in Cawker City, Kansas, if you care) and other roadside amusements on America's forgotten highways, your spouse may have been pining all along for national parks and major cities. Suddenly, pursuing either dream over the other becomes a major disappointment for one of you.

Of course, you can compromise—that's ultimately the goal—and take in the twine on your drive toward Colorado's Rocky Mountain National Park and nearby Denver, for instance. The point: To compromise, you first have to know what each other wants. Making a list of your retirement desires, expectations, and concerns is a perfect way to begin designing your road map for retirement.

The worst thing you can do is keep your desires pent up. Linda, my financial planner friend, was working with a couple who had come into an inheritance and wanted to determine whether they had enough of a nest egg for the husband to retire immediately, followed by his wife five years later (he was 11 years older and approaching retirement age). Linda ran the numbers and determined that, with the wife still earning a paycheck, everything would work out. That's the path the couple pursued.

Yet every time the wife stopped by Linda's office, she was unhappy. "The reality," Linda says, "is that she hated her job, but she didn't speak up about her wants when we ran their retirement plan. So we asked her what she really wanted to do." Turns out she wanted to be a librarian. Linda told her to research the education needed, the schools that offer the necessary degrees, and the financial assistance that's available. The woman did and found there existed a strong demand for librarians on U.S. military bases around the world. Linda recalculated the couple's retirement projections to determine the feasibility of the wife taking two years off to obtain a degree.

"The numbers worked," Linda says, "because after getting a degree in something she loved, she knew she wouldn't want to retire in five years. They wanted to travel the world letting her be a librarian, and they could continue to earn money longer. That's what stepping back to look at what's important in your life can do for you, if you just talk about it."

You also need to step back and take in the costs of health care. The average retiree in 2002 spent about $3,700 on out-of-pocket medical costs, including co-pays, deductibles, outright medical payments, medical equipment, pharmaceuticals, and hospital stays.[12] That doesn't sound like much, but it represented roughly 22 percent of the average retiree's income, according to the Urban Institute, a nonpartisan economic and social policy research organization. But remember, these retirees generally have decent insurance coverage. The cost of future medical expenses increasingly is shifting onto your back.

You might have insurance coverage when you retire, but the way the world is headed—with health care costs continually escalating and corporations continually seeking ways to separate themselves from their obligation to their workers—there's a pretty good chance you'll be responsible for a large chunk of your medical costs in retirement. For a ballpark estimate of the heath care costs you will likely face in retirement, the Employee Benefits Research Institute has a Retiree Health Savings Calculator (www.choosetosave.org/tools/rethlth.htm) that can give you an inkling of what you may be on the hook for one day.

There are way too many insurance plans and options to summarize here. Instead, I want to share with you three options to keep in the back of your mind that can help you foot the bills when that time arrives. You might want to consider these options today if you have parents struggling with medical bills right now or whom you expect will need financial assistance as they age and grow increasingly frail.

Long-Term Care. People generally assume that if you have health insurance or you're eligible for Medicare, you're pretty well set. That's not so, particularly when it comes to nursing home or in-home care. Traditional insurance policies and Medicare just don't cover these expenses to any real degree. Medicaid does, though you generally have to be impoverished to qualify. Worse, as far as I'm concerned, Medicaid reimburses at such a low rate that the best nursing homes typically refuse to accept Medicaid patients, focusing instead on private-pay patients who can afford a higher caliber of care.

This is where long-term-care insurance comes in. Long-term-care coverage provides the dollars needed to pay for nursing home and in-home care. On a private-pay basis, such services can be extremely pricey. Northwestern Mutual, a big life insurer, says that the average nursing home payout for its long-term-care customers is between $65,000 and $70,000 annually, depending on where you live in the country.[13] (The AARP study mentioned earlier cites a lower number because it includes Medicaid patients in the mix, which reduces the average.)

Long-term care basically provides a predetermined amount of dollars per day to cover the costs of care. The policies can last as long as you live, or can be structured similar to a term life insurance policy and expire after a set number of years. Most policies are offered with some form of inflation protection built into the plan, so that the $100 worth of coverage you buy today equals whatever that same coverage costs X number of years from now when you need to rely on the insurance.

People generally think of long-term-care insurance as something only old folks buy. Though that was the case several years ago when the products were new, it's no longer so. The age of the average policyholder is falling rapidly as people better understand what they're buying. Northwestern Mutual's average policy buyer is 57, on par with the industry. Even some people in their mid-thirties are buying policies because the prices are so much more affordable then. That might seem to some to be entering the game a bit too early, but consider that 42 percent of adult Americans who are receiving long-term care are under the age of 65, according to a March 2001 report by General Accounting Office (the audit, evaluation, and investigating arm of Congress). The average age of policyholders making claims, however, is about 76.

If you decide to buy long-term-care insurance just before you need it—say, in your late sixties or seventies—your premiums could be substantial, possibly more than you can afford. Here's a very rough estimate that illustrates the point: If you buy lifetime coverage benefits at age 40, you might pay about $450 a year, or less than $40 a month. Wait a decade until you're 50, and your premiums go up to between $600 and $700. Hold out until you're 60 and you're paying $1,400 or more. In your late seventies, the premiums could well exceed $6,000 annually, depending on your coverage.

You must take numerous factors into consideration, such as how much coverage you need or want and whether you desire lifetime coverage or just a set amount of benefits, say six years' worth. You may not even need long-term-care insurance, given that two-thirds of men and one-third of women over 65 never spend a day in a nursing home.[14] Talk to a financial planner who has knowledge in this area, or find a fee-only insurance consultant who will work for you rather than an agent who works on commission from the insurance company. Fee-only insurance consultants are tough to come by, so any advice you receive from an agent should be run by a trusted attorney or CPA, both of whom have a fiduciary obligation to you. I certainly don't mean to knock all agents, but fee-only consultants generally don't push any particular product, since they're not being paid to, so they typically work for your benefit. (The same logic applies to financial planners; those who charge a set or hourly fee are generally better for your pocketbook. Those who are paid on commission by an investment-products company may offer slanted advice, because their paychecks depend on how much product they can sell you.)

If you want to do a little homework on long-term-care insurance, the Health Insurance Association of America has a Guide to Long-Term Care Insurance that you can download from its web site, www.hiaa.org/consumer/guideltc.cfm. Meanwhile, the American Health Care Association and its sister entity, the National Center for Assisted Living, jointly operate a web site, www.longtermcareliving.com, that is stacked with consumer information and resources. Nolo, a Berkeley, California, publisher well known for easy-to-read books on self-help law and other topics, offers *Choose the Right Long-Term Care,* by Joseph L. Matthews. You can find it at Nolo's web site, www.nolo.com.

Reverse Mortgages. As the name implies, a reverse mortgage works in reverse. Instead of paying a lender as you do when you buy a home, a lender pays you. Basically, you're tapping the illiquid wealth residing in your home. Many people sell their houses and move into smaller, less expensive digs in order to unlock some of that wealth. That can be a fine strategy since a smaller house or a condominium requires less money to maintain. Still, if you want to live out your days in your current home and generate cash you need to finance health insurance, daily living expenses, or just to travel and enjoy life, then you might take a look at a reverse mortgage.

You have to be at least 62 years old to apply for a reverse mortgage. The amount of money you can obtain from a lender varies based on your age, the value of your home, and where you live. Younger seniors generally are eligible for a smaller percentage of their home's value, because they statistically have more years left to live, and lenders want to ensure that there's enough equity remaining to cover the repayment one day. As with a traditional mortgage, you pay interest on a reverse mortgage; the cost accrues over time and must be repaid when you die or sell the house.

Reverse mortgages can be structured so that you receive a lump sum immediately or monthly payments for life. If you choose the latter and live far longer than expected, you'll always have the income coming in, even if it ultimately exceeds the value of your home. In that case, the lender simply made a bad bet; neither your estate nor your heirs are on the hook for the extra money. Also, your heirs can repay the loan with other assets in your estate if they wish to keep the home. If they sell, they repay only what is owed; the rest of the proceeds return to your estate. You can even obtain a reverse mortgage if you still owe money on your home. In fact, some seniors go for a reverse mortgage to pay off their current mortgage, in turn freeing up cash they can use for necessities or wants. The money you receive is tax-free and does not impact Social Security or Medicare benefits, but it could affect eligibility for certain government assistance programs. The U.S. Administration on Aging (www.eldercare.gov) is a good resource for information on assistance programs in general and on how a reverse mortgage could impact eligibility.

For more general information on reverse mortgages, check out the National Reverse Mortgage Lenders Association (www.reversemortgage .org), which offers consumer information as well as a state-by-state list of lenders. Meanwhile, AARP has an abundance of consumer information at www.aarp.org/revmort.

Life Settlements. If you own a life insurance policy, particularly a term policy or a universal life policy, you might consider selling the policy for cash. With term policies, in particular, most policyholders just assume the contract has little value outside of the death benefit and so let them expire. Since term policies have no cash value, unlike whole life or universal life policies, people often see term policy premiums as just another drain on their resources when the money could better be used elsewhere. But life insurance policies do have value to investors who are willing to buy them. The purchaser becomes the beneficiary of the policy, continues making the premium payments, and collects the death benefit when you die. The upside for you is the ability to turn an asset that you might otherwise abandon into cash that you need for some immediate purpose.

You generally must be at least 65 years old to sell a policy, and the policy must have a face of value of at least $250,000, sometimes $500,000 or more. The type of insurance contract you have, your health, and your actuarial life expectancy will determine how much money you receive. In general, universal life policies are worth between three and four times the underlying cash value, sometimes a little more. Term policies, meanwhile, generate between 10 and 30 percent of their face value. That income can help pay for long-term-care premiums or cover other medical or daily living expenses you might not otherwise be able to afford.

Be careful, though, because there are trade-offs you must be aware of. If you truly need insurance coverage to provide for your spouse or your heirs, then don't sell your insurance, since replacing it could be more expensive or, in some cases, impossible. Also, while death benefits go to your beneficiaries tax-free, the proceeds from selling a policy are taxable. Be sure heirs and spouses know what you're up to since they ultimately are impacted by your decision. In fact, reputable life settlement companies (and yes, some aren't very reputable, so look for those that are licensed) generally require that beneficiaries sign off on the transaction to ensure that everyone is clued in.

Financial planners usually are a good source of information on life settlements and can help you determine whether selling your policy really makes sense, so check in with a professional before making a rash decision. The Orlando-based Viatical and Life Settlement Association of America (www.viatical.org) has some information on its web site for consumers, though www.viatical-expert.net is aimed directly at providing policyholders and investors with the pros and cons of these arrangements.

Ultimately, what I want you to take away from this chapter and from my and Amy's exercise in listing our visions for retirement is this: Know what both you and your partner want from retirement before it arrives, understand the expenses you'll likely face when it comes to health care, and know the options you have for paying some of those costs if your savings and retirement income can't cover the price tag.

These steps can help you better prepare for retirement and, just as important, give you the sense of well-being that comes in knowing you're doing something proactive to plan for your future—not just living life blindly, hoping that retirement is palatable and affordable once you get there.

CHAPTER 19

College Savings 101

Pass or Fail

Most parents I know no longer dream of a college degree for their new-borns as did parents in previous generations. . . . Modern parents downright *expect* it, starting from the moment of conception.

We all want a better life for our kids, and, as everyone knows and as every study seems to prove, college is almost always the path to that brighter future. As soon as our kids join the world, and sometimes while they're waiting to be called into the game, we rush out and open some kind of investment account and immediately begin saving for the day Harvard, Stanford, or Rice comes calling.

Just like all eager new parents, Amy and I first began saving for our son's education just months after he was born, investing in an aggressive-growth mutual fund that, with any luck, we hope will balloon into a beefy pot of cash for his future educational needs. And, just like lots of parents, Amy and I stopped saving for our son's college education shortly thereafter.

When your life is filled with dirty diapers and your infant son is spitting up creamed corn down your back and you're trying to remember whether you paid the mortgage on time and you're worried you forgot to deposit your paycheck and the dog just dragged a dead frog into the kitchen and . . . the last thing on your mind is funding college, which, at that moment, seems eons away. There's plenty of time to save later.

Then one morning you drop off your son at school and wonder how he got to be six years old so quickly. As a parent, time doesn't fly when you're having fun; it evaporates like morning mist. You realize you're spending all this time planning your own retirement, still some 30 years away, and doing little to prepare for the huge expense looming much sooner. In my heart I know why: He'll always be a kid to me, my little buddy. It's so hard—and painful—to imagine him growing up when you just want to hang onto his youth as long as you possibly can.

In my head, I know that ignoring the future to cling to the present will one day leave me lamenting my past. As much as I hate it, I know the next 12 years will slip by and my son will graduate to a new chapter in his life. When that day arrives, Amy and I want to know we'll have the money he needs to pursue a college degree.

Many parents I know with older kids have yet to begin saving, or have saved only marginally at best. Finding yourself late in the game can be incredibly taxing. With only a few years to go, you just know there's no way you'll meet the hurdle. You're frustrated at not having saved enough, anxious about meeting your goal, guilt-ridden at not planning sooner, and worried about how you'll accumulate what you need for a teenager already talking about favored schools and fancied degrees.

No matter where you are on the parental timeline, though, you face the same two quandaries every parent confronts when talk of college prep rolls around: You not only have to find the dollars to set aside, you have to figure out where to invest to get the biggest bang without going bust.

Such a challenge it all is that preparing for college can feel like walking into a final exam without having read the notes—and this is one class you really don't want to fail.

Everyone faces a unique situation when it comes to college costs. Families have different income levels, different abilities to save, and different expectations of their children's contribution to the effort. You may feel peachy about your kid ultimately pursuing a state school education; then again, you may dream of nothing but a tony private school diploma. Some parents want their kids to pay part of the bill and work through college, or you may be like me and Amy and hope to muster the resources to cover the entire cost as a gift to your child.

For that reason, there's no one right answer when it comes to how much you need to save, though you can be certain it won't be insignificant. Four years at the average public university, including room and board, requires roughly $40,000 in 2003. Upgrade to the average private school and it's closer to $80,000. For each year until your kid enrolls, add about 7 percent annually to account for college-cost-related inflation.

How much you need to save is enough of a bugger, but *where* to save is where the real homework begins.

That homework can be a real chore, I know, because I did it. I spent several weeks dissecting as many practical options as I could find, and trust me, options are bounteous. Worse, each has its own quirks that can affect your child's ability to obtain financial assistance if your family needs to follow that route one day, and the options have various tax consequences for you and your kid, depending on the savings plan you choose. Waiting for you is everything from savings accounts to savings bonds to zero-coupon bonds, certificates of deposit, brokerage accounts, custodial accounts, Coverdell education savings accounts, 529 plans, your own 401(k), and probably a couple that I've wiped from memory. After wading through it all, I have to say that I understand why parents become confused and frustrated and just fling up their hands, pick a plan, and hope for the best. Sometimes, decoding the mysteries of saving for college seems to require a degree in finance and tax law.

In short, I nixed savings accounts, CDs, and savings bonds; they might help pay for some books when the time comes, but the long-term returns simply will not meet the funding needs of a college degree. That leaves investment options such as custodial accounts, Coverdell accounts, 529 plans, a 401(k), and a Roth IRA. Amy and I ultimately chose a hybrid approach—a 529 plan with a high-octane mutual fund in a standard brokerage account in our name. I'll explain in a minute our rationale. First, though, let's address the problem that really haunts parents—the future cost of college, an expense that can seem so mind-boggling that you think there's just no way you can ever get there from here without selling a body part on eBay.

Amy and I are lucky: Our parents covered our college bills. Thus, we never struggled with finding scholarships or student loans, nor did we have to deal with years of repaying loans (a very good thing, given that nursing, Amy's gig, and journalism, mine, certainly aren't known for their excessive paychecks). We hope to provide to our son that same gift, though we're far from certain of our ability to do that.

I don't expect many folks keep up with inflation news, but I have to, so let me tell you that inflation on the college campus is running at an athlete's pace. Tuition and fees at public universities averaged $4,081 nationally for the 2002–2003 academic year, according to the College Board, a nonprofit agency.[1] That doesn't include room and board, which ran to nearly $5,600 a year. In 1990–1991, tuition and fees amounted to $1,908. The difference: Basically a 7 percent annual increase, substantially faster than everyday consumer-related price inflation.

Of course, every school is different. There's a wide gulf between, say, the University of Michigan and the University of Wisconsin Waukesha—and I don't mean Lake Superior. A national average is pretty useless; I want to know what real costs might be for schools my son might attend. That provides a better gauge against which to measure our progress in saving for his future. Cruising the Internet, I found a college-cost calculator (run by T. Rowe Price, at www.troweprice.com) that provides specific cost estimates years into the future for an education at any of hundreds of individual schools across the county. Four years of college at the time my son will head off to school are projected to cost between $53,500 at my alma mater, Louisiana State University (absent housing costs, assuming we return to our home state before he goes to college) and something just shy of the gross domestic product of a small island-nation if he decides on a private school like, say, Dartmouth College, where the price tag for an education likely will run north of $400,000.

Amy and I are pretty sure we won't be able to afford the priciest end of the spectrum, no matter how hard we try. Reaching for that ring means we'd need to save roughly $1,650 a month and generate investment returns of 8 percent a year. We can't pull that kind of money from our budget and still meet all the other goals we have, including building our own retirement nest egg. We don't want to mooch off our son when we're old and out of cash because we spent it all on his art history degree.

Based on the median household income—vaguely $42,000 in 2001, according to the census—I'd guess most families can't stretch that far, either. It's frustrating, I know. You so badly don't want to disappoint your kids. Honestly, you don't want to disappoint yourself, as did a New Jersey woman I know. The years slipped by, and all too soon her little boy was applying for college, "and we realized we had only half of what was required to pay for four years" at his dream school, which accepted him.

The problem: His request for financial aid was denied. (The family had kept his college money in his name—a potentially big mistake I'll discuss in a moment.) "We suggested he take out a loan, but he declined because the idea of graduating with that kind of debt was frightening," she says. Her son enrolled in a less prestigious institution "and when the day came that we had to notify his dream school that he would not be attending, I sat down and cried, feeling like a complete and utter failure."

The obvious answer to meeting the outrageous costs of college is to save— early and often. I know that's easier said than done, but it's the only safe bet. You can hope that your daughter's prowess behind the three-point line will win her a free ride at the University of Connecticut, that your son's academics will get him into Princeton on the no-cost-to-you plan, or that drumming will land your child a prime role on the Florida A&M Marching "100" Band. Those are great dreams, but when you wake up, you really need to have some money set aside—just in case. That means a bit of sacrifice on your part.

In the early 1970s, few college-savings plans existed. In that environment, Tim and his wife, Love & Money readers, began stuffing $100 a month into a credit union savings account. (Just to give you some per-spective, that $100 would be the equivalent of about $240 a month today; then again, $100 worth of college would exceed $1,000 today.) The cou-ple's goal was "to do whatever was reasonable to ensure that our kids would have every opportunity to complete a bachelor's degree at one of the state universities."[2]

Most of the couple's friends, Tim says, "did not share our thoughts about this, and often questioned our inability to enjoy vacations similar to theirs and some of the other niceties that our saving for college would not allow. Without exception, all of our friends have commented in the past few years that they wish they would have spent a little less and planned better for college expenses." Neither Tim nor the kids have any college debt to pay off. "It will be five or ten years before any of our friends are in a similar position," Tim says. The moral: The short-term sacrifice of plan-ning for the future pays significant long-term dividends.

I hear many parents fret about how they'll never be able to accumulate enough money to cover the cost of college before it arrives, while also sav-ing for their own future years from now. The simple answer: You don't have to accumulate it all. While you most certainly need to amass enough cash to cover the cost of your retirement, there's no rule that says you must have your child's entire tuition ready to go the day high school ends. That's an assignment more daunting than memorizing a Shakespearian soliloquy; little wonder parents sometimes never get started.

Pamela, a financial aid administrator at a private Midwestern college, says parents often fail to overlook at key source of funding: current income. College often coincides with your peak earning years, "and if you have lit-tle or no consumer debt and haven't overcommitted on your housing, you often can afford a substantial portion of college costs from current income."[3] Indeed, Pamela and her husband paid about 80 percent of their third child's college costs on the pay-as-you-go plan and took advantage of low-rate student loans. "When she's done," Pamela says, "we can pay off those loans in about a year by making the same effort we're making now."

A kid can help, too. If Amy and I ultimately cannot save enough to pay for four years at whatever university our son picks, then we will encourage him to seek scholarships, financial aid, and a part-time job. I don't have nearly enough room to detail the scholarship opportunities available, but the value of those scholarships totals nearly $3 billion annually, according to the College Board, which has online tools at its web site (www.collegeboard.com) to help locate scholarship dollars.

If my son is adamant about his academic selection and has no funding alternatives, student loans may be his only option. The way Amy and I see it, we're making a sacrifice to save for his future and ours, and while I think it is incumbent on parents to help provide a university education, it's not a mandate that parents must finance the best college education money can buy. At some point, it's not the school that produces the achievers, but rather the student who achieves no matter the school. What we parents can't afford financially we can provide philosophically—namely, the conviction that our kids have the gift to make of their world what they seek, if only they apply themselves.

Jeff, an Ohio reader, began saving in a 529 plan just after his son was born. Not only do he and his wife have 18 years to build a college fund, Jeff expects that in the long run the couple "will be above-average earners" because of their careers. Combined, he reckons, years of savings and years of larger-than-average pay increases will make the cost of college much easier for him to manage. Yet Jeff still wants his son "to borrow some reasonable amount of money for school, and be responsible for paying it off" when he enters the workforce. Jeff and his wife both paid their way to bachelor's and master's degrees at private schools, in large part through debt.

"There is a lesson to be learned in doing so," Jeff says. "We want our children to have a strong work ethic and understand the value of a dollar."

Some parents who have plenty saved would rather see their kids strive to achieve the education they want, if only because doing so builds character. Amy's friends in Louisiana offered their son a proposition I particularly like. Dee and her husband began saving for their son's college tuition just after he was born in the early 1980s, estimating they'd need roughly $30,000 by the time university life arrived. They reached their savings goal. When their son began high school, though, they told him of the college savings awaiting him, enough to cover expected tuition at the University of Alabama, where he longed to attend. Then they tossed in a sweetener: Any money remaining in the account after graduation was his. If he strived in high school to earn an academic scholarship, he'd have a sweet chunk of money for himself at the end.

Their son did in fact win a scholarship covering all four years at Alabama. The result, says Dee, is that "the majority of the funds remained in his savings, and he will have a nice down payment on a new home when he graduates."[4]

As I mentioned, Amy and I opted for a hybrid approach. We chose to invest largely in a 529 plan, sticking a smaller contribution into a mutual fund account in our name but earmarked for our son's education. We started off funneling $50 a month into the 529 plan, an amount that increases by $10 monthly each year, meaning that by the time he's 17, we'll be saving $160 a month. Those dollars are flowing into an aggressively managed portfolio that grows more conservative as our son ages. Meanwhile, we're contributing $100 a month to an aggressive mutual fund. By doing all that, Amy and I likely will have accumulated $55,000, enough to see our son through a school such as LSU—as long as he lives at home. (These calculations are based on average annual returns; I've never checked the probability that we will make it, because when it comes right down to it, there are ways to finance college if you don't quite hit your financial target, so I'm not as concerned as I am when it comes to retirement.)

Here's the rationale for our approach: Assuming our boy does enroll in college one day, the 529 plan will have allowed the biggest portion of our college savings to grow tax-free. That means we won't lose a hefty chunk of assets to the U.S. Treasury, which will give us substantially more dollars to spend on college. If he doesn't go to college, or if it turns out he's a brilliant scholar or athlete or musician and lands a free ride, then we'll let the money grow for our future educational wants or for those of any future grandchildren. (I'll explain in a moment why all of this can happen only in a 529 plan.)

As for the mutual fund, if he does need the money to pay for school, chances are the aggressive fund we're in will outpace the 529 plan because of the plan's increasingly conservative slant. So the mutual fund will juice our returns a bit and, hopefully, give us a bit more money to draw on. If, however, he never needs the money, then we'll have a pot of cash that we can gift to him tax-free over a few years. Doing so with cash in a 529 plan would subject us to taxes and penalties, and I see no useful reason to share with lawmakers any money I don't have to. If by chance our son decides to run off and join Hell's Angels instead of Harvard, well, Amy and I will have a nice stash of dollars for one heck of an around-the-world journey.

Honestly, I still don't know if Amy and I will reach our goal, despite the planning. Who knows what financial hurdles await us? Who knows how our investments will perform? But I do know this: I don't want to wonder how my son got to be 12 years old and then start thinking about his college fund.

Dollars & Sense

I had a physics teacher in high school who prefaced really difficult chapters with, "Are you guys ready for the hard stuff?" We never were. Here's hoping you are. We need to dissect the various savings plans to reveal the inner workings. Like most hard stuff, it's important to know these basics so that you don't mess up and years from now find yourself in a place you didn't want to be.

So, are you guys ready for the hard stuff?

Remember, these are the savings plans I find most practical for a broad swath of people, though not necessarily for everyone, since circumstances vary and may be better addressed by a financial planner who can take the time to scrutinize your particular situation.

At interest rates prevalent in 2003, savings accounts, money market mutual funds, certificates of deposit, and savings bonds just won't get you where you need to go unless you're kicking in large sums of money. They're certainly safe, but you'll be sorry when you don't accumulate what you need. For instance, if you want to accumulate $56,000 for college 15 years from now and you can save $100 a month in some form of savings account that pays about 3 percent a year, you'd need to seed that account with $21,247. That's not realistic for most families. (By the way, you'll have saved nearly $39,250 to reach your goal.) Of course, interest rates change over time, so these numbers are ballpark estimates at best; still, they show the magnitude of the hurdle you must surmount.

Zero-coupon bonds were a decent option when interest rates were much higher. These little creatures are issued by the U.S. Treasury. You buy them at a discount from their face value, and when they mature you get the full amount. To reach that same $56,000, you could buy fourteen $1,000 bonds this year and for each of the next three years. Assuming interest rates are a static 8 percent, you would pay each year just $4,413 for those 14 bonds—a grand total investment of $17,654 over four years. Over the intervening years, the bonds would grow at the 8 percent rate, leaving you with $14,000 as each new year of college begins. That approach is less easy as I write this; bond yields are so low that it would now cost nearly $8,500 each year in up-front payments to achieve the same result. The tricky part with zeros is that you must pay taxes on the interest earned every year, even though you don't physically receive any of that money—it all just accumulates in the bond's price. Zeros do make a lot of sense, however, if you generally have accumulated what you figure you'll need and you have just a few years remaining before your kid's college expenses start. In this case, you can buy zeros that mature exactly when you need the cash.

In choosing where to invest, my financial planner friend Linda says, you should consider which plan will:

• Save you the most in taxes
• Allow your child to qualify for the most financial aid

- Impose income limits that may make you ineligible to contribute
- Limit the amount of money you can save yearly
- Give you adequate investment choices
- Offer the most flexibility on how withdrawals are used in the event your child receives a scholarship or doesn't attend college

Following are my notes of the pros and cons of the accounts with the most promise, according to the homework I've done.

Custodial Accounts. These are accounts you own at a brokerage house or mutual fund company. They have the most flexibility because they offer a wide range of investments, with no limits on the amount of money you can save each year. Moreover, you face no early-withdrawal or other penalties if your family needs the money in an emergency or if your child skips college.

For all the flexibility, though, these accounts have some disadvantages. First, they offer no long-term tax breaks, and because they are held in your child's name, he or she could owe meaningful income taxes at some point if the account grows to any real size.

In addition, it could affect a child's ability to obtain financial aid, because federal financial aid formulas consider 35 percent of a student's assets as being available to pay tuition. However, those same formulas consider at most 5.6 percent of the parents' assets. If you save between $50,000 and $100,000 in the child's name, as any parent will likely need for a youngster who hits college in 10 or more years, your kid could be eligible for substantially less assistance. In our case, Amy and I would need assets of between $312,000 and $625,000, excluding the value of our home and retirement accounts, before 5.6 percent of what we own would equal 35 percent of our son's account. If he ultimately needs financial aid, I'd hate to have this account out there, possibly screwing things up.

Coverdell Accounts. These are structured much like individual retirement accounts, so they usually have a broad range of investment options. Contributions are not tax deductible, though withdrawals are tax-exempt if used for qualified educational expenses. One benefit: Coverdells can be tapped to pay elementary- and secondary-school expenses as well as college costs.

Here's the rub, though: Annual contributions are capped at $2,000 *per beneficiary*. You cannot contribute $2,000, then get grandparents to kick in $2,000, too. The net effect: If Amy and I dumped the maximum into a

Coverdell for a dozen years and counted on average annual returns of 8 percent, we'd amass just $38,000. That isn't nearly enough. Also, be aware that eligibility to contribute to Coverdells phases out at $95,000 in income for a single taxpayer and $190,000 for a married couple.

Worse, to me, is that the cash remains in the beneficiary's name. If our son chooses college, these funds count as student assets when it comes to financial aid, so they could muddy the water again—a real concern, since we likely will need more money than we can realistically accumulate in a Coverdell. If he chooses Hell's Angels, he retains control of a potentially big wad of cash. We cannot put the money back into our names. Moreover, the money must be completely withdrawn by the time a beneficiary is 30 years old, or else the remaining amount is forcibly distributed and subject to taxes and a penalty equal to 10 percent of the earnings.

529 Plans. Named for the section of the IRS tax code that legitimizes them, 529 plans allow you to save a total of more than $200,000 per beneficiary, so you can save substantially more than with a Coverdell account. Contributions are not tax deductible, but earnings grow tax deferred, and if used for qualified educational expenses, you can withdraw the money tax-free; if withdrawn for other purposes, you pay taxes on the earnings and a 10 percent penalty.

The downside is that 529s typically have limited investment options, usually a small selection of mutual funds or a prearranged mix of investments managed to match your risk tolerance: conservative, moderate, aggressive. However, the money remains an asset of the parents, so it does not have nearly the same impact on financial aid unless you have a large liquid net worth.

Moreover, 529 plans have no set distribution date and the beneficiary can change. That means if our son earns a full scholarship or bags college completely, we can let the account continue to grow and use it for any grandchildren years later—or even for our own educational desires if Amy or I want to return to school at some point, which both of us do.

The hardest question is which 529 plan to choose. Just about every state has at least one. Some are better than others; some offer better investment options; some avoid state taxes if used for an in-state school but incur taxes if used out of state. Your own family's personal circumstances play into this choice. The best bet is to do some online research at a site such as www.savingforcollege.com, which offers educational information about 529 plans, as well as practical data on each state's plans. It also includes information on Coverdell accounts, too.

There's one wrinkle to be aware of: A sunset provision in 2011 may rob 529 plans of their tax-exempt status unless Congress extends the exemption. Sunset, though, seems unlikely. From Maine to Hawaii, there were 3.1 million individual 529 accounts at the end of 2002, holding some $20 billion for future college expenses, according to research and consulting firm Cerulli Associates.[5] Cerulli estimates the cash stash will hit $140 billion by 2008.[6] Certainly, some of that money is earmarked for older kids who will be hitting college before the sunset provision weighs in, but it seems to me that politicians aren't likely to quash a provision so widely relied on by a nation of soccer moms and dads saving for college. No doubt killing the program would kill some political careers. My bet is that the 529 plan will continue with its exemption, or, at worst, the accounts in place by 2011 will be grandfathered in and continue to grow tax-free long enough to see your kid through college.

401(k) Plans. IRS rules allow borrowing from these accounts as long as the money is paid back. The benefit is that if you're already saving here, you don't need to worry about saving as much elsewhere. Maybe you just increase the amount you're saving in your 401(k) plan. Better yet, if you're going to borrow anyway to pay for college, at least you'll be paying interest to yourself instead of to a bank.

Yet there are some potential flaws. The lesser evil is that a possibly large portion of your nest egg suddenly will be earning bondlike returns, possibly not the best use of your cash in the run-up to retirement. The bigger evil comes if you lose or leave your job. Most 401(k) plans are structured so that employees have just 30 to 90 days to repay a loan if you leave your job, are fired, or get laid off. Otherwise, the remaining balance is considered a partial withdrawal. That would subject you to onerous tax penalties. Raising tens of thousands of dollars—or more—in such a short period could be challenging. By the way, a 401(k) loan isn't really a loan; you're not literally borrowing money. Instead, you're liquidating a portion of your account and taking control of the cash, so that money grows only at the rate of interest you're paying yourself, which in the current environment is negligible. That will impact how much you save for retirement.

I'll leave you with some statistics to throw at your kids one day when they're bemoaning the thought of college. This comes courtesy of the College Board and shows median household income in the year 2000, based on educational achievement:

- Bachelor's degree: $65,922
- Master's degree: $77,935

- Doctorate degree: $92,361
- Professional degree: $100,000
- High school graduate: $36,722
- High school dropout: $22,753

Hopefully, that's motivation enough to convince an even mildly thoughtful teenager that life is indeed brighter when looked at through a rolled up college diploma.

CHAPTER 20

When Parents Need Money

Deciding When You Can Say No

A day will arrive in your life when you must confront the inevitable: Your parents' retirement.

That marks a day many people rue years in advance—not parents, mind you, but their kids. For on that day the reality of Mom and Dad's financial planning begins to surface. Either your parents saved admirably through the years and have plenty money to see them through to their dying day, or they planned poorly and instead will have little to live on other than their Social Security checks. Or possibly, they just expect that *you* will help them afford some of the niceties they seek in retirement but can't quite stretch to fund—much as they helped you buy all that stuff you just had to have as a kid and teenager all those years ago.

No matter the reason, facing the possibility that you might be called on to finance a parent's life often breeds much angst, because whether you ultimately want to help your parents or whether you want to banish that very thought, questions and worries and concerns swarm around this issue like a flock of angry finches flitting about your head.

To what degree should you be responsible for your mom and dad's financial well-being? Are their financial needs your liability? Is it okay to say no if helping your parents means you must, by necessity, draw money away from your and your spouse's retirement dreams or your child's education fund? If you do want to help, does that mean you have to provide your parents with the luxuries you have or the luxuries they think they deserve? At what point do you shut off the spigot . . . or can you ever? And what's your obligation if your parents did a slipshod job of preparing for their future and instead spent foolishly all these years, living for the moment—should it be incumbent on you to repair their mistakes years after the fact?

None of those questions are easy to answer—and dozens more just like them are waiting to be addressed, too. I know. I've lived this angst for years as I've watched my mom's financial life erode, largely by way of her own actions and inactions. She won't have much in retirement, save for Social Security. By her own admission, she's never been one to routinely save, when instead she can take a trip or buy some shoes or redecorate the house. I know a day will come when my phone will ring and I'll hear my mom's voice asking the question I've dreaded for years: Can I borrow some money?

Not all situations with parents are so extreme. The scenarios we all face individually span a wide continuum—from the parent who has demonstrated financial irresponsibility over a lifetime to parents who have sacrificed their own future to provide you the opportunity for a better life to the parents who have enough to live on but not enough to splurge on items they might think they deserve because you have them in your life, such as travel, new furnishings, or a home theater system. Whatever the case, if the nest egg that your mom and dad have amassed is insufficient or non-existent, a good chance exists that you will emerge at some point as your parents' personal banker.

Coping with your mom or dad's inadequate finances, I've learned, is one of the toughest challenges you or your family will confront—a financial, emotional, and sometimes psychological tug-of-war playing out in your head and in your relationship with your spouse. If ever there were a monetary motive behind a divorce, this is likely it. One of you might feel compelled to help, out of a sense of duty, obligation, or guilt. The other just as often feels angry and annoyed, maybe even a bit betrayed, that the needs of an extended family member come before the needs of the immediate family.

No matter whether your parent is an unrepentant spendthrift or a sympathetic soul who never caught a break, this matter always boils down to one common denominator: Can you say no to any family member in need, especially a mom or dad?

You'd think the simple, caring answer is, "No, I can't refuse a parent's needs." Where love and money is concerned, though, no answer is that unencumbered. If you blindly open your wallet every time Mom or Dad stumbles into a financial bind, you're taking away dollars that otherwise could build a better life for the most important people you know—your own family. Chances are, you don't blindly open your wallet for your child's every want, so what makes your parents any different?

Funding a parent's small-scale desires is probably okay, but few things with parents ever happen on a small scale when it comes to money. Mom and Dad's problems usually necessitate big financial solutions that require either a sizable one-time payment or relatively tiny repeated payments strung out over a number of years for everything from the monthly electric bill to insurance payments to overdue credit card statements to their desire for a new car.

"I have watched my spouse struggle with this problem for 10 years," says Joan, a reader in Texas. She sees, she says, how a financially needy parent "will drain you and ruin your marriage, and still happily keep spending."[1]

When you're snared in this situation in your own life, you typically don't talk about the problem publicly. You know how easy it is to inadvertently paint yourself as an ogre, too willing to sacrifice the people who raised you for your own financial motives. Friends often wonder why you, so heartless, don't unquestionably rush to Mom or Dad's aid. That's an understandable criticism, but it's much too naive, and usually it's a sentiment voiced by someone who never has lived this mess. The only people who really understand are those who have experienced this in their lives, or siblings who share your woes. Or, if you're like me, siblingless, you just bottle it up inside and pray it vanishes.

Adult children everywhere live with this all-but-unspoken fear, not because we're selfish, not because we're money hungry, not because we're heartless. We fret because we have our own families to support. We know our money can't stretch that far, and that if it's forced to then something must give somewhere else. That something is usually the quality of life our own families live today or, more likely, the quality we hope to live tomorrow. Dishing out dollars to our parents, either willingly or grudgingly, jeopardizes opportunities that we, our spouses, or our children might otherwise benefit from. That creates resentments and guilt all around.

A woman I know has already assumed her parents' mortgage payments and paid off their $30,000 credit card bill. Even with that, her mom and dad refuse to cancel their credit cards, won't record the details of the checks they write, and continue to rack up huge expenses, often needlessly and carelessly, such as $300 in bank overdraft charges in a single month. It's not as if money is no object; Social Security and a small pension are the only income they have.

"It is a constant struggle to explain to them what they need to do to get a handle on their expenses," she says. Her parents' profligacy continually eats through the money she and her husband set aside for their own retirement. The upshot: She now wrestles with "feelings of doom and hopelessness" because of "the guilt of taking money from our retirement to pay for all of this." She's also robbing herself today because, she says, "I find myself not spending money for me so that I can justify the money being spent monthly on my mom and dad."

For as far back as I can remember my mom has struggled with financial independence. I joke that she has never met a dollar she couldn't spend. In fact, I vividly recall as a fourth-grader sitting in my mom's car on Post Oak Boulevard, on our way to the Galleria mall in Houston, Texas, as she dispensed her financial motto: "If money was made for saving, God would've made everything free." I used to think that was funny, particularly when it benefited me.

It's not so funny now. I've watched my mom flounder financially though the years, and I realize that her inability to manage a dollar, her demands for immediate gratification, and her failure to help herself financially have had drastic impacts not just on her own finances but on those of family members around her. That's unfair to everyone sucked into the vortex unwittingly. My mom's lack of financial planning means that, far from one day being her beneficiary, I will instead likely be called on to be her benefactor. It's not a title I relish. Without a doubt, I want my mom to be happy and not want for anything as she ages, but I do not think the bills for that happiness should be funded with my paychecks. She assures me she won't be a burden—that between Social Security and an expected small inheritance from my grandmother, she'll be fine.

I know she won't. I know what she stands to inherit and what she's likely to receive from the government. Knowing how poorly she manages money, there's just no way she'll have enough to cover her needs. Worse, I know who will be called on to cover the gaps when they arise—over and over again.

It's that whole ant-and-grasshopper fable from a family finance point of view. The ant works all summer and the grasshopper doesn't. When winter comes, the hungry grasshopper knocks on the ant's door. I'm the ant. That's the way it goes, though—those who plan ahead always end up being the savings account of last resort for those who don't. That raises a big question: To what degree should a child be responsible financially for parents who have shown no responsibility for themselves? I asked my dad that question. He and my mom divorced when I was two, and their lives could not have tracked more dissimilarly. His response: "A child has no responsibility to a parent. We're the ones who brought you into the world, and that was our choice, not yours. We're the ones who have all the responsibility; you don't owe either of us a dime."

That's the advice offered by countless Love & Money readers—from clergy members (who say your first obligation is always to spouse and child) to counselors (who say that feeding a parent's money needs only enables their neediness) to parents on the receiving end of family largess.

"I'm one of those divorced moms who went from job to job and made no plans for my future, retirement, senior aging, or possible medical issues," says Sharon, a 65-year-old reader in New England. "I guess I thought I was invincible and that . . . it'll all work out. Yes, it has worked out—much to my dismay." Sharon says she lives "with constant guilt at how, by not taking better care of my body, being more realistic, and planning ahead, I have put my daughters in this position.

"Although my family members are quite gracious and generous," Sharon continues, "at my age they should not have to be doing so much for me—and spending so much of their hard-earned money on me. Had I only planned ahead during my younger adult life . . . I might have prevented or at least postponed the sacrifices they are now forced to make to ensure that I have the prescriptions and medical supplies I need, enough food to eat, and money for rent and utilities. I never would have believed that I'd find myself at this crossroad." The point, Sharon says, is "a plea to younger parents of the importance of planning ahead for this time in life— a much healthier alternative than living with regrets."[2]

When I look forward a generation to my son, my dad's sentiments and Sharon's plea make a lot of sense. My son will never owe me anything. I raised him out of love, and by my choice, and I don't want him ever to feel that he needs to care for me financially. Yet when you *are* that child, looking back a generation at your own parents, it's hard to take that view. Your emotions are clouded by a sense of obligation and, to some degree, guilt. A spouse just adds to the complexity; suddenly your spouse is intimately tied to this issue, too, and not by desire. Thus, navigating this three-way relationship is rarely easy.

Amy is naturally loath to split her paycheck with someone she believes is capable of fending for herself. Moreover, Amy's first priority will always be her immediate family's financial security, and in particular the needs of our son. Amy has told me in no uncertain terms that our marriage would suffer greatly if I divert family money to my mom's upkeep.

Such emotions, or ones very similar, are common when spouses are swept up in the histrionic drama of a financially needy parent. Emilie, a reader in Minnesota, says her mother-in-law had a history of repeatedly seeking bailouts from her son, Emilie's husband. When Mom needed a major bailout the year Emilie was pregnant with her first child, it became clear very quickly that "if there was going to be a choice between my unborn child and my mother-in-law, my mother-in-law would have received sincere regrets—only—because if I had to spend on her and deny my child, I was going to be resentful sooner or later. Probably sooner."[3]

It's not that the costs of a financially needy parent are always large—it's the frustration that parents often just seem oblivious to the ramifications their actions have on their kids. Seemingly, they either don't care or simply expect you to pay their way. Becky, a reader in Virginia, says that just before her dad died more than 10 years ago, "he told me to 'look after your mom's money because if you don't she'll spend all her money on knickknacks,' his description for frivolous, unnecessary purchases."[4] Becky says that during her parents' 40-plus years of marriage, her dad always gave her mom an allowance for everything from groceries to clothing to household items, which Becky thought "was very condescending and demeaning."

Becky agreed to the deathbed request, but then let her mom control her own money. "Big mistake!" Becky says. "Within two months her checking account was overdrawn, her charge card was at its maximum limit, and the bills were not being paid." Becky took control of the finances again. Yet planning her mom's financial future proved fruitless because "my mother throws a monkey wrench in my plans every so often." One year that meant that Becky's mom used an insurance check earmarked to repay her hip surgery bills to buy a mink coat instead. Becky paid the hospital bill out of a sense of moral obligation.

Against Becky's advice, her mom sold a condo she owned free and clear, liquidated her assets, and bought an expensive home in a planned community that she otherwise could not afford. "I'll give you three guesses, and the first two don't count, as to who pays the monthly maintenance fee of $280, the increased property taxes and all the 'knickknacks' she guilts me into buying." There are other instances, Becky says, "where my self-gratification-seeking mother has taken advantage of responsible me to buy her a new car, new window treatments for her home, and multiple other items I am trying to expunge from my memory.

"How do I feel about all of this? I am angry, bitter, and resentful. My husband and I have worked for 25 years, lived frugally, and invested wisely. We began planning for our retirement the day we got married. We have saved a sizable sum of money. [Several years ago] we semiretired, but I have returned to the corporate rat race because I refuse to spend my retirement savings on my mother's extravagances." To her mom, Becky says, "I am Becky the bank."

In all fairness, not every situation is dire. Parents are just people, and sometimes they make bad choices along the way that leave them unable to fend for themselves adequately. Up crop health problems or natural disasters that they simply cannot manage alone, despite their planning.

Christy, in Illinois, has always known that she and her husband one day would have to take in her mom. That day came when Mom was diagnosed with terminal cancer and had no health coverage and almost no money to cover the costs. Christy quit her job to care for her mom as well as her own young children. Financially, Christy knew this would not be easy. Her husband "worked nearly around the clock," she says, to support the family and "was very understanding even when he did not agree."[5]

Looking back on that year, Christy says, "It was a financial burden. We struggled to give my mother anything she wanted. I remember the last meal I cooked for her; it was one of her favorites—a T-bone steak, baked potato, and some shrimp cocktail. Yes, bills went unpaid, and yes we're still recovering, but in the end, do I consider it a burden? I would trade anything I have to do it again. My inheritance was beyond value . . . the love of my mother."

Situations such as Christy's demand a degree of empathy, particularly from your partner, and solutions generally come easier because feelings of resentment, anger, guilt, and entitlement aren't bubbling inside everyone involved. Far more problematic are those instances in which Mom and Dad face a self-inflicted quandary due to self-indulgence and a refusal to take responsibility for their own finances. Lots of adult children deal with this issue precisely as I dealt with it for years—they avoid it and just hope an answer materializes when life presses upon them later.

To date, I have watched my mom's pending implosion from afar. Her financial needs so far have been my grandmother's cross, which my grandmother has borne throughout my mom's adult life with mixed amounts of love and loathing. My grandmother grew up with nothing in a Mississippi orphanage, so she revels in giving her daughter everything. Yet, frustrated, she continued working into her eighties, partly, she told me one day, "because I've got to help your mom."

My grandmother and I have talked about this issue throughout my adult life. I've tried many times to get her to wean my mom off the family dole so that, through tough love, my mom might reclaim a sense of financial self-sufficiency to shape the destiny she ultimately seeks. Yet while agreeing in principle to that course of action, my grandmother concedes she simply doesn't have the heart to say no to her daughter. The question, as Amy routinely asks, is: Do I?

All of this has become a running joke in my family: Everyone teases me about my pending role as my mother's keeper. I laugh, but it's no joke. I've battled this concern internally for years, tormented by a decision I do not want to make, unsure of how I'll ever be able to finance my family's life as well as my mom's, all the while wondering if I could ever really say no to

Mom—and, if so, how. It's like watching an unavoidable, head-on colli-
sion—and I'm in the driver's seat. Even though this wreck is looming, I've
done my best to ignore it because the terrain is so difficult to steer. Choose
one option and you're a terrible son; choose the other and your family suffers. Either way, people get hurt.

How do you talk to a parent about any of this without coming off as callous, and how do you get Mom and Dad to plan for their own needs so
that you aren't forced into the role of parental banker? Bonnie, a Love &
Money reader in Florida, calls her mom "a financial mess" who is "always
behind the power curve in terms of debt."[6] Mom stands to gain a chunk of
money from Bonnie's grandmother, but Bonnie expects that her mom "will
blow through her inheritance in a year, maybe two." The biggest frustration, Bonnie says, is that "it is unlikely my mother will want to participate
in any plan that inhibits her behavior." Bonnie and her husband have spent
numerous hours through the years trying to fashion a solution to her
mom's pending destruction. All to no avail, though.

"We have wrung our hands," Bonnie says, "over the inequity of our
'work hard, save your pennies' mentality when it most likely will be blown
away by my mother's propensity for financial disaster."

For the longest time, I wanted to talk to my mom about my worries. I
rehearsed silently for years the speech I wanted to deliver . . . encouraging
her to alter her course, to find work she enjoys, to build a savings account,
and to gain health care coverage she most certainly will need as she ages,
particularly given her back and blood-pressure ailments.

Instead of delivering that speech, I continually dodged the conversation
because I was scared to express my feelings for fear of sounding unsympa-
thetic or hurtful. That avoidance has led to heated arguments at times with
Amy, who increasingly grew annoyed watching me back away from a confrontation she knew had to happen. As tough as it is to talk to a spendthrift parent, it can be tougher still to communicate with a spouse the
difficulty you face. Unless you've lived with this worry, you simply cannot
fathom the internal torment of trying to figure out how to tell a parent to
shape up financially because you can't—won't—be his or her bank one day.
You wonder if, in uttering the words that need to be said, you're sending
the unintended message that your money is more important than your
parents' well-being.

Then again, unless you've lived the life of your partner, watching all of
this unfold, you don't have the perspective and aggravations of an outside
observer. Amy's concerns are just as valid as mine. "Isn't your own family's

well-being and future just as important?" she asks. In other words, is it fair to finance Mom or Dad if doing so takes away from your child's educational opportunities? Is it fair to rob a spouse of a better life and your shared retirement dreams?

In the end, the confrontation came. I told my mom of the worries I've harbored all these many years. She was pleased to discover I loved her enough to challenge her and express such concerns. Substantially more upsetting to her was learning she had caused such angst. Still, she told me not to fret, insisting she'll be fine without my help and that she'd never seek such assistance anyway.

I hope that she is going to be fine. Unfortunately, I know that's not the case.

I know the phone one day will ring. So like so many adult children, here I wait, caught literally between love and money.

Dollars & Sense

When it comes to parents struggling financially, there's no solution that is painless. Somebody will feel hurt; somebody else will feel slighted. And you get a front-row seat for the fireworks. It's natural to feel tormented by dueling concerns for parents who are financially adrift and a spouse who likely is annoyed with the whole affair. You're not alone with those emotions. People that I've talked to all across the country share in your worry and misery. Those folks, along with family counselors and even clergy members, insist that you can—and must—say no to parents who have demonstrated no discipline in their own spending. After all, it's your life and your money, and no one outside of your partner or your dependent child has a right to impose financial needs on your family's resources.

More important to your home life: "Your first obligation is to your spouse and child," says Joan, the Texan who watched her husband battle this dilemma for years. If you ultimately choose a parent over your family, Joan says, "you will regret it long after the parent is gone" because your spouse may be gone, too, and the funds for your future long since siphoned away.

Of course, that doesn't mean you have to say no if helping is what your heart tells you to do. You might recognize that in assisting your parents you're giving back just a little of all they provided for you through the years. Maybe you just feel obligated, or maybe you see that because of circumstances beyond their control Mom and Dad simply cannot get by without your help. How much you give, though, should be based on your means, not on your parents' wants or your feelings of obligation and guilt.

If you have no problem giving Mom and Dad that flat-panel TV they want to hang on their wall, and you can afford to, fine. If you can't afford it yet they still expect it, that's something entirely different. You should not jeopardize your own financial security to provide a parent—or a financially wayward sibling or child—some material luxury. Moreover, you should not feel guilty about saying no to such a request when the expense will have detrimental impacts on you. Worse, you set a dangerous precedent because, as Becky learned, parents come to see you as their money supply.

Before offering to give any money, explore your motives. Are you throwing money at an impossible situation simply to paper over the angst you're feeling? If so, the better solution is talking to your parents about taking responsibility for their own lives. That's particularly true if either of your parents is still working; they still have time to do something about their situation. Otherwise, footing the bills for your parents may prove counterproductive. Once you establish the pattern, they'll return repeatedly, straining further your relationship with them and with your spouse. Better to help by getting them to focus instead on their own money, maybe by giving them the gift of a few hours with a financial planner who can assist in righting their finances.

In planning to care for your parents' financial needs in the future, or even in providing for them in little ways today, you're rewarding them for not taking care of themselves. Additionally, you're potentially placing your parents' financial interests above those of your family, such as saving for your child's education, your and your partner's future retirement, or even an adequate emergency fund your family might one day need to rely on. By not funding your own family's needs first, you potentially perpetuate the legacy you now loathe. Ask yourself this question: Will I one day call upon my children to bail me out because, in paying for my parents, I never prepared for myself? If so, imagine your children years from now facing exactly the same financial and emotional jam you confront today. Will your kids feel toward you what you feel now toward your parents? If so, how is that going to make you feel?

Sharon, the reader in New England who says she lives with constant guilt for putting her daughters in this position, looks back on her life and realizes that with just a little "financial planning and saving rather than only living in the moment" she would not be in her situation.

If you are leaning toward financing Mom or Dad, you and your spouse must make that decision jointly. Partners often see the situation as we can't, as detached outsiders looking in. When they question our desires to help a parent—or even a needy brother or sister—it's easy to fault them for not understanding. In reality, they often have a much clearer view, unobstructed by history and pangs of guilt. Remember, too, that the money you ultimately bestow on a parent belongs partly to your spouse, even if you keep your dollars in separate accounts. Spouses have equal say in how money is spent because at the end of the day you both live off your combined income. You must both be on board with the plan and agree to all facets of it, including the limit of money you will offer, either in one lump sum or over a period of time.

Make clear to Mom and Dad the extent of your generosity if you choose to help. Stress that you will not be a personal ATM to raid every time money grows tight. Look, too, for creative solutions that preserve your family's assets. Emilie, the woman in Minnesota who faced a needy mother-in-law and a child on the way, says she knew there was no way her husband could turn away from his mom. The family, Emilie says, needed a plan that would provide Mom some financial security, allow Emilie's husband to meet what he considered an obligation, and yet preserve Emilie's peace of mind in knowing her family's money wasn't being diverted from her child's future financial requirements.

The couple's solution: Buy an inexpensive house for Mom to live in and care for until their newborn son started college, at which point the sale of the house or its rental income could help pay for or defray tuition costs. The arrangement worked all around: Mom felt like a partner in protecting the investment for her grandson's future; Emilie's husband provided for both Mom and his family; and Emilie knew her family's money ultimately would benefit her child.

"You owe it to your spouse," Emilie says, "to put him or her first. And you owe it to your children to put them first, to give them the best start in life you can."

CONCLUSION

When all is said and done, *Love & Money* comes down to this: Talk is cheap. It's the silence that's expensive.

In Chapter 4, the one on emergency savings accounts, I related the story of the $15,401.99 that Amy and I had in our savings account one particular month. The point of that story was the idea that each of us has our own definition of what constitutes a feeling of financial security, and the goal is to find ways to compromise so that both partners agree a fair balance has been struck between safety, covering a possible financial emergency, and investing for a secure future. There's another piece of the story that embodies everything *Love & Money* stands for—namely, that communicating about your money will better your financial life and help you and your partner build not just a stronger bank balance, but a more robust relationship.

The rest of the story starts right after I announced to Amy our account balance. Pleased that my math matched the bank's, I wrapped up the exercise by nonchalantly announcing the balance and telling Amy, "We're good to go."

"Hmmph," she grunted.

As you might recall from many pages back, Amy really wanted our account to hold at least six months' worth of expenses; I reasoned that three months was fine. It would have been convenient to let the discussion drop at that point and just stick to the status quo, or argue with one another about why my position makes more sense than your position. Instead, I asked her why she was so unhappy with our savings account balance. So we talked—well, more like I interviewed her to try to better understand why she was so bent out of shape.

For 30 minutes we talked about why she thought six months was a smart idea for all sorts of perfectly logical reasons. Finally, I asked her, "What is it about the number $15,401.99 that makes it so bad that you go 'hmmph?' " She blurted out: "Because our account is *always* around $15,000. I don't feel like we're going anywhere. We should have more money."

There it was—the emotional root of this entire argument. Amy wasn't mad about the money; money was just the outward expression of a much more deep-seated relationship concern she silently has harbored all these years. She was mad because more than a decade into this marriage she didn't see our life progressing. She just never knew how to communicate what she was feeling and I'd never asked. It took me talking to her and trying to probe her concerns for the underlying rationale to get her to dig deep enough to pull out the truth.

Amy's comment made me realize how ill prepared she felt financially and how clueless she was about our financial life. I'm not saying that condescendingly. Indeed, part of it is my fault. Our nest egg grows bigger with every paycheck, as bits of money flow into retirement accounts and savings accounts and, occasionally, investment accounts. We have plenty of money to meet an emergency. I've just never communicated that to Amy very well, just assuming she knew that we were okay. Aside from writing the occasional check or recording a deposit in the checkbook, she never really interacts with our finances. That has been my self-appointed job, an arrangement similar to so many marriages I've come across.

Look at your own life. Perhaps one person, maybe you, serves as the financial gatekeeper, handling the bills and checkbook and monitoring all the various accounts you have. You might keep all the information in your head; you might track it all on Quicken or Money; you likely know exactly where all the paperwork is filed. You don't share the information with your partner because, after all these years of silence, you just assume your spouse isn't really interested. Maybe you just don't want to have to explain everything you've done with the family's money.

The other person, maybe that's you, simply goes through life not really clued in to what's happening inside those various accounts. Maybe you're not really content with that setup, but you say nothing, because after all these years you're not sure how to even talk about money. Whatever your reason, you just accept the status quo and all the while grow silently anxious and angry—and you don't know why.

That's a problem in any relationship. Success, and I'm not just talking financial success, depends on both partners openly confronting the issues that arise in life. In terms of money, that means both must be knowledgeable participants in the family's finances. That doesn't mean that a spouse who has no interest in money and bills and all the drudgeries of investing and retirement planning should be thrust into something he or she despises. If you hate all that stuff, there's no reason to muck about with it if your partner is willing to take on that role. But you owe it to yourself to know what's going on. You must make it your business to know. And the spouse who handles all these duties must make it his or her business to share this information regularly.

Not long after our Sunday discussion, Amy was sitting at the kitchen table, and I presented to her my laptop showing our financial tracking program, which highlighted all our various accounts, the money in each, and their cumulative value. I detailed how much cash flows into each account every month and showed her that our net worth really is improving, that we're far better off than we were when we got married and even better off than we were just a year ago.

She soaked it all in for a few minutes, silently scanning the numbers as I explained where each account was and where all the paperwork could be found if she ever needed it.

"Does this make you feel better about where we are?" I asked her.

"Yep," she said, and sauntered off. The added benefit was that Amy agreed that we don't need as much in our savings account as she originally thought, because she saw that we have enough money for her to feel safe. To be fair, I did start funneling a few more dollars into our savings account every month to boost its size as small proof to Amy that I take her financial concerns to heart. And now I share this breakdown with her quarterly, or as often as she wants an update.

The point is that financial compatibility, as I hope you recall from Chapter 5, isn't about meshing perfectly with your partner all the time. No relationship is like that, not even the most successful ones you know. We all have money quirks; you just rarely pay attention to them until you're back from the honeymoon and begin to settle into what will become your life together. Instead, compatibility grows because you learn to take the time to talk to one another about your money, about each other's needs, wants, fears, desires, hopes, dreams, and concerns. Compatibility grows because instead of acting apart, you learn to plan together, through something as simple as a retirement wish list, or something as necessary as a spending plan, or something as unifying as joint financial accounts. Proof of compatibility appears when you suddenly realize one day that you're helping each other work toward shared and individual goals instead of thinking only of your financial wants.

Remember this: If you can create the road map to where you want to go, you can drive to any destination you can foresee.

From all that I have learned in my own experiences, and all that Love & Money readers across the country have taught me, that road to success is a four-letter word—but it's not *cash*.

It's *talk*.

In the day-to-day flurry that is life, it's way too easy and substantially more convenient to just skip the talking and get on with the spending. We're a culture so on the go (or at least we like to think we are) that we've learned to communicate in sound bites and verbal snippets. We let an affirmative grunt replace "Yes, I paid all the bills last Thursday and we have $1.97 left in the checking account." That doesn't foster open communication, and more often leads to pent-up frustrations and resentments that silently undermine your finances and your relationship.

Barry, a friend of mine in San Diego, called me one day to tell me that his wife, Lisa, "always tells me after reading one of your columns, 'Why can't you be more like Jeff? He communicates with Amy.' " The implication, Barry says, was that Amy and I talk so much about our finances and our life together that it makes him look like a slacker by comparison. "You're not real. I told Lisa, 'Yeah, but he's a fraud; he *has* to talk to Amy to get material for the column.' "

Barry is absolutely right. Talking to Amy is mandatory in order to get material for the Love & Money column. That is precisely why we began to talk. That is not, however, why we've continued to talk. Before I began writing the column, I was just like everyone else. I didn't make it a habit to share with my spouse everything going on in our financial life. What did she care? I figured. The bills are paid, the checking account has money in it, and we're saving a bit for the future. What more is there to say?

Similarly, she didn't make a habit of talking to me about stuff she was concerned about or just interested in, figuring I wouldn't have the time or patience to detail everything she wanted to know. She figured, "Why put up with that hassle?"

All these years, though, we were simply doing it wrong. I realized this while writing the column and learning so many things about money and my partner about which I previously had no clue. "Now," I told Barry, "I'm standing up to tell everyone out there who's lost but doesn't know it yet that, 'Hey, the path is over here.' "

In talking to Amy about her thoughts on the various financial issues that have impacted our relationship, I began to see behind the facade that we all erect to hide our money from view. I saw all the ways money plays on our emotions and the ways we all compartmentalize those feelings, shunt them off to the side, lock them away, or confront them only when they're forced into the open . . . and hopefully, we pray, they never see the light of day.

Hiding in the dark, though, is just a means of avoidance. For months when I was a child I thought there were alligators under my bed at night (remember, I grew up in south Louisiana, home to gators). I was convinced that if I let my foot slip out from under the covers and dangle over the side the gators might snap it off. Hot and frustrated one night, I jumped out of bed and onto the floor to scare the gators away. I was tired of avoiding the issue—a fear of being alone at night—and confronted my concerns directly. I'm happy to note that I still have both feet.

Financial silence is just another way of avoiding those gators. We're all raised with certain money beliefs that, in turn, create the money memories we subconsciously rely on as adults to help us navigate the financial affairs of our lives. Why confront the scary stuff if you don't have to? Just keep the covers on and you won't lose any toes.

Often, though, that's like putting a child in charge of a Mack truck—it's just a disaster waiting to happen. Regardless, we avoid our financial lives in a vast array of ways. For some, it's stashing unopened bills so that you don't have to confront the reality of your debt and the problems of an untamed charge card. For others, it's never balancing your checkbook or knowing what you have in the bank because, that way, you don't have to deal with the reality of what you can't afford in your life. For my friend Melissa, way back in Chapter 1, it means avoiding a budget because it makes her feel poor. For still others, it's never having a discussion with your partner about the family's money and, instead, spending it as though it is yours alone.

Denise, my counselor friend in California, recalls a client who grew up in the ghetto with much tension, anxiety, and arguing about money in his family. As an adult he sought to avoid that possibility by avoiding any discussion about money with his wife. His rationale: Talking about money means you're probably going to fight about money, so why talk about it in the first place?

Yet not talking about money doesn't prevent the tension, it actually exacerbates the tension, because while one person retreats, the other over-compensates by wanting to talk more and pushing money matters into the open. That, in turn, pushes the avoider farther away, leading to increasing overcompensation. It's like a game of rock-paper-scissors—you know that no matter which you choose, something can beat you, so why play?

"As you become more conscious about your money, though," Denise says, "you very quickly begin making better decisions about how to spend and save your money, and you're more open to talking about it. You don't have anything to hide. You don't have any shame. But to become more conscious about your money, you first have to learn to talk about your money."

Here's what I've learned in talking about my money that I hope anyone who reads this book will take away: By opening your financial life to each other's scrutiny, you're forced to confront everything that's wrong with your finances—and for me and Amy there were plenty of things wrong with our finances, from too many individual accounts to secretive spending to a lack of knowledge about what we both seek from our future. In turn, by dragging these issues out of the shadows and into the sunlight, you're forced to address the problems. When you keep your finances hidden, not necessarily from the world but at least from your partner, it's easy to rationalize the moves you make financially, no matter how misguided, illogical, or boneheaded. No one can question you because no one can see what you're doing with your money. You're safe—temporarily, at least. Ultimately, you're rationalizations are destructive because you're lying about your money to yourself and to those you love the most. Ultimately, those rationalizations will surface. They always do, and sometimes in not so pleasant ways. You'll end up with a suffocating load of debt, maybe facing bankruptcy, unable to save for the life you really want, possibly headed toward divorce (or, at the very least, many long months in costly marital counseling) because you have destroyed the trust your partner once placed in your care.

When you're open about your finances, though, you simply cannot hide behind anything. It's like trying to conceal a crow in a bucket of milk. You just can't do it. When your finances are transparent, you cannot con anyone because a partner sees the holes in your logic and the flaws in your excuses. Better yet, your spouse calls you on it, compelling you to confront the harsh reality of your money and the poor decisions you're making. In essence, openness forces honesty; honesty forces you to change your ways; changing your ways forces you do the right thing. And if you're doing it right, you simply can't screw it up because you can't turn truth into a misdeed.

You might never make a million dollars doing the right thing. You might never afford that beach house doing the right thing. I might never get that 1966 Mosport green Corvette doing the right thing. Yet you will be happier, and your partner will be happier, and you'll both know that you have a better grasp on your financial life than you ever had before. And you'll both know your relationship is stronger. I know all of this to be a fact because I have lived it and I have experienced firsthand how my relationship and my financial life have improved noticeably.

I asked Amy once if she thought our life was any better because of the Love & Money column and the time we now spend talking about our money, putting together our spending plans, and generally being more cognizant of our financial life. Without hesitating, she said, "Absolutely. You have become more open with me about what you're thinking, and you've taken more time to consider what I'm thinking. We talk about issues we never talked about before, and we've come up with joint solutions that we're both happy with. I truly feel like we're closer."

Ultimately, I hope these pages help you grow closer with your partner and your finances.

This book began with a simple question: What is personal finance if not personal? Let me end with my answer: Personal finance is nothing if not personal.

Shine a little light on the dark recesses of your money and share your financial life openly with your partner and you'll both be amazed at how your wealth improves—in terms of money . . . and love.

Notes

Introduction
1. Bonnie, Florida, e-mail to author, July 22, 2002.

Chapter 1
1. Melissa, Louisiana, interview with author, November 2002.
2. Denise Hughes (financial counselor, San Carlos, California), interviews with author, various dates.
3. Andrea, New York, interview and e-mail exchange with author, May 2003.
4. Jack, Seattle, interview with author, June 2003.

Chapter 2
1. Debbie, New York, interview with author, June 2002.
2. Becky, Minnesota, e-mail to author, July 23, 2002.
3. Gina, California, e-mail to author, March 16, 2003.
4. Christie, California, e-mails and interviews, various dates, 2002–2003.
5. Melissa, Louisiana, interview with author, July 2002.
6. Hughes interview.
7. Becky, Minnesota, e-mail to author, July 2002.

Chapter 3
1. John, Rhode Island, e-mail to author, November 3, 2002.
2. Jim, Louisiana, interview with author, August 2002.
3. Lou, New York, e-mail to author, November 3, 2002.
4. Hughes interview.

5. David, Toronto, e-mail to author, November 25, 2002.
6. Margaret, California, e-mail to author, November 4, 2002.

Chapter 4

1. Laura, New Mexico, interview with author, March 2003.
2. Stan, Colorado, e-mail to author, February 10, 2003.
3. Carol, e-mail to author, February 10, 2003.

Stage Two

1. Terry, California, e-mail to author, March 2003.

Chapter 5

1. Glenn, Rhode Island, e-mail to author, March 30, 2003.
2. "Financial Problems as Predictors of Divorce: A Social Exchange Perspective," Jan D. Andersen, California State University, Sacramento, 2001.
3. Hughes interview.
4. Michelle, New York, interview with author, February 2003.
5. Statistical package, Association of Bridal Consultants, 2000.
6. "Time, Sex and Money: The First Five Years of Marriage," The Center for Marriage and Family, Creighton University, Omaha, NE, 2000.

Chapter 6

1. Hugh, Texas, e-mail to author, May 22, 2002.
2. Andrea, New York, interview with author, May 2003.
3. Jack, Seattle, interview with author, March 2002.

Chapter 7

1. Melissa, California, November 24, 2002.
2. Zack, Texas, e-mail to author, November 25, 2002.
3. Hughes interview.
4. Melissa, Louisiana, e-mail to author, November 12, 2002.
5. *Other People's Money: And How the Bankers Use It*, chap. V, Justice Louis D. Brandeis, 1914.
6. Maria, New Jersey, interview with author, November 2002.
7. MaryAnn, Wisconsin, e-mail to author, November 27, 2002.
8. Mike, Minnesota, e-mail to author, November 24, 2002.
9. Bob, Iowa, e-mail to author, November 24, 2002.
10. Charles, Colorado, e-mail to author, November 24, 2002.

Chapter 8

1. Nikki, Minnesota, e-mail to author, October 28, 2002.
2. Karen, California, e-mail to author, October 31, 2002.
3. Hughes interview.
4. Colleen, Seattle, interview with author, October 2002.
5. Jack, Seattle, interview with author, October 2002.
6. Holly, Connecticut, e-mail to author, October 28, 2002.

Chapter 9

1. *Expenditures on Children by Families,* U.S. Department of Agriculture, 2002.
2. *Student Fiscal Fitness Survey,* Phoenix Home Life Mutual Insurance Co., 1996.
3. Nancy, Arizona, e-mail to author, October 7, 2002.
4. Rhonda, Minnesota, e-mail to author, October 1, 2002.
5. Darlene, Texas, e-mail to author, October 1, 2002.
6. *Expenditures on Children by Families,* U.S. Department of Agriculture, 2002.
7. *Great Expectations—Unexpected Baby Costs Bring Financial Blues,* American Express survey, Great Britain, March 2003.
8. Ibid.

Chapter 10

1. Connie, Florida, e-mail to author, July 2002.
2. Gay, Florida, e-mail to author, June 30, 2002.
3. Ashraf, Bahrain, e-mail to author, June 30, 2002.
4. Lorrie, South Carolina, e-mail to author, June 30, 2002.
5. Sheila, Washington State, e-mail to author, June, 30, 2002.
6. Alison, Texas, e-mail to author, June, 30, 2002.
7. Lori, Texas, e-mail to author, September 9, 2002.

Chapter 11

1. Harris Interactive, interview with author, May 2003.
2. Stacy, Louisiana, interview with author, September, 2002.
3. Melissa, Louisiana, interview with author, September 2002.
4. Alex, New York, interview with author, May 2003.

Chapter 12

1. Marty, Alabama, interview with author, February 2003.
2. Julia, Missouri, e-mail to author, March 4, 2003.

3. Linda, e-mail to author, March 2, 2003.
4. "Young Investors Survey," conducted for Stein Roe by Harris Interactive, December 13, 2000.
5. "Money Talks," Girls Inc., 2000.
6. Dan, North Carolina, e-mail to author, March 3, 2003.
7. The Young Americans Bank, "Customer Statistics," as of December 2002, www.theyoungamericans.org.

Chapter 13

1. U.S. Bureau of the Census, "Two Married Parents the Norm," press release, June 12, 2003.
2. Kids Count Project, Annie E. Casey Foundation, unpublished data provided in interview with author, July 2003.
3. Hughes interview.
4. Colleen, Seattle, interview with author, February 2003.
5. Jennifer, Texas, e-mail to author, August 8, 2002.
6. Al Franken, Class Day Address, Harvard University, June 5, 2002. Text of speech available at www.commencement.harvard.edu/franken .html.
7. Ibid.

Chapter 14

1. Laura, New Mexico, interview with author, March 2003.
2. Janet, Minnesota, e-mail to author, May 25, 2003.
3. Mike, California, interview with author, June 2003.

Chapter 15

1. Cassandra, California, e-mail to author, October 6, 2003.
2. David, Florida, e-mail to author, October 7, 2002.
3. Ginger, California, e-mail to author, October 7, 2002.

Chapter 16

1. Karen, California, e-mail to author, March 30, 2003.

Stage Five

1. Calculations run by T. Rowe Price for the author. The results are based on a portfolio allocated 40 percent to stocks, 40 percent to bonds, 20 percent to cash, assuming a 3 percent annual rate of inflation in the cost of living, and calculated to ensure a 90 percent chance of having a nest egg to supply adequate annual income for 25 years.

Chapter 17

1. "The Distribution of Financial Wealth Among Baby Boomers," a paper presented at the Western Economic Association International Meeting, Denver, John Gist and Kebin Wu, AARP Public Policy Institute, July 2003.
2. Ibid.
3. Centers for Disease Control, National Center for Health Statistics, "Life Expectancy," Final Data 2000, www.cdc.gov/nchs/fastats/lifexpec.htm.
4. T. Rowe Price Retirement Income Calculator, www.troweprice.com. Monthly income based on an asset allocation of 60 percent stocks, 30 percent bonds, 10 percent cash, and an 80 percent success rate of reaching income target.
5. Social Security Administration, interview with author, July 2003.
6. "Revisioning Retirement," a survey conducted for AIG SunAmerica, by Harris Interactive and gerontologist Ken Dychtwald, April 2002.
7. Ibid.
8. "2003 Retirement Confidence Survey," Employee Benefits Research Institute, April 11, 2003.
9. Michael, Arizona, e-mail to author, January 26, 2003.
10. "Will My Nest Egg Last? Probability theory, an old math technique, is providing new—and better—answers to the question," Jeff D. Opdyke, *The Wall Street Journal*, Encore Special Report, page 7, June 5, 2000.
11. Marilyn, e-mail to author, January 26, 2003.
12. Margie, Ohio, e-mail to author, January 26, 2003.

Chapter 18

1. Jack, South Carolina, e-mail to author, February 7, 2003.
2. Linda Lubitz (president, Lubitz Financial, Miami, FL), interview with author, June 2003.
3. Hillery, Florida, e-mail to author, January 29, 2003.
4. *National Vital Statistics Reports*, vol. 51, no. 3, table 1. Life table for the total population: United States 2000, National Center for Health Statistics.
5. *National Survey of Employer-Sponsored Health Plans*, Mercer Human Resource Consulting, New York, various years.
6. "Health Insurance Cuts Hurt Retirees," *USA Today*, Money Section, based on research by Kaiser Family Foundation, Mercer/Foster Higgins, Watson Wyatt Worldwide, October 1, 2002.

7. Ibid.
8. Ibid.
9. AARP Public Policy Institute, interview with author, July 2003.
10. Ibid.
11. *Who Will Pay for the Baby Boomers' Long Term Care Needs?*, American Council of Life Insurance, 1999.
12. Urban Institute, interview with author, July 2003.
13. Northwestern Mutual, interview with author, July 2003.
14. Joseph L. Matthews, *Choose the Right Long-Term Care*, 4th ed. (Berkeley, CA: Nolo, 2002).

Chapter 19

1. *Trends in College Pricing*, The College Board, 2002.
2. Tim, e-mail to author, February 16, 2003.
3. Pamela, Minnesota, e-mail to author, February 24, 2003.
4. Dee, Louisiana, e-mail to author, February 2003.
5. "Is it time to 86 the 529 Plan?" MSNBC.com, June 15, 2003.
6. Ibid.

Chapter 20

1. Joan, Texas, e-mail to author, July 21, 2002.
2. Sharon, New England, e-mail to author, July 2002.
3. Emilie, Minnesota, e-mail to author, July 26, 2002.
4. Becky, Virginia, e-mail to author, July 23, 2002.
5. Christy, Illinois, e-mail to author, July 21, 2002.
6. Bonnie, Florida, e-mail to author, July 22, 2002.

Index